Distant Thunder

**Third World Conflict and
the New International Order**

Distant Thunder
Third World Conflict and the New International Order

Donald M. Snow
University of Alabama

St. Martin's Press
New York

Senior editor: Don Reisman
Managing editor: Patricia Mansfield-Phelan
Project editor: Amy Horowitz
Production supervisor: Katherine Battiste
Maps: Maryland CartoGraphic
Cover design: Michael Jung
Line art: Hadel Studio, Inc.

Manufactured in the United States of America.
76543
fedcba

For information, write:
St. Martin's Press, Inc.
175 Fifth Avenue
New York, NY 10010

ISBN: 0-312-06666-X (paperback)
        0-312-08684-6 (cloth)

Library of Congress Cataloging-in-Publication Data

Snow, Donald M., 1943–
    Distant thunder : Third World conflict and the New International
Order / by Donald M. Snow.
        p.   cm.
    Includes bibliographical references.
    ISBN 0-312-06666-X (pbk.), 0-312-08684-6 (cloth)
    1. International relations.   2. Developing countries—Foreign
relations.   I. Title.
JX1395.S595   1992
327'.09'048—dc20

                                                    92-50022
                                                    CIP

To Howard B. Gundy, without whose good advice this book probably would not have been written.

Preface

Some of the most obvious changes in response to the end of the Cold War are occurring in the Third World. The developing countries in Asia, Africa, and Central and South America have not shared in the general prosperity of the industrialized nations known as the First World, nor have they experienced the disintegration of the Second, or Socialist, World. They were often sideshows in the international scene during the Cold War, places where the contestants could wage surrogate competitions relatively safe from the dangers of direct confrontation.

With the end of the Cold War our interest in the Third World is likely to increase, as it becomes the major source of instability and violence in the international system. The disintegration that occurred in the Second World, as suppressed nationalism gained strength in the former Soviet Union and Yugoslavia, is likely to be seen as well in many Third World nations as democratization progresses. Instability and violence are nothing new in the Third World, of course; these problems are now merely more vivid because the Cold War is not here to overshadow them.

All this is reviving an interest in the Third World that was visibly dampened by the Vietnam War. The 1950s political and economic arguments about developing the Third World are becoming relevant again, as is the literature on revolutionism and the conduct of insurgency and counterinsurgency.

However, there are new concerns as well. Nuclear, biological and chemical (NBC) weapons capabilities are now possessed by numerous Third World states, some of which have or are developing ballistic means of delivery. At the same time, the interest of the United States and other Western countries both in staunching the flow of narcotics from the Third World and in keeping terrorism at bay adds new dimensions to relations with the Third World.

The idea for *Distant Thunder* was the product of my stay at the U.S. Army War College as a visiting professor from 1989 to 1991. It was an exciting time from any vantage point, and an especially yeasty time to be around senior military leaders responsible for the nation's defense. Together we watched the Berlin Wall fall and were part of the process leading to major reductions in military spending as well as major reformulations of military roles and missions. The experience was a traumatic one for my colleagues and students as lifelong roles and missions dissolved before them, but it was also very stimulating intellectually. Most notably, I was able to interact with individuals responsible for formulating and executing the very kinds of concerns included in these pages. This text would have been far less rich without the discussions we had.

There are numerous thanks to be accorded. The Army War College graciously provided the setting for my research and writing. I would like to extend my thanks to the chair of the Department of National Security and Strategy, Colonel Dave Hazen, for giving me the time and "space" to write; to Colonel Jim McCallum and the other members of the faculty for their support; and especially to my officemate and fellow visiting professor, Dr. Gene Brown, for his support and perspective. I am also grateful to the students in my advanced course, Low-Intensity Conflict in American National Policy, who served as the guinea pigs first for my ideas and then for my raw manuscripts. Their insights and suggestions were crucial to the quality of this book.

Thanks also go to my colleagues who reviewed and provided valuable suggestions on the manuscript: William H. Baugh, University of Oregon; Scott L. Bills, Stephen F. Austin State University; Donald L. Hafner, Boston College; Richard A. Melanson, Brown University and Kenyon College; Gregory A. Raymond, Boise State University; and Paul R. Viccotti, U.S. Air Force Academy.

I owe special thanks to my editor at St. Martin's Press, Don Reisman, for encouraging the project, and to the excellent production staff for their professional handling of the manuscript. Finally, thanks are due as usual to my wife, Donna, and my son, Ric, for putting up with me throughout the writing of the book.

Donald M. Snow

Contents

CHAPTER 1 **The Changing Face of Violent Conflict**   **1**

The Revolutions of 1989: Causes and Effects   2
The Disintegrated East-West Confrontation   8
Third World Conflict without an East-West Overlay   13
South-South and North-South Conflict and the
    New World Order   19
Conclusion   22

CHAPTER 2 **Third World Problems in a First World–Dominated**
Global System   **25**

The Crisis of Legitimacy and Authority   27
Economic and Social Causes of Conflict   33
Patterns of Third World Conflict   43
Conclusion   55

CHAPTER 3 **The Venerable Foe: Insurgency**   **57**

The Roots of Insurgency: Underlying Causes   59
The "Poor Man's War": A Historical Perspective   66
Mobile-Guerrilla Warfare   72
Insurgency as Conventional War Inverted   77
Conclusion   82

CHAPTER 4 **The Intractable Nemesis: Counterinsurgency**   **85**

The Basic Difficulty: "There Is a Problem Here"   87
The Political Dimension: Centers of Gravity and
    Hearts and Minds   93
The Military Dimension: Shooting the Symptoms
    and the Brushfire Corollary   99

The American Approach to Counterinsurgency 105
Conclusion 108

CHAPTER 5 **The New Challenges: Counternarcotics,**
Counterterrorism, and Peacekeeping **112**

Different Problems, Different Solutions 115
Counternarcotics: "Fighting" the War on Drugs 117
Counterterrorism: The Frustration of Ends and
Means 125
Peacekeeping and Peacemaking: Who, Where, and
Why? 131
Conclusion 135

CHAPTER 6 **An Old Problem with New Teeth: Regional Conflict** **136**

Old Roots: Regional Rivalries in the Cold War
System 137
The Cold War Factor: Then and Now 145
New Dimensions: The Rise of the "Weapon" State
with New Capabilities 149
Managing Regional Conflict in the Emerging
International Order 158
Conclusion 165

CHAPTER 7 **Cases in Point: *Sendero Luminoso* and Desert Storm** **167**

Shining Path and Coca: The Battleground for the
War on Drugs 169
Operation Desert Shield: Regional Conflict in the
New World Order? 181
Conclusion 193

CHAPTER 8 **Distant Thunder or Siren's Call?** **195**

Features of the New International Environment 197
Ongoing Third World Problems 202
The "New World Order"? 206
The American Response to the New Order 208

Bibliography **214**
Index **221**

Distant Thunder

**Third World Conflict and
the New International Order**

CHAPTER 1

The Changing Face
of Violent Conflict

Change is inevitable in the international order; no part of the globe is exempt from the process or consequences of change. Today's altered political world is most striking in the center of Europe, where the revolutions of 1989 toppled the authoritarian reins of Communist rule. But the pace of change sweeps the entire world. The "new world order," of which President George Bush speaks, will differ significantly from that which preceded it.

The major purpose of this book is to look at one aspect of international change and its consequences for the United States. The Third World has long been the center of instability and unrest in the international system. During the Cold War confrontation between the First World—the industrialized countries of the West—and the Second World—the Communist or Socialist countries—the Third World was at the margins of the international system. At that time, the developing countries of the Third World acted as supporting players. In today's evolving international system, however, the developing world may move to center stage. Therefore, it is important to understand the Third World's problems, including its patterns of violence, and to search for solutions.

The ongoing collapse of the Second World is changing the political priorities of the world. Certainly, concerns about the restructuring of the former Soviet Union—politically, economically, and physically—will continue. The map of Central Europe is also likely to change, possibly accompanied by violence, as in Yugoslavia. Generally, peace is more likely to characterize the Northern Hemisphere now than at any other time in the twentieth century. Unfortunately, the same is not true of the Third World.

It is misleading to speak of the Third World as if it is a single place with one defining set of characteristics. It is not. Most of the world's population resides in—and the overwhelming percentage of that population's growth occurs in—the incredible diversity of places we call the Third World. Furthermore, most of the world's poverty, misery, instability, and violence are also found in the Third World.

In terms of national security, the developing world is likely to remain an area of great concern throughout the rest of this century and in the beginning of the twenty-first century. This is partly because most of the threats to international peace will occur in the Third World, thereby providing opportunities for military involvement. The opportunity to do so, of course, has been present ever since the Third World began to decolonize in the 1940s. During the Cold War era, the superpower competition occasionally brought the United States into Third World situations (for example, in Vietnam, Grenada, and the Dominican Republic). In the post–Cold War world, however, other interests and events will draw the United States toward the sounds of distant thunder. It is our purpose here to determine what those interests and occasions are likely to be.

In order to understand why the Third World is likely to become increasingly important in the future, it is first necessary for us to examine how the international system is changing, what those changes are, and how those changes affect the international system in general, as well as so-called interactions between the First and Third Worlds.

THE REVOLUTIONS OF 1989: CAUSES AND EFFECTS

Since the end of World War II, international politics has been dominated by the political and military confrontation between the United States and the Soviet Union. That competition, known generally as the *Cold War,* developed with the restructuring of the international system after the war.

The prewar international system had been dominated by the major European powers—Great Britain, France, Germany (especially after the rise of nazism in the early 1930s), Italy, and to a lesser extent, the Soviet Union. Outside Europe, Imperial Japan was a major force in Asia, and the United States was isolated from a Europe whose power politics it found distasteful. Most Third World countries were either under colonial rule (for example, much of Africa, the Middle East, and Asia) or isolated from the international mainstream (such as Latin America).

World War II changed the international order significantly. The major European powers, whether winners or losers, were no longer able or willing to reconstruct and operate the international system. Britain and France, on the winning side, were physically and economically reduced to regional power status. During the next two decades, they retreated from their empires, thereby helping to create the Third World. Germany and Japan, of course, were conquered and occupied.

Only the United States and the Soviet Union emerged from World War II with residual strength, though it was uneven. By gearing its Depression-idled economy toward becoming an "arsenal of democracy," the United States emerged from the war physically stronger than before. It had suffered relatively light casualties (300,000) and was the only nation in 1945 with the atom bomb. The Soviet Union, in contrast, bore the physical brunt of World War II. An estimated twenty-eight million Soviet soldiers and civilians died during the war; millions more were killed by Stalin during the purges of the 1930s. In addition, two-thirds of Soviet industry was destroyed, as were many towns, cities, and villages. What the Soviets retained, however, was their huge Red Army of twelve million.

In the post–World War II international climate, the major concern was reconstructing the system so as to prevent another world war. The key question here was whether the two major powers (not yet called "super-powers") could maintain the wartime collaboration. If they could, the United Nations Charter provided a vehicle for them to organize peace around the principle of collective security (the provisions are found in chapter VII of the Charter). If they could not maintain the wartime collaboration, the Charter allowed them to form competitive alliances through Article 51, which provided for the individual and collective self-defense of the members.

What would determine collaboration or competition was whether the two major powers could agree on a mutually acceptable world order that could be enforced. They could not. America's world of liberal democracies conflicted with Stalin's world of socialism and communism. The result was the Cold War international system, in which the competition between communism and anticommunism became the central international concern.

The Cold War did not emerge instantly in 1945 as a dominating feature of the international system. Rather, it took several years for the collaboration to break down and for the competitive system to emerge. Collaboration was dead by 1947, though the hardened rules of Cold War competition were not firmly in place until June 1950, when North Korea invaded South Korea.

The Cold War system now lies shattered. The most dramatic symbols of its end include the revolutions of 1989 in Eastern Europe, the destruction of the Berlin Wall, and ultimately, the demise of the Soviet Union. In retrospect, the revolutions were not so much the cause of change as they were the consequences of forces from the Cold War period. In turn, the revolutions of 1989 provided a momentum to events that will help shape the post–Cold War order that is evolving today.

Two major sets of dynamics came together to make the end of the Cold War inevitable: (1) the East-West military paralysis that was caused largely by nuclear weapons, and (2) the international economic revolution of the 1980s that was linked to unprecedented advances in technology. Both situations focused on the East-West confrontation and were particularly important to the Soviet Union, which helps explain the importance of Soviet President Mikhail Gorbachev's role in promoting change.

East-West Military Paralysis

The heart of the Cold War international system was the expensive conventional and thermonuclear military competition between the Eastern and Western alliances led by the United States and the Soviet Union. At the end of World War II, the United States rapidly demobilized its armed forces but remained the sole possessor of the atomic bomb. In contrast, the Soviet Union lacked this awesome weapon but maintained a huge army of occupation in Eastern Europe.

As collaboration turned to confrontation and the Cold War system emerged, the armed competition gradually became more permanent and symmetrical. In 1949, the United States joined the major Western European states to form the North Atlantic Treaty Organization (NATO)—the first major peacetime military alliance in U.S. history. Its purposes were to ensure a continuous American commitment to Europe and develop permanent forces to face the Soviets. Faced with the prospect of an independent Federal Republic of Germany army in 1955, the Soviets reciprocated with the Warsaw Treaty Organization (WTO, or the Warsaw Pact) in 1956.

The nuclear relationship between the United States and the Soviet Union also became symmetrical. In 1949, the Soviets produced their own atomic (fission) bomb. In 1952, the Americans exploded their first thermonuclear (hydrogen) weapon, a feat replicated by the Soviets in 1953. The Soviets were the first to test a successful intercontinental ballistic missile (ICBM), in 1957, followed shortly by the United States.

With these developments in nuclear weaponry, the military competition between the superpowers took its form and symmetry. It was extremely costly and raised the lethal capacities of the opposing sides. Ralph Peters's 1989 novel *Red Army* depicts graphically the lethality of a so-called "conventional" (that is, non-nuclear) war in Germany—it would leave Germany so devastated as to be a dubious prize of war. But it was in the area of thermonuclear weaponry that the lethality of the weapons increased most.

At the end of the 1950s, the nuclear arsenal of each superpower included hundreds of weapons deliverable only by highly inaccurate rockets or aircraft. Intervening technological and deployment developments later expanded the strategic inventories of the superpowers to around seven to eight thousand weapons apiece as a result of the Strategic Arms Reduction Talks (START) agreement of 1991. Virtually all of these weapons could be delivered by ballistic systems that, by contemporary technology, cannot be prevented from reaching their targets. (The moribund Strategic Defense Initiative—SDI—was an attempt to develop the capability to defend against such missiles.)

A funny thing happened along the way to expanded military capacity. The nuclear arsenals grew so large and so deadly that they became virtually unusable. What gradually emerged was a state of necessary peace, for to use nuclear weapons that could devastate both societies—and possibly the rest of the world—was clearly not in anyone's best interests. In *The Illogic of American Nuclear Strategy* (1984), political scientist Robert Jervis describes the potential outcome of a nuclear war as "assured destruction"; that is, regardless of what intentions each side had for entering a nuclear conflict, the outcome would be the destruction of both sides. The United States and Soviet Union gradually came to realize this and became self-deterred to avoid the disastrous consequences of a nuclear war.

The political leaders of the two superpowers were aware of the dangerous nuclear situation well before nuclear theorists and military planners. American President Dwight Eisenhower and Soviet leaders Nikita Khrushchev and Leonid Brezhnev knew that nuclear weapons could not be used under any circumstances. During the succession process following Brezhnev's death, his successors—Yuri Andropov, Konstantin Chernenko, and Mikhail Gorbachev—all stated firmly the impossibility and unacceptability of nuclear conflict.

Thus, huge nuclear arsenals make nuclear war inconceivable not only between countries that possess them but also because they can destroy societies worldwide. *Any* war between the superpowers has the potential of being a nuclear war and so has to be avoided. Furthermore, the caution exercised by a country with a large nuclear arsenal, such as the United States, may not be true of countries with a small arsenal, such as those of the Third World.

According to Marshal Igor Sergeev, head of the Soviet Strategic Rocket Forces that controls most Soviet nuclear forces, "It was precisely nuclear parity, the existence of nuclear weapons on both sides, that has preserved the peace. In my opinion, it is the guarantor of the impossibility of a world war."

Nuclear paralysis thereby deters both nuclear and conventional military confrontation. The standoff between the Warsaw Pact and NATO was gradually reduced to a hollow ritual whereby arms were placed in arsenals and plans were exercised in the absence of any real anticipation of use. Nuclear weapons, the archetype of the Cold War, created the stalemate, and the START reductions did not change it. Although the limits were lowered to between seven thousand and nine thousand weapons apiece, the deadly effect remains. The rubble may not bounce as high or as often as before, to paraphrase Sir Winston Churchill, but it would still assuredly bounce just the same.

The military competition between the superpowers became expensive, especially in terms of conventional arms. In the late 1980s, NATO-related costs for the United States represented 60 percent of the U.S. defense budget. Defense expenditures, much of which were devoted to East-West matters, consumed 25 percent of the Soviet gross national product (GNP).

Mikhail Gorbachev and his associates realized the need to end the competition, particularly in light of the troubled economic times in the Soviet Union. The most reasonable solution was to dismantle as much of the nuclear arsenals as possible. For the Soviets, that meant jettisoning the Warsaw Pact and reducing their conventional armed forces. Gorbachev, of course, saw the need to take these actions. Political analysts disagree on whether anyone leading the Soviet Union in the 1980s would have reached a similar conclusion.

Economic Change

Another major factor tied to the inevitable end of the Cold War was the economic revolution of the 1980s, a phenomenon with opposite pulls and effects. On the one hand, the economies of the West—North America, Japan, and the European Community (EC)—experienced unprecedented growth and prosperity during this time, which extended to certain Third World countries known as NICs (newly industrialized countries), many of which are clustered around the Pacific Rim. On the other hand, the economies of the countries of the Second World (especially in the Soviet Union) failed to expand during the 1980s. As their economic performance flattened, the gap between the First and Second Worlds, as well as the gap between the First and Third Worlds, became a chasm.

The reasons for the extraordinary growth in the West are complex and controversial. Three factors, however, did play important roles. The first, the *high technology revolution,* brought great increases in the generation, transmission, and application of knowledge to economic purposes in the 1970s and 1980s. With high technology came advances in computing and telecommunications as well as a series of derivative fields, such as fiber optics and new materials science. Each of these areas was applied increasingly to commercial activity, and redefined productivity and economic competitiveness.

The second factor related to the West's growth during the 1980s was the *internationalization of economic activity.* Global communications in the 1980s increased well beyond the bounds predicted in the 1960s and 1970s that had suggested growing economic interdependence among the world's nations. The multinational corporation (MNC) of the 1960s—a corporation that is located in one country but produces and sells products in numerous countries—became the "stateless corporation" in the 1980s—one so international in ownership, management, labor force, and product derivation and mix that it is, for all practical purposes, beyond identification with any single nation-state. Moreover, basic science and technological application became similarly international as high-speed telecommunications allowed the sharing of scientific information rapidly and massively across national borders.

The third and most controversial factor tied to the prosperity of the West was the *global privatization of the international economy.* During the 1980s, the governments of several First World countries deregulated economic activity, especially in the high technology areas. Deregulation created the incentive for massive investment (as well as the accumulation of great debt), which helped fuel the growth of the 1980s (and may slow recovery in the 1990s as the debts are being repaid).

The privatization of the economy, largely confined to the European Community, Japan, and North America, resulted in great wealth and prosperity. The Soviet economy had been excluded from the international economy (for instance, Soviet currency was not convertible to other currencies because it was feared that its low value would be weakened to the point of worthlessness.) The Soviet social net meant subsidies on consumer goods that, when exposed to the market, would result in wholesale rises in prices.

Soviet socialism was failing. The Stalinist command economy, which had been the envy of the world in the 1930s, was declining. The Soviet Union's problems were obvious to some within the Soviet government in the early 1970s, but it wasn't until Gorbachev came into power that the 1970s and early 1980s were described as the "era of stagnation." Thus, the Soviet economy and the economies of the Eastern European countries declined as the West grew. And the gap became more obvious as the Western media penetrated the East.

In addition, the Soviets were excluded from the high technology revolution that might have stimulated their economy. The reason for their exclusion was that most of the technologies were "dual use," with both civilian and military applications; the Soviet Union remained a military threat, so the technologies were not shared with them.

The economic imperative thus provided a two-pronged incentive to end the Cold War. The success of the Western market model and the failure of the Soviet command model eventually led to the idea of *perestroika*. At the same time, access to Western technology and resources was crucial to development in the Soviet Union and required that the Soviet military threat be lowered.

Hence, military stalemate and economic necessity combined to produce the end of the Cold War, the political and military division of Europe, and the "enslavement" of Eastern Europe. During the summer of 1989, Gorbachev and Foreign Minister Eduard Shevardnadze visited the Warsaw Pact capitals with a simple message: Reform your systems or face the wrath of your own populations, for there will be no Soviet tanks to save you this time. The Poles were the first to test the proposition. When the Soviets did not interfere in the ascension of an anti-Communist government in Poland, the floodgates of change were opened. The revolutions of 1989 destroyed the Communist regimes of Eastern Europe as well as the facade of the Cold War.

THE DISINTEGRATED EAST-WEST CONFRONTATION

The Cold War ended because Gorbachev knew his country could not win the confrontation militarily and because he realized the hollow competition had become ruinously expensive.

The most important effects of the end of the Cold War include not only the termination of the military confrontation between the former Soviet Union and the United States but also the fact that the old competition is highly unlikely to reoccur. Even so, we must still address two vital questions concerning the changes brought about by the Cold War: (1) What are the changes and (2) How permanent are the changes?

A word of caution is necessary here. Although it is universally recognized that we are in the midst of fundamental change, our perspective is limited in a way similar to that of the framers of the post–World War II system shortly after the end of that war. Like the framers, we can only make assumptions about the outcome we will later encounter.

What Are the Post–Cold War Changes?

At least four major changes in the international system stem directly from the revolutions of 1989. The first and most obvious change was the *decommunization of the countries of Eastern Europe.* Given the opportunity, the peoples of Central Europe cast aside communism and its leaders with a ferocity and velocity that caught the world aghast. What has begun in these countries is a process of democratization, nationalism, and economic transformation to the Western system. The revolutions of 1989 revealed that Eastern Europeans sought to be more like those on the other side of the Iron Curtain; they wanted the freedom and prosperity that was not available to them under Communist rule.

Yet the Westernization process is not likely to occur without problems. Democratization is the easier task, though it is more advanced in the "northern tier" or Central European countries (Poland, Czechoslovakia, and Hungary) than in the "southern tier" or Balkan states (Romania, Bulgaria). Transforming command economies into market economies is difficult, and different states have chosen more or less precipitous paths toward that end. Ultimately, however, the success of Westernization is likely to hinge on economic betterment.

The most important systemic effect of Eastern European independence was that it severed the alliance relationship between the former Soviet Union and its "allies." The Soviet Union and the Warsaw Pact no longer exist, and the successor states to the Soviet Union no longer have a military alliance or allies facing the West. In fact, the Commonwealth of Independent States no longer has a unified military.

The second change brought about by the revolutions of 1989 was the *transformation of the Soviet Union itself.* Under Gorbachev's leadership, the Soviet Union had significantly Westernized. The degree of political participation and freedom that existed in the Soviet Union under Gorbachev's rule, though modest by Western standards, was unprecedented there. The attempts to reform the economy were catastrophic, and political freedom included nationalist demands for independence among conquered peoples who were forcefully a part of the "union." The result has been the dissolution of the Soviet Union into a series of independent, loosely confederated states. Working out new relationships between these states will preoccupy the former Soviet Union for the rest of the century.

Gorbachev's Soviet Union became a more "normal" state within the international system. Previously, the country's Marxist-Leninist philosophy made it an outsider to the rest of the world. Under Gorbachev, the Soviet Union abandoned the political and economic systems of communism. In international terms, the Soviets moved to join the mainstream. Most of the successor states are likely to try to continue this process.

The third change was the *reduction of Soviet offensive military capability.* A major part of Gorbachev's "new political thinking" (his philosophy of international relations) was the reduction of the offensive capabilities of conventional (non-nuclear) forces. This included large-scale reductions in Soviet troops and, through the Conventional Forces in Europe (CFE) agreement, in offensive weapons (such as tanks, armored personnel carriers, and mobile artillery pieces). The effects of these reductions were twofold. From the Soviet viewpoint, the reductions lowered costs—especially those associated with stationing troops in Eastern Europe—and reassured NATO that the Soviet Union was no longer a threat and therefore eligible for Western assistance. From the Western perspective, the reductions meant that it would be virtually impossible for the Soviets to launch an attack on the West without a long and observable mobilization. A Soviet invading force would have to fight its way across the territory of its former allies (Poland or Czechoslovakia), meaning there would be plenty of time to prepare for the attack. Thus, fewer forces had to be stationed permanently in Europe, a cost-saver for the United States. Soviet nuclear forces were also affected by the reductions through START and other agreements. The breakup of the country has accelerated this trend as former Soviet forces pledge loyalty to the successor states.

The fourth change came in *Soviet foreign policy toward the Third World*. Before the rise of Gorbachev, competing for influence with the United States in the Third World was an important part of Soviet policy— a means for promoting communism and reinforcing Soviet power worldwide without significantly raising the specter of military conflict between the superpowers.

But all that changed. New thinking renounced the Brezhnev doctrine, which asserted the right of Soviets to intervene on behalf of beleaguered Socialist movements worldwide. It was replaced by the assertion that the sovereign rights of nations should be honored without interference. One result was to reduce the competition between the East and West in Third World countries. Problems remained in areas of long-standing competition (such as Afghanistan, Angola, and Mozambique), though there were attempts to work them out. Neither side looked for new commitments or opportunities.

The Soviet motivation appeared to be dual. On the one hand, the competition was usually costly and the benefits of it short-lived. The competition failed on cost-gain grounds, an especially important consideration in hard economic times. On the other hand, East-West competition in the Third World was just another irritant in overall relations. Faced with the need to reduce tension in order to gain access to Western assistance, backing away from losing propositions was a mild price for the Soviets to pay.

How Permanent Are the Post–Cold War Changes?

The end of the Cold War initially created exaggerated feelings of euphoria and optimism. However, as historian Crane Brinton explains in *Anatomy of a Revolution* (1965), the progression of a revolution is never linear. All revolutions create negative reactions and require some readjustment to the new state of things, whether good or bad. In this respect, the revolutions of 1989 were no different than any other. However, we can tentatively assess the four changes discussed earlier in the chapter.

The independence of Eastern Europe from the Soviet Union was the least reversible outcome of the events of 1989. First, communism could be imposed in 1945 because of unique circumstances—the liberation of Eastern Europe from Nazi occupation during World War II—that would be virtually impossible to repeat. Soviet domination could have returned only by blatant aggression, an act that would likely have triggered World War III. Second, the completeness with which the nations of Eastern Europe threw aside all remnants of communism suggested that it was extremely unlikely that they would choose voluntarily to emulate their former rulers in the future.

However, this is not to suggest that the process of change in Eastern Europe will be smooth or even successful. Westernization, the apparent goal of most Eastern Europeans, will be a difficult process, especially in the most backward states in the southern tier (Romania, Bulgaria, and Albania). Soviet-imposed dictatorship did contain ethnic and nationalistic differences among peoples that were evident and unleashed in Yugoslavia, for example. It is uncertain whether all of the residual nationalistic problems will be solved readily or without bloodshed. Yet Eastern Europeans will benefit from their desire to attain Western prosperity as well as from the willingness of Western Europe to assist in the transition.

It is difficult to predict positive outcomes of change for the successor states in the former Soviet Union. Reform is more difficult in the former Soviet Union for at least two reasons. First, there was the question of whether any attachment remained to the old system. Eastern European communism was not homegrown; it was an imposition that could be discarded without remorse. For the former Soviet leadership (including Gorbachev), change was more traumatic because it required renouncing their own system. Gorbachev almost certainly had as his initial purpose the improvement of a Socialist system that he believed was fundamentally healthy and good. Discovering instead that it was the system that was the problem had to be traumatic and difficult for him. And the often hesitant, even halfhearted pace of attempted reforms that plagued the process was probably linked to his difficulty.

The second problem has to do with scale. The former Soviet Union was the physically largest nation in the world as well as one of the most diverse. Transforming a command economy based on socialism, and that remained essentially feudal in some regions, would be a difficult task in even ideal circumstances. Moreover, there were no tested guidelines for transforming a command economy into a market economy. The breakup of the political union also interrupted economic integration, exacerbating the problem.

The potential for reaction to reform was thus stronger in the former Soviet Union. The nationalities problem made secession by at least some of the republics inevitable. The nationalities problem was the underlying cause of the peaceful and voluntary total breakup of the Soviet Union—an unprecedented event in history. The successor Commonwealth of Independent States is no more than a shadow organization that lacks a constitution, authority, and leaders. The ongoing economic crisis was a serious problem; if things did not improve, parts of the populace would question and reject reform.

If the reforms failed, might some of the successor countries revert to authoritarianism or greater radicalism? On one side of Gorbachev were those—principally in the Communist party of the Soviet Union (CPSU) and the military—who believed that reform bred chaos and needed to be replaced by order and authority. On the other side, those led by the Russian leader Boris Yeltsin believed that reform was too timid; they called for more radical democratization and economic change. Moreover, some states may pursue reform while others revert.

Regardless of the outcome of the change process, *a return to an aggressive offensive conventional capability is unlikely* for several reasons. First, such a change of policy would sour East-West relations, revive Western interest in NATO, and cut the republics off from economic and political support. Lacking an alliance with Eastern Europe, the republics would be militarily isolated and disadvantaged.

Second, such a change would be extraordinarily expensive and could only be mounted by abandoning any serious effort at economic development. A reversion to a large, offensively configured force would place the millstone back around the economy's neck and reverse defense reductions apparent by 1992. Third, such a change would be most unlikely to engender public support. As the 1991 demonstrations, violence, and attempted coup demonstrated, the military was already held in dubious regard; increasing its role and numbers (including generous numbers of conscripts) would almost certainly have been resisted.

Fourth, what remains of the military is likely to be busy at things such as maintaining internal order. The Soviet military does not relish this role, as its leadership has made known since the Army was involved in suppressing unrest in Armenia and Georgia. Fifth, it is uncertain if there will even be a centrally controlled military in the future. Among the eleven former Soviet republics that have joined the Commonwealth, several—notably the Ukraine—have rejected the idea of even having a centrally controlled military. The old Soviet armed forces are rapidly becoming little more than militias controlled by the republics—with accordingly diminished capabilities.

Finally, *it is unlikely that Commonwealth policy toward the Third World will return to activism in the near future.* First, the former Soviet Union simply cannot afford to subsidize Third World movements; in fact, they were cutting loose as many of their old clients as possible, including Castro's Cuba, before the Soviet Union dissolved. Second, noninterference in the Third World helps make Russia and the other republics appear as responsible members of the international system. Third, there is simply not much Third World interest in the former Soviet system. The old Soviet system is not something to emulate; rather, it is something to avoid at all costs.

THIRD WORLD CONFLICT WITHOUT AN EAST-WEST OVERLAY

The revolutionary forces that are restructuring the international system have centered almost exclusively on the developed world—the First and Second Worlds. The only real exception was Saddam Hussein's invasion of Kuwait, which took place because the system's rules were in flux in August 1990 (for a more detailed appraisal, see Chapter 7). Given the world's dependence on Persian Gulf oil, the West had no real choice but to turn its attention to the war.

Conflict and instability characterize much of the Third World. Repressed under colonial rule, the problems that exist there today were created in part by decolonization. The North-South debate about who is responsible for the ills that beset the Third World, as well as the degree to which the North owes the South the assistance it needs to achieve economic and political stability, endures.

In the Cold War system, the attitudes of East and West toward the Third World were largely instrumental. Some Third World countries, such as parts of southern Africa and the oil-producing regions of the Middle East, gained value because they possessed needed resources. Those countries with resources of a military or strategic value (such as metals) were highly regarded. At the same time, the Third World countries, especially

Latin America, appeared to be a good place to invest and make money, and so private capital flowed.

However, much of the interest in the Third World stemmed from the Cold War competition. In 1961, Khrushchev publicly formalized that competition in his dual support for "wars of national liberation" (Marxist insurgencies, in most cases) and "the peaceful road to socialism," whereby Marxist movements could come to power legally.

Thus, the Communists and non-Communists competed for influence in the Third World. At one level, the purpose was to ensure that the other side did not gain undue influence in any one country or region.

The symbols of the competition were familiar enough. Within certain developing countries, the East and West competed to recruit potential leaders. When instability devolved to internal violence, one side sponsored and supported the government while the other backed the insurgents. In regional conflicts, each side tried to nurture at least one state, usually offering armaments as an inducement.

This pattern is likely to change in today's altered environment. Concerns in the North are likely to be introspective, so as to encourage adjustments to the new conditions. This may include a reduced level of competitive involvement in Third World problems. As a result, much of the East-West overlay may no longer characterize how Third World problems are considered.

The Process of Adjustment

One early conclusion of the Gorbachev regime was that the Third World competition was an unaffordable luxury. In some cases, Soviet influence gained only a fleeting advantage that was easily countered by the United States. In other cases, victory meant being saddled with a long-term dependent (such as Cuba's Fidel Castro).

Although a controversial issue, it can be argued that the Soviets' Afghanistan adventure provided their focus for reassessment. In December 1979, the Soviets invaded Afghanistan in order to place a loyal Communist in power as well as to help the government put down a rebellion led by a loose coalition of Afghan tribes known as the *mujahadin* ("freedom fighters"). The intervention was not a military success, and it gradually soured Soviet opinion as the casualties were made known.

The Soviets' involvement in Afghanistan has been compared to the U.S. experience in Vietnam. For example, the Soviets initially believed that they could end the war quickly and easily against a primitive foe. Instead, the military conflict, which began in 1979, did not end until 1988.

Further, Najibullah, the leader the Soviets installed in power in Afghanistan, remained in office for four years after their departure.

The Soviet withdrawal from Afghanistan was symbolic of the general malaise of the Soviet system and the need to withdraw from the Third World. Although some residual Soviet involvement, as well as American counterinvolvement, continued in places of long-standing competition (for example, in Afghanistan and Angola), the Soviets were anxious to end Third World involvements either by negotiation (as in Namibia and Angola) or by de facto acceptance of adverse changes (such as the election of Violetta Chamorro as president of Nicaragua).

Disengagement will likely continue for at least two reasons, both of which are related to the pressures toward introspection in the former Soviet Union. The first has to do with resources. At one level, both the United States and the former Soviet Union have considerable reasons to redirect their resources toward domestic problems. Funds for Third World adventures and commitments are likely to be among the first items to fall under the budget deficit-reduction axe in the United States. In the former Soviet Union, the internal economic disaster will be expensive, so there will be little left to subsidize Cuban sugar, for instance. Moreover, the adjustment to the political reality that the Soviet Union is now effectively fifteen independent states will dictate great effort and adjustment.

This phenomenon is likely to influence Western Europe as well. Because of colonialism, most West European countries have a special relationship and concern for the Third World. At the same time, European resources are likely to be directed toward healing the postwar division of the continent. Germany, the country with the deepest pockets, is certain to devote its attention to making the former East Germany more like the West. Once that is accomplished, Germany and the rest of the European Community are likely to direct their resources to the peaceful and democratic evolution of the fledgling Eastern European democracies.

Another reason for introspection is to redirect resources to institutionalizing the new post–Cold War international system. Two concerns will have to be addressed here. First, regarding the new structure of security within Europe itself, the major issue involves how or whether to include the United States and the Soviet successor states in the new arrangement and how to make the transition amidst the turmoil and instability in Eastern Europe and the former Soviet Union. Second, it will have to be decided how to replace the collective defense system of opposing military alliances (NATO and the Warsaw Pact) of the Cold War. At the international level, the collective security principles enunciated in the United Nations Charter may replace the Cold War structure; certainly the Desert Storm coalition was loosely organized around that principle.

Yet another question concerns the role of the Third World in the new international arrangement. The majority of United Nations members are Third World countries, so a United Nations-based collective security system cannot ignore the feelings and opinions of Third World leaders. At the same time, the great majority of threats to and breaches of the peace will continue to be in the Third World. Thus, the question arises whether the Third World will be an active participant in enforcing collective security actions that take place in the Third World.

In addition, there is the question of who will enforce a collective security world if that is what evolves. If the United Nations Charter provisions are followed (they never have been), enforcement would be the responsibility of the permanent members of the Security Council (the United States, Russia, Great Britain, France, and China). Other states would be largely disarmed, with the primary responsibility for providing host conditions such as bases for United Nations peacekeepers. Except for China, of course, all the members are from the First World, making the enforcement mechanism inherently northern.

United Nations practice has, of course, been quite different. Most United Nations actions have been in peacekeeping (trying to enforce a peace that already exists) rather than in peacemaking (using force to create peace between warring parties). Peacekeeping is a comparatively passive activity not requiring any great force in terms of soldiers or equipment. Such actions are typically carried out by the lesser powers of both the First and Third Worlds, including those nations distinguished by their reputation for objectivity and with forces dedicated to United Nations duty (such as Canada and Norway).

The pattern selected will help determine what kinds of actions the collective security instrument engages in. If it is confined to reactive peacekeeping, the use of smaller powers will suffice, and both the First and Third Worlds will be major players. If peacemaking becomes its major role, the system will have to include the major powers of the First World and possibly impose order in places like Bosnia.

The Magnitude of Involvement

Limited resources for competitive purposes, declining ideological competition, and the incentive for introspection are likely to mean less First World involvement in Third World conflicts and problems. Yet this is nothing new. Third World countries, after all, do not have constituencies in Western voting districts, and so they are often the target of budget reductions.

Certain factors are exacerbating the temptations to further marginalize investment in Third World conflicts. The lack of sufficient interest for the major powers to involve themselves is one. The Cold War created an interest in containing communism or spreading Leninism that no longer exists. With ideological incentives stripped away and other bases of interest nonexistent, the incentives for involvement are insufficient.

However, that two-thirds of the world's known petroleum reserves are in the Persian Gulf creates a strong interest in peace and stability in that region. Instability in the economically booming Pacific Rim would pique Western concern, and a case can be made for opposing instability in parts of Latin America and resource-rich southern Africa. These interests are not, however, as vital as maintaining a free Western Europe was during the Cold War.

Also important to Third World involvement is ethnocentrism. Americans lack a colonial past associated with the Third World. They know little about what goes on there and lack a cultural appreciation of the problems that exist. This lack of understanding of the historical and cultural roots of the Third World causes Americans to assume that their perceptions and values can be transferred to others. When that transference has not produced positive outcomes, the result has been to shy away from involvements lacking a containment theme.

Removal of the East-West Overlay

The various trends and forces developing today will remove much of the East-West Cold War flavor and influence from what goes on in the Third World. The old East-West overlay was largely extraneous to real problems, so there will be some benefit to removing the distortion. However, there remains a real danger that the North will simply lose interest altogether.

On the positive side, the Cold War distortions of Third World problems may be overcome, thereby facilitating the settlements of problems that were worsened by the East-West competition. The Middle East situation illustrates this point well. Communism and Islam are fundamentally opposed belief systems, which is why the Soviets faced such difficulty in the region. The only real interest that any states, notably Syria and Iraq, had in the Soviets was in a steady supply of arms. The Soviets knew the basis of their appeal and that their continued basis for influence required the continuation of at least latent hostility in the region. If the Arabs and Israelis solve their differences peacefully, this could mean a lowering of the armaments in the various states.

The end of the Cold War raises the positive prospect of changing the basis of alignment in the region. In a post–competitive world, the former Soviet Union will need Middle Eastern oil more than Middle Eastern armaments revenue, which will be a major force of stability. This was obvious in the Soviets' support of the United Nations resolutions underpinning Desert Storm in 1990. American and Soviet sponsorship of negotiations on the Palestinian issue in 1991 and 1992 also reflected the changed atmosphere of the post–Cold War environment.

The effect of the former opponents acting to calm rather than stir up regional problems will likely be positive, but there is a negative side to receding involvement. In at least three ways, a reduced role could adversely affect what goes on in the Third World in the 1990s.

First, a decline in American or Russian presence may result in fewer Western resources flowing into the region. As noted earlier, internal concerns predispose the North to redirect its resources—especially its investments—closer to home. The North-South economic gap may still widen substantially even if large transfers of wealth from North to South occur (reversing the current South-to-North flow); the reduction of presence can only accentuate the differences in economic performance.

Second, a lessening commitment will mean a decline in the ability— and probably the willingness—of the Cold War opponents to restrain conflicts within and between Third World countries. In many cases, one or the other was the sole source of arms in various countries, providing a good deal of leverage for the suppliers, especially because of the need for spare parts, ammunition, servicing, and the like. Historically, a central purpose of arms transfers has been to gain leverage over the recipient. If the superpowers cease to be the major suppliers to the Third World, then the buyers will benefit from more market-oriented arms trade.

Soviet actions in Jordan in 1970 and in Iraq in 1990 illustrate this problem. In 1970, Syria, which received almost all its arms from the Soviets, planned and began to execute an intervention into Jordan during that country's civil war to protect the Palestinian refugee camps that had come under attack by King Hussein's Arab Legion. The intervention was never consummated. Mindful of the volatility of the situation and its prospects for escalation, the Soviets simply told the Syrians to end their intervention; dependent on Soviet resupply, they did. In contrast, when Iraqi President Saddam Hussein contemplated the invasion of Kuwait in 1990, he already possessed a formidable arsenal of Soviet arms obtained from non-Soviet sources, as well as international sources of resupply. It did not matter if the Soviets disapproved of his actions.

In the absence of major power actions to restrain regional conflicts, controlling these types of conflicts will be more difficult in the future.

Efforts to do so will probably have to be multilateral—building international consensus against certain actions and developing multilateral ways to respond to transgressions, including means such as economic sanctions. The way in which the international community eventually mediates a settlement of the Cambodian situation, monitoring Vietnamese withdrawal without allowing the murderous Khmer Rouge of Pol Pot to return to power, will give some indication of how international efforts will evolve.

Third, the absence of superpower competition is likely to stimulate the rise of hegemonic Third World regional countries. The idea is that individual countries in various parts of the Third World would like to be more than a part of the regional balance of power, aspiring instead to dominance of their small part of the world. During the Cold War, the struggle to balance influence restrained these countries; today, there are no restraints.

The hegemonic phenomenon was an important aspect of the Persian Gulf crisis. Saddam Hussein is a prototypical regional hegemon, and his ultimate fate will encourage or discourage others' actions. At the same time, the attempt to frustrate his hegemonical desires raises questions about what kinds of regional outcomes are sought when a hegemon is thwarted. If Saddam's power was reduced significantly, the other candidate for hegemony, Iran, would become the most powerful Gulf nation. It is doubtful that the world's interests would be well served if Iran's Ali Akbar Hashemi Rafsanjani adopted the role to which Saddam aspires. Other potential regional hegemons include Vietnam, India, Nigeria, Brazil, and Argentina.

SOUTH-SOUTH AND NORTH-SOUTH CONFLICT
AND THE NEW WORLD ORDER

Three factors reasonably ensure that instability, conflict, and violence in the Third World will continue as the new international order evolves: (1) the continued presence of internal grievances both within and between Third World states, (2) the absence of formal restraints (such as those imposed by the superpowers during the Cold War), and (3) the limited available resources needed to ameliorate the conditions that cause conflict.

The First World's policy for dealing with the ongoing crisis in the Third World will need to be reformulated because the removal of the Cold War overlay has left the absence of a guiding concept for driving foreign policy toward the Third World. The new policy will face three different kinds of situations: traditional conflicts between and within Third World countries (South-South conflict); newly emerging problems, such as the narcotics flow that affects the North directly and unavoidably (North-South conflict); and the continuing North-South debate over economic and political development.

The South-South Dimension

There is little reason to expect the pattern of violence in the Third World to abate in the upcoming decade. Grievances still exist, and their political and economic solutions remain elusive. With external restraints either absent or problematic, the situation may even worsen.

The stability of internal governance is not well established in much of Asia and Africa and in parts of Latin America. As a result, numerous instances of internal violence continue there, usually in the form of insurgencies against vulnerable ruling groups. Espousing communism or anticommunism will not generate much outside assistance in the future; the new problem for dissidents, then, will be finding sponsorship for their activities.

Regional conflicts between historic rival states are also likely to occur. The most obvious examples include the Persian Gulf (Iran-Iraq-Saudi Arabia), South Asia (India-Pakistan), Southeast Asia (Vietnam-Thailand), Northeast Asia (the Koreas), and, slightly less plausibly, South America (Argentina-Brazil-Chile).

The Cold War restrained these types of conflicts. Typically, the Soviets backed one side and the United States the other. To maintain control, a balance was created between the parties and neither side gained dominance. That control has dissipated. Partly due to superpower policies, Third World regional powers are heavily armed with lethal weapons, such as chemical and biological warfare agents and ballistic missile means of delivery. Moreover, Third World states increasingly produce these deadly weapons, further diminishing the prospects for outside influence and control.

How will the North deal with these problems? The most advanced states may define their vital Third World interests more narrowly than before, making them less likely to interfere, especially with armed force. At the same time, however, there may be times when involvement is deemed necessary—the imminent fall of a close associate (the success of the New People's Army in the Philippines), the likely moral tragedy of noninterference (Pol Pot in Cambodia), or the geopolitics of disorder (the secession of Shaba province from Zaire) could all provoke response.

The danger in the massive escalation of regional conflicts raises serious concerns. Many states that possess chemical weapons ("poor man's nuclear weapons") are near nuclear weaponry capacity. Consider, for instance, the world's response to a possible India-Pakistan war over Kashmir that threatened to go nuclear, or to Saddam Hussein's threat to attack Israel with nuclear weapons, thereby provoking a nuclear response. How the First World reacts to these kinds of potential situations will greatly influence the pattern of Third World instability in the future.

New North-South Challenges

Two factors are likely to be important in the First World-Third World relationship. First, in most instances, First World interests are not fundamentally affected by Third World events. Who controls Cambodia does not really affect the daily lives of most Americans, for example. However, control of Persian Gulf oil by a hostile state and a regional conflict escalating to a nuclear exchange are among the exceptions. Second, the states of the South lack the power, militarily or economically, to force Northern compliance with their positions.

However, there is a new category of interactions in which the North cannot ignore the South—*transnational problems* are issues inherently international in character and beyond solution by any single state. Moreover, in the current context, many of these problems affect both the First and Third Worlds and can only be solved by mutual interaction.

Some transnational problems are peaceful, such as environmental degradation (pollution, ozone layer depletion, and the like). Similarly, deforestation of the Amazon Basin creates problems for both worlds. Other transnational concerns involve more direct national security problems with military and paramilitary overtones. For example, countering the narcotics trade is a North-South problem because most narcotics are produced in the Third World (coca in South America, opium in Southeast Asia) but consumed in the First World. One approach to solving the drug problem involves eradication of source supplies and interdiction of the supply heading north. Such actions require cooperation between First and Third World governments.

Another example of a transnational problem is counterterrorism. The grievances that give rise to terrorist organizations occur mainly in the Third World, making it the "source" of the terrorism problem. Most terrorist acts are carried out against other Southerners, though there are occasions, especially in the Middle East, when First Worlders are the victims, as in kidnappings, airplane bombings, and the like. If terrorist acts spread more generally northward, cooperative means of dealing with them will be necessary.

The North-South Developmental Dialogue

Third World problems will not disappear in the absence of the substantial economic and political development of the region in ways compatible with the various cultures in which such development must take place. Development will not guarantee the end of instability and violence; while it is a necessary condition, it may or may not solve the problems of the Third World.

The gap between rich and poor countries is widening for two reasons. First, although the high technology revolution is transforming the global economic system, most of its benefits are confined to the First World. There are exceptions, such as the new emerging economic powers called the "Four Tigers" (South Korea, Taiwan, Hong Kong, Singapore), but these may not necessarily provide role models for others to follow. Second, the debt accumulated by several Third World countries, especially in Latin America, is coming due, and the flow of resources from North to South has reversed as a result. Since the mid-1980s, the interest and principal on loan repayments from Third World to First World countries has physically exceeded (by $10 billion or more annually) the capital flowing into the Third World for developmental purposes.

Historically, rich countries have been able to view such problems as regrettable but not so compelling as to demand a response. Developmental assistance has not been a high priority, and there has been little that the Third World could do to force attention to its problems.

There are two possible sources of change for the evolving world order. First, the Third World is likely to be the exclusive source of instability in the world. If the successor states of the Soviet Union continue to Westernize, the new order is likely to place a much higher value on stability than before, thereby creating a greater incentive to decrease instability and violence wherever they occur.

Second, a stabilized Third World will provide good business opportunities for the new market-based international economic order. All the great undeveloped markets are in the Third World, which is also where the bulk of the world's population resides. The dynamics of the economic revolution suggest that transferring certain parts of the global production process to the Third World—where labor is cheaper and will probably remain so—may result in positive-sum economic outcomes that will benefit all.

CONCLUSION

This chapter introduces the significant changes in international politics, highlighted by the revolutions of 1989, as well as their impact on the developed and developing worlds. As such, it provides the context for understanding the causes and kinds of Third World conflict with which the new international system will have to deal.

The international system is in the midst of its most fundamental change since 1945. The change began in and has had its greatest impact on Central Europe, but its effects will reach people worldwide. The outcomes of change in various parts of the world, and especially in Eastern Europe and the former Soviet Union, are uncertain.

One aspect of change is immutable: the end of the Cold War competition between communism and anticommunism symbolized by the Soviet-American political-military confrontation. Regardless of how reform in the former Soviet Union evolves in the future, the Marxist-Leninist philosophy is no longer an intellectual competitor to political democracy and the economic marketplace. The only true Marxists left are in Cuba, China, and North Korea. In this sense, we have reached political analyst and former State Department official Francis Fukuyama's "end of history," in that there are no longer any intellectual alternatives to the Western notion. This does not mean challengers will not return; for now, fundamentalist Islam is the only potential challenger.

Uncertainty about how the new international system will evolve in the First World is amplified in the Third World. To the extent that it was not already the case, the Third World will experience ongoing instability and violence in the new order. This is nothing new, for the vast majority of wars since around 1950 have been in the Third World, as have the overwhelming majority of First World interventions and military engagements.

Third World conflict is likely to occur in the context of general tranquillity—or at least in the absence of major conflict—elsewhere. There are residual sources of potential violence in the political adjustment to the breakup of the Soviet Union and the process of territorial adjustment in Central Europe and the Balkans. The Balkans have a long history of producing political problems bigger than they can handle themselves, and nowhere is this clearer than in the tragic nationalist-religious breakup of Yugoslavia. However, there is a universal desire for the common goal of political and economic Westernization.

During the Cold War period, the existence and severity of Third World conflicts were muted because of the centrality of the military competition in nuclear-armed rockets and the conventional balance in Germany. To the extent that the Third World was a concern, it was because the Cold War spilled over into Third World problems. With the Cold War ended, Third World conflict will move into the spotlight.

The centrality of Third World conflict for the war regulation system marking the new order makes the handling of Third World conflict critically important to how that order evolves. The historic approach of neglect will not cure the underlying causes of Third World violence, which are rooted in inequities and deprivations both within and between nations of the region. These will continue to worsen if left untreated.

The alternative to dealing with the causes of problems is to find an effective way to deal with the symptoms—in this case, the Third World's pattern of instability and violence. It is likely that internal wars will continue to plague the region in the forms of insurgencies, terrorism, and other types of disruption. In addition, the withdrawal of superpower involvement in the Third World may result in hegemonic behavior among some countries.

CHAPTER 2

Third World Problems in a First World–Dominated Global System

The problems in the Third World that periodically give rise to violence are deep, varied, and fundamental in nature. An understanding of them, therefore, is crucial to any attempt to find solutions and end the violence. Many Third World problems are rooted in the colonial experience that began after World War II, particularly in the Middle East, Africa, and most of Asia. Much of Latin America, while politically independent since the nineteenth century, has remained economically and otherwise dependent on the North.

The major problem in the Third World is development. Although the First and Third Worlds are divided by their many differences, most of these differences are related to development. Generally, the First World developed politically through evolving governmental systems that are broadly representative and generally supported by their populations. This is not true of most of the Third World. Furthermore, the developed world experienced the First Industrial Revolution (basic industrialization), progressed through the Second Industrial Revolution (the orientation of the economy to service and consumer functions), and is now in the Third Industrial Revolution (the information-based economy). In contrast, much of the Third World has not even entered the First Industrial Revolution.

As a result, there is an enormous gap between the rich and poor nations of the world, and it continues to widen. In addition, the disparities between the wealthiest and poorest people within many Third World countries are becoming greater. In some Third World capital cities, for example, the contrast between gleaming steel-and-glass high rises and cardboard shanty homes is striking indeed. This disparity has become increasingly difficult to mask because of the growth of the mass media. Fifty years ago, people living in the Asian countryside may have realized their situation was hard, but they probably did not know that their life-style was neither universal nor irreversible. Urbanization has revealed these disparities, and the mass media, particularly television, have made the differences apparent to all.

Given its situation, then, the Third World looks to the First World for assistance in development. Its cry for help goes back to the period of decolonization. At that time, the countries granted independence by the European powers were desperately poor, structurally ill-prepared to help themselves out of poverty, and almost totally unprepared for self-governance. That they turned to the countries that left them that way is not surprising.

In terms of structure, the Third World's problems are similar to those facing the former Soviet Union today. Both areas of the world are facing crises that are political, economic, and ethnic or national in nature.

Politically, most Third World problems stem from a lack of legitimacy and authority in government. There is no real political loyalty to the nation-state or its government, which has ethnic (national), historical, linguistic, religious, and cultural bases. Economically, there is a physical inability to provide adequately for all of the society's members, thereby creating the situation in which some groups prosper at the expense of others. The ethnic dimension reflects the multinational nature of most Third World nation-states (that is, they contain various population segments of different nationalities). The political struggle, therefore, is often between national groups seeking political control and economic power.

It is difficult for Westerners, especially Americans, to understand the types of problems facing the Third World. In a stable political system, Americans can debate government policies. There is usually no question about the legitimacy of the system, since economic adequacy is available to most Americans. And while ethnic problems still exist, they do not threaten to undermine the American life-style. Furthermore, the United States has faced crises similar to those confronting Third World countries today: Some examples include the bloody Civil War that determined the form of the political system as well as the difficult period of economic development during the latter part of the nineteenth century. In addition, the U.S. civil rights struggle for equal access to the political system continues today.

But what does this have to do with the conflict in the Third World, especially that which can potentially disturb the international system and draw the United States into military action? The answer is clear: The problems of political and economic development are the underlying *causes* of the conflicts in the Third World. Those conflicts, in turn, are *effects* of the underlying causes. As long as the causes go untreated, conflict will continue.

THE CRISIS OF LEGITIMACY AND AUTHORITY

The most basic political problem in the Third World is a lack of stability. Although there are several interrelated dimensions to the instability, they all stem from the absence of nationalism in the Third World.

At the political level, the Third World has difficulty with authority (the power to govern). The crisis of authority is present at both the state and government levels. The constitutionally defined institutions that formally make up the state, or the individuals who hold positions of power created by the state (the government), or both, may not be acceptable to certain segments of the population, who, in turn, refuse to accept their rule.

In contrast, the developed world has usually overcome problems of authority. Over time, the population comes to accept a system of governance that it deems appropriate, fair, and worthy of its support. As a result, the state is accepted as having legitimate authority; its power to govern is based on consent.

This process has not occurred in much of the developing world, where consent is absent and authority is placed in the hands of some charismatic figure or is dominated by the tradition of subservience. Again, the authority problem is related to the absence or weakness of nationalism in the Third World. *Nationalism*—a shared sense of identity with one's nation—is the basis on which authority develops.

Multinationalism and Irredentism

Much of the crisis in Third World countries stems from the fact that they are *artificial nation-states*. To understand what this means and why it is a problem, we must first discuss the term *nation-state* and why its application to the Third World situation is difficult. The hyphenated word *nation-state* refers to two separate concepts. *Nation* is an anthropological term that means loyalty to a group. *Nationality* refers to a person's identification with a certain group or nation. Most nations are distinguished by such characteristics as ethnicity, language, history or myth, and religion.

State is a legal and political term. It refers to legal jurisdictions within which some state apparatus claims exclusive jurisdiction over maintaining order, to de facto control of territory, and to diplomatic recognition by other states. A common problem arises when state jurisdictions are not the same as the habitation patterns of various national groups. State boundaries may do one or both of two confounding things: (1) They may incorporate several national groups within one state (as in the African nation-states, where nationality is often expressed tribally) or (2) They may separate national groups so that the members of a nation inhabit several states.

The first situation, called *multinationalism,* affects Africa, most of the Middle East, parts of Asia, the former Soviet Union (including most of the newly independent republics), and much of Eastern and Central Europe. Multinationalism poses two problems in terms of state authority. First, in multinational states, people tend to be more loyal to their own national group than to the nation-state. This occurred in Nigeria in 1960 when it was granted independence: most people did not suddenly consider themselves Nigerians but continued to identify with their own tribal groups. Thirty years later, the authority process in the Nigerian state is still incomplete. There are still many who think of themselves as more Ibo or Hausa-Fulani than Nigerian.

The other problem with multinationalism is that the political struggles within states tend to be between national groups. In these states, national groups rule at the expense of other nationalities and without official legitimacy. In the early years of Nigerian independence, for example, the political struggle was between the largely Islamic Hausa-Fulani of the northern region and the Christian Ibo of the eastern region. When the Hausas' control became oppressive in 1967, the Ibo attempted to secede and form the independent state of Biafra.

Multinationalism attacks the authority of both state and government. Until there is loyalty to the state, the state is not viewed as worthy of its citizens' identification with it. In this case, the government is usually accepted only by those groups in power and is considered illegitimate by the groups whose loyalty rests elsewhere.

The absence of loyalty to the national government is common in much of the Third World, especially in Africa and the Middle East. It was clear after Desert Storm in 1991, for instance, that many Kurds identify more with Kurdistan than with Iraq. In central Africa, where nationalism is largely based on tribal identification, the small state of Rwanda-Burundi broke apart into the separate states of Rwanda and Burundi in 1962.

Another problem arises when state boundaries divide national groups. These divisions tend to create a universal drive among the members of the divided nations to unite and form their own independent national state at the expense of the larger state. Such movements, known as *irredentist,* exist worldwide. In the Horn of Africa, for example, ethnic Somalis living in the Ogaden region of Ethiopia have long fought to become a part of adjacent Somalia. Similarly, the Kurds of Iran, Iraq (where many Kurdish tribespeople were killed by the government with chemical weapons in 1988), Turkey, and the former Soviet Azerbaijan have sought since the end of World War I to form Kurdistan. In Central Europe, there remains postrevolutionary tension about the Romanian province of Transylvania, which is ruled by Romania but whose citizens are primarily Hungarian. In the former western Soviet republic of Moldavia, now known as the Republic of Moldava, the population is overwhelmingly of the same ethnicity of Romania, and may seek union with Romania. The former Soviet Republic of Azerbaijan and the Iranian province of Azerbaijan provide another example.

Because nationality is so enduring, it will remain a source of friction, instability, and violence in the Third World as long as its nation-states ignore national realities. In the former Soviet Union, the problem was the forceful inclusion of nations into the state via conquest, a process reversed by the implosion of the Soviet state. In others, the culprit has been receding colonialism. The maps of most Third World states, drawn by Europeans, do not represent the national realities that existed prior to European rule. Rather, the maps created multiple or divided individual nationalities within and among states, which has led to internal violence and conflict. Much African internal violence can be traced back to a contest between the major tribal groups within the state. Similarly, the imperfections of postcolonial maps can be used by someone like Saddam Hussein to justify "reclaiming" Kuwait as the nineteenth "natural" province of Iraq.

There are only two possible solutions to the problem of state boundaries. One is to realign the state boundaries on the basis of nationality and statehood. This would permit all members of a nation to live within a single state, and no state would contain more than one nationality. The problem with this solution, however, is that there are too many national groups for each one to be given a state. The result would be thousands of tiny nation-states, few of which could be economically viable. Another problem is the considerable movement of peoples across former boundaries into areas where they are now a minority. Matching up nationalities with state territories would require mass migrations, which are usually accompanied by considerable hardship and suffering.

The first solution, then, is clearly impractical. The other possible solution involves encouraging the transfer of loyalty from more parochial bases to the state. This is likely to be a difficult and lengthy process for most Third World states, but there are no other practical alternatives.

Authority and Legitimacy

One major dimension of the problem of loyalty transfer is reconciling the different values of different national groups. Legitimacy requires that

Table 2.1   Bases of Authority

	Authority	
Basis	Legitimacy	Coercion
Outcome	Justice	Injustice
Nature	Stable order	Unstable order

a state's authority be based on a set of commonly accepted values. When several sets of conflicting values exist within a state, national groups become distrustful of one another and it becomes extremely difficult to define a mutually agreeable set of values on which to base the state's authority.

This brings us to the central point about the basis of authority. As shown in Table 2.1, authority can be based on legitimacy or coercion. The major distinction is how the authority of the state is derived. Legitimacy refers to the right to rule via popular consent; thus, a regime is legitimate to the extent that its people consider it deserving of support. In turn, the public's judgment is based on the belief that both state and government rule follow an accepted set of doctrines and values. In many Third World countries, attachment to a charismatic leader or a tradition of obedience may form the consensual base.

In contrast, coercion is the imposition of force intended to compel compliance with the political system and government. The need for coercion, of course, presumes that compliance would not occur if people were free to act on their own. Government systems based on coercion are illegitimate; they are viewed as unjust by much of the population.

The authority problem in Third World countries, then, is linked to both authority and legitimacy. In the developed world, governments are widely viewed as legitimate: most people willingly associate with them and, with the exception of criminal elements, comply with their rules. In much of the Third World, however, at least some portion of the population views the state or the government as illegitimate and not worthy of support. Where the perception of injustice exists, there may arise individuals and groups who promise justice through the overthrow of unjust, illegitimate rulers. Thus, the absence of legitimate authority is directly related to the potential for violence in the Third World.

Another way to view the situation is to examine the power and strength relationship between a society and its state in terms of cohesiveness. As shown in Figure 2.1, a strong society is characterized by cohesion; its members basically agree on the values that determine governance. In a strong society, the majority of the population has conferred

Figure 2.1   State and Society

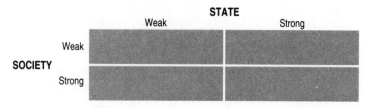

legitimacy on and willingly accepts the authority. In contrast, a weak society is characterized by population segments that do not support the authority (the larger this group is, the weaker the society will be). A state's strength refers to the amount of coerciveness it has (or needs) to maintain control of the population (or to enforce its authority).

In most First World societies, the state is weak (governance does not depend greatly on coercion) because the society is strong. This is generally not true of the Third World, where the imperfect combination of nation and state results in weak and fragmented societies. When a society is weak, the state must be strong or the result is chaos. One compelling example of this is Lebanon, where internal control is weak and Syrian occupation forces are the vehicles of Lebanese coercion.

Many developing countries have chosen a compromise—a high capacity for government coercion while development builds consensus and creates legitimacy. The problem is how to form national consensus within the state's boundaries, a process known as *nation-building.*

How can these countries create loyalty transfer to the state? Coercion can mask the public's lack of identification with the state, as was successfully done in Eastern Europe during the period of Soviet occupation. Yet coercion cannot bring about conversion. The extent to how the changes in Eastern Europe and the fractiousness, latent and actual, of the successor states to the former Soviet Union occur, will help or hinder their development into legitimate states, and may be instructive for the nation-building process in the Third World.

Third World states face loyalty transfer problems as well. Unlike the Third World, however, Eastern Europeans at least have something in common—a desire for political freedom and economic prosperity through the transformation of their economies. Their road to success will also be made easier by their more educated populations, skilled labor forces, and government workers who can aid the movement to prosperity. Success will be far more difficult for the Third World. In order for its populations to transfer their loyalties to national governments, they must first see some benefits in doing so. Whether political or economic, the benefits must be demonstrated for the transfer of loyalties to occur.

One dilemma has hindered efforts at development intended to facilitate nation-building in the Third World. It has to do with where change or reform should occur first—by granting political freedoms (weakening the state's coercive mechanisms) or introducing economic reform that would make conversion possible. The problem is that doing one may make the other more difficult to execute.

If reform begins by weakening state coercive mechanisms, two negative outcomes are possible. First, for the society divided into antagonistic nationalities, freedom will only exaggerate the divisions as well as secessionist desires. Second, freedom will allow the expression of discontent with the economic order, whose lack of development and provision of well-being to the vast majority are parts of the definition of underdevelopment.

The alternative approach is to begin the nation-building process with economic modernization while maintaining tight political control and strong state coercion (as in China). This approach also has several drawbacks, however. First, underdeveloped societies are usually oligarchical; that is, a handful of people in power maintain the economic control of production and the coercive reins of the state. Most economic changes that could strengthen the society would adversely affect these people, so they are unlikely to respond in a positive way. Second, economic development typically requires outside assistance, but governments and private investors are increasingly reluctant to provide funds to repressive and inherently unstable developing countries.

The former Soviet Union is a classic example of a strong state with a weak society. The country contained an amalgam of conquered peoples who largely had not abandoned their national identities. The society was weak, and the classic Imperial Russian/Soviet Communist response was highly coercive in order to suppress societal differences. The system brought about the economic crisis that began in the 1970s and came into public view in the mid-1980s. The strong Soviet state both controlled dissent and stifled economic growth. In order for the economy to recover and compete, it had to be freed from the shackles of state control. The state's (Communist party's) control of the economy had to be loosened. Gorbachev and his followers were forced to weaken the state so that economic rejuvenation could be given a chance to create legitimacy for the system. It was a gamble, and it failed. The process of economic transformation reduced the quality of life in the Soviet Union. As a result, the loosening of state coercion only exacerbated the unraveling of the society.

Gorbachev started by weakening the state and learned that freeing the people allowed them to express their national aspirations. The result was the collapse of the Soviet state and its replacement with a series of independent states that are more nationally defined.

If development is to occur in the Third World, the Soviet case may serve as an example of how not to proceed. Many Third World countries with a weak society have sought to compensate for that weakness with authoritarian rule. Such rule, however, tends to stifle economic initiative and growth, as it did in the former Soviet Union. The key is balancing the political and economic dimensions of development in a way that will enhance legitimacy—and avoid Soviet-style disintegration.

ECONOMIC AND SOCIAL CAUSES OF CONFLICT

Developing and maintaining broad-based public loyalty to the nation-state is relatively easy in areas where the quality of life is high and people are able to improve their lives. This is generally true of the advanced world, where problems of nationalism and state authority and legitimacy are relatively rare.

The same cannot be said of the Third World. A variety of structural and human problems related to limited material resources combine to create a wretched existence for most people living in developing countries. These problems include accumulated foreign debt and debt service, population growth and its demographic effects, inadequate and maldistributed food supplies, crushing poverty, disease, inadequate medical care, economic underdevelopment and maldistribution, underdeveloped human and material infrastructures, religious divisions that manifest themselves in violence, battles over environmental degradation, and many others. Some of these problems are more or less severe in certain countries. The relatively affluent countries located around the Pacific Rim, for example, have overcome many of their problems and are poised to join the First World. In other countries, though, these problems continue to hinder the support needed to create political stability. Until most of the problems are overcome, the violence will remain.

Debt and Debt Service

During the 1960s and early 1970s, public and private sources from the West began to invest massively in selected parts of the Third World. The public sources (such as national foreign aid and multilateral developmental assistance) invested in the hopes of aiding development and the transition to stability; the private sources (mostly banks) had a profit motive. A great deal of money was loaned to the most developed Third World countries (such as Brazil) and to those with valuable natural resources (such as oil). The revenues from the resources were to be used to facilitate repayment (as in Nigeria and Mexico).

However, some of the investments were not made wisely. Rather than investing borrowed funds in self-liquidating projects (those with profits that could be used to repay loans), the investments were made in non-self-liquidating ways, leaving the question of sources of repayment unanswered. In the worst cases, loans were used for social welfare payments to prop up the popularity of governments. In other cases, the ability to repay was based on overly optimistic projections about national revenues (as in steadily upward projections for petroleum prices in light of the oil "shocks" of 1973 and 1977).

Before the binge of lending ended, many Third World nations found themselves deeply in debt to foreign private creditors demanding repayment. Bad investment decisions, ignorance or malfeasance on the part of governments, and corruption added to the problem of how to meet payments. The answer often was to tap funds targeted for development.

Debt-service burden is the ratio of the amount of foreign currency owed in interest payments on past loans divided by the amount earned in foreign trading. The lower the ratio is, the healthier the economy and the more resources are left for investment. As the ratio rises, and especially as it approaches unity, there is progressively less left for developmental (or any other) purposes, much less for retiring the principal on loans.

The individual and cumulative effects of the Third World's debt burden are overwhelming. Brazil, the largest debtor nation after the United States, had a foreign debt of about $95 billion in 1982. In the ensuing five years, Brazil made payments of $70 billion against its loans, but its overall debt rose to $115 billion. The current situation is so bad that Brazil has to borrow additional money to pay the interest on its accumulated debt (the new loans, of course, add to its debt-service burden). The cumulative effect has been to reverse the flow of capital from North–South to South–North: There is now more money being sent from Third World countries to the First World than the other way around, a kind of reverse development. For the overall international financial system, the net flow from South to North in 1988 was $43 billion.

As a result of the debt-service burden, banks are increasingly reluctant to loan money to Third World countries. Many countries have had to restructure their debts (by negotiating more lenient and longer repayment schedules), while others have threatened to renege on the loans (by declaring the national equivalence of bankruptcy). The First World banking industry has been weakened by these potentially uncollectable loans. In addition, many Third World countries fear an overall reduction in available capital as the First World redirects its investment capital to the emerging former Second World countries of Eastern Europe and the former Soviet Union. Finally, fluctuation of the commodity prices of products that Third World countries sell and buy makes financial management difficult (this is known as the *terms of trade* problem).

The debt problem will hinder development in the Third World. In order to qualify for available funds, Third World countries are asked to institute economic austerity programs so as to demonstrate their responsibility and solvency. These programs require enforced savings and sacrifices from the citizenry that are politically difficult and seemingly hypocritical when compared to the economic profligacy of the First World during the 1980s. The problem is circular: To get the money necessary for the economic development on which political development is based, Third World countries are asked to take actions that threaten their political stability.

Until the debt problem is solved, other types of developmental progress are unlikely as well. Money may not solve all problems, but its absence reasonably ensures that the major problems facing the Third World will remain unsolved. This is why the debt problem is high on the North-South agenda. Its solution may require the determination in the North that solving the debt burden is cheaper than dealing with the political violence and instability that underdevelopment creates.

Population

The Third World population problem is multifaceted and controversial. Its facets include the pace and pattern of population growth, the demographics of Third World population and habitation patterns, and population movement both within and between Third World countries. It is controversial because substantial disagreement exists about what causes the population growth problem, how serious it is, and what to do about it.

The dynamics of population growth are straightforward. For any country, changes in population size (the population growth rate or PGR) can be calculated by this formula: birthrate (BR) minus death rate (DR) plus or minus net migration ($Mig.$) ($PGR = BR - DR +/- Mig.$). For the world population, the migration figure drops out (no one migrates off the globe). When the birthrate exceeds the death rate, the result is population growth; when the death rate exceeds the birthrate, the result is contraction.

Population growth is a problem both because the overall world population is growing and because it is growing faster in some places than in others. The world's total population was 4.4 billion in 1980; by the year 2000, it is expected to rise to about 6.2 billion. After climbing at a slower rate during the first quarter of the twenty-first century, most experts expect the numbers to stabilize.

However, population growth is differential. Of the 1.8 billion people added to the world's population by the year 2000, 1.6 billion of them will reside in the Third World. Moreover, the populations of the People's Republic of China and India will reach 1.2 billion and 1.1 billion, respectively, by the year 2000, meaning that more than one out of every three people living will reside in one of those two countries. The year 2000 population of Mexico (130 million) will be half that of the United States (260 million). Brazil's population of 200 million will represent almost two-thirds of the total population of South America in 2000.

We know what causes population growth in the Third World. Starting about one hundred years ago, the death rate began to decline dramatically because of the introduction of sanitary procedures and rudimentary health and medical care in places previously lacking them. The death rate also declined because of reduced infant mortality, while the birthrate remained reasonably static. The result was growth in population. This had happened in Europe following the great plagues, but it was welcomed then because the population had been depleted. In the Third World the result was over-population.

The only solution to overpopulation is to decrease the birthrate to the gross reproduction rate (GRR) of one so that the population merely replaces itself in numbers. But this will be difficult at best. In the areas where population growth is greatest, cultural or religious taboos against contraception often exist. In some cultures, for instance, having many children is a sign of virility and status; in others, children are needed to care for elderly parents. Still other countries view calls for population limits as a geopolitical ploy to keep them (or their ethnic and tribal groups) small and weak.

Population growth, however, is only one aspect of the Third World situation. Demographic composition is also a consideration. For instance, while First World populations are aging because people there are living longer, the populations of the Third World are becoming increasingly younger because of the high birthrate. It is not uncommon in developing countries for more than 50 percent of the total population to be aged fifteen years or younger. For the First World, an aging population means that more people are living beyond their productive ages, thereby creating a shrinking work force and greater demands on social services. For example, people in the First World typically make over 80 percent of their demands on the health care system during their last two years of life. In the Third World, the younger population creates two problems: (1) there are too many people looking to enter a work force plagued by inadequate employment opportunities and (2) these people, of child-reproduction age, are adding to the overpopulation problem.

Population movement both within and between developing countries is also a problem. Within many Third World countries, people migrate from rural to urban areas in search of job and other opportunities not available to them elsewhere. The cities, however, are usually not prepared for the influx, resulting in frustration and the potential for instability.

Third World populations are also migrating across borders, such as from the impoverished South to the rich North. Recently, a net influx of people moving to the First World from the Third World has begun. For the United States, for example, the influx has been largely from Central America and Asia (especially Vietnam).

In addition, there is considerable migration within the Third World. Sometimes people migrate out of economic necessity (for example, foreigners who work in the Persian Gulf oil fields). More often, though, people in the Third World migrate for political reasons—war and violence cause them to flee their countries for neighboring lands, where they become refugees and a burden on the new countries.

Population growth clearly strains a Third World already faced with so many other problems. In areas where population growth exceeds economic growth, the economy is largely absorbed by the costs of caring for the growing population. In the 1980s, the combination of low economic growth and high population growth resulted in a net decrease in the standard of living for many Third World countries. At the same time, certain demographic trends (such as urbanization) made the potential for discontent and violence even greater.

Food Supply

The food supply available to much of the Third World is inadequate in terms of both quality and quantity. Dietary deficiency debilitates people by robbing them of their ability to perform adequately. For example, if crucial nutrients like protein are not part of a child's regular diet, the result can be diminished mental capacity for life.

The food problem in the Third World is not the result of a global shortage. As a result of the "green revolution" of the 1960s as well as later scientific discoveries, there is plenty of food available to feed every person on earth. Moreover, anticipated breakthroughs in biogenetics are likely to expand food production to levels that will sustain predicted population increases well into the twenty-first century. It is how the food supply is distributed around the world, however, that is the problem. It does not reach those who need it most, such as those in the Third World. This was also a problem in the former Soviet Union, where in 1990 three-quarters of the potatoes never reached consumers because of the inadequate transportation system, a problem certain to worsen as the newly independent states struggle to establish new commercial relationships among themselves.

In addition, it is difficult to produce or grow food in areas that are marginally suited for agriculture. For example, poor soils or inadequate or overabundant rainfall can create problems. Cultivating in the Sahel region of Africa uprooted vegetation and contributed to the loss of topsoil and creeping desertification. Similarly, the ongoing destruction of the Amazon rain forest, which has very poor soil, is promoting global warming. And the use of chemical fertilizers is polluting the ecosystem.

Finally, food is withheld from the Third World for political purposes. The most dramatic examples of this occurred in the Horn of Africa, and especially in Ethiopia, during the 1970s and 1980s. Until recently, the Ethiopian government had been in a thirty-year civil war with Eritrean separatists (the Eritrean Liberation Front, or ELF). The Eritreans, who are Muslims, sought to establish their independence from the Christian-dominated government. A long draught depleted foodstuffs in Eritrea, and relief efforts intended to provide food to the Eritreans were routinely interrupted by the government. The Islamic government of neighboring Sudan was accused of doing the same to its Christian minority in the south.

Poverty

Poverty in the Third World is a long-term problem. The traditional agrarian societies that predated colonialism had a very low standard of living. Today's Third World poverty is different in many ways. For example, the desperately poor are no longer in the countryside, where extended families can provide support in bad times. There has been a massive movement of Third World populations to large urban centers that are unprepared in terms of housing and employment. As a result, large, very poor, young, unemployed or underemployed populations exist in the cities. Mexico City, for instance, is projected to have thirty million inhabitants by the year 2000.

Furthermore, the plight of the poor in the Third World continues to deteriorate. The growth and prosperity that characterized the First World in the 1980s did not occur in the Third World. Population increases, rising energy costs, and the reverse flow of capital back to the First World combined to drive per capita income down in many developing countries.

In addition, the global revolution in telecommunications has made world conditions transparent. Previously, people living in desperate poverty usually did not know that their condition was not universal. Today, the mass media, especially television, make the discrepancies between the rich and poor known to all.

Finally, as poverty in the Third World deepens and becomes more obvious, it also becomes less tolerable and acceptable. Of course, the unacceptability of poverty does not pose a direct threat to the First World because the Third World is too poor and weak to try to seize its wealth. The discrepancies between rich and poor, however, will continue to ensure instability and violence in many developing countries. Also, an increasing response to poverty is to escape it through illegal immigration across porous borders.

Disease

Although improvements in basic health services helped to trigger the population explosion, good medical care remains the exception for many people of the Third World. Diseases long eradicated in the First World, such as child blindness preventable by simple vitamin dosages, still prevail in many developing areas. Good health care remains the exclusive preserve of the wealthy and privileged.

In recent years, much of the Third World, especially Africa, has experienced an epidemic of sexually transmitted diseases. This may be explained by the youthfulness of the population; young people are among the most sexually active yet the least educated on sexual matters.

The greatest threat is AIDS. It is estimated that as much as 20 percent of the youthful male populations in some African nations are infected by the virus, and the numbers are growing. In the absence of a cure, many African nations are facing the prospect of a lost generation to provide leadership for their countries. Most developing countries refuse to discuss the problem openly, in part because preventive efforts have been largely ineffective and the prognosis is so bleak.

Economic Underdevelopment and Maldistribution of Wealth

Most Third World nations suffer from two major economic difficulties that frustrate their political and economic stability: economic underdevelopment and maldistribution of wealth.

Underdevelopment means that there are inadequate resources to sustain growth and improve the overall economic competitiveness; thus, most Third World countries remain poor compared to First World countries. Second, most of the available wealth is in the hands of a few whose commitment to investing that wealth for the betterment of the public is often limited or suspect.

The level of underdevelopment in the Third World varies considerably among countries. Some states, especially those who export petroleum and are hence quite wealthy, are modestly developed in political terms (for example, the Persian Gulf sheikdoms). The NICs of the Pacific Rim are not far behind. In some cases, such as in the Republic of Korea, Brazil, and Argentina, a future claim to First World status is not implausible if their debts can be repaid.

Although several other developing countries have experienced some progress, they are so overwhelmed by debt that their future is questionable; Nigeria is an example. Some states, such as Indonesia, have industrial potential but lack the infrastructural development or resources to succeed without substantial outside assistance. Finally, those states at the bottom lack the human or natural resources to rise from poverty (such as Bangladesh and the West African Sahel region).

Most Third World countries, however, experience some level of economic misery, but the portions of the populations who suffer the most are increasingly less willing to accept their misery. Moreover, poor states no longer accept their poverty willingly; they expect and demand help in escaping it. At times, this puts them at odds with the First World, as is the case with Peru. The Peruvian economy has essentially collapsed; its only major base of foreign exchange is the revenue it generates from growing coca (the plant from which cocaine is derived). The United States seeks Peruvian assistance in eradicating this crop; though the Fujimori government in Lima is sympathetic, their sympathy is tinged with the reality that destroying coca also undermines the fragile economy and even more fragile democracy, as the suspension of the Constitution in April 1992 demonstrated.

Another problem is the maldistribution of wealth within Third World societies. Typically, wealth is concentrated in the hands of the elite, who control economic resources, land, and the political system, either directly or through surrogates. The result is incipient instability. Third World masses are increasingly unwilling to accept great disparity in the standard of living; they demand change, including democratization and land reform. Those in power often oppose reform because they would lose at least some of their wealth in the process. Maldistribution also can have an ethnic base; in Pakistan, for instance, the Punjabis disproportionately control the lion's share of resources.

Economic maldistribution and elite opposition to reform help to create the Third World insurgencies that bring the United States into possible involvement. In these instances, a major source of frustration is the intransigence of the elite to the kinds of changes that would undercut support for the insurgency. One example of this problem was the American relationship with President Ngo Dinh Diem of the Republic of Vietnam before his assassination. Another is the decade-long U.S. assistance program to El Salvador that culminated in 1992, when the goverment agreed to negotiate on the issues—especially land—that energized the insurgency.

A confounding aspect of maldistribution is capital flight. Because the resources of most Third World societies are concentrated within the hands of a few people, they are the only internal source of funds for development. However, underdevelopment and economic instability have caused many wealthy Third Worlders to invest in the First World or to stash their money into First World banks to avoid expropriation. The resulting capital flight from South to North aggravates the reverse capital flow associated with debt servicing.

Infrastructure

The two general sources of external funding for Third World economic development are public and private. Public funding includes bilateral developmental assistance (foreign aid) as well as assistance from multilateral lenders (such as the agencies of the World Bank). Private funds include loans and private investment by foreign (including multinational) corporations.

Ideologically, there is a strong First World preference for private investment. This arises from the experience of the 1980s, where deregulation and privatization helped fuel the great economic expansion worldwide, as well as from a widespread First World adherence to the principles of market economy. Private investors are naturally most attracted to those places where they can maximize their profits. For many, this means that a Third World nation is attractive to the extent that it has a policy and physical environment most conducive to private enterprise—that is, governmental policies that minimize interference in business activities and that maximize advantages like tax breaks and a strong infrastructure base.

The infrastructure base consists of both physical and human components. Physically, things such as road and railroad networks, port facilities, and sources of consistent and economical energy are necessary for manufacturing facilities to operate efficiently. An example of human commitment is the government's dedication to producing an educated population that is capable of performing more than unskilled or semiskilled labor. Those Third World countries able to provide such a profile, such as the NICs of the Pacific Rim, have successfully attracted large amounts of foreign investment.

However, many developing countries lack an adequately developed infrastructure to attract foreign investors. Here infrastructure projects are generally not self-liquidating (for example, a loan targeted for educational purposes is not a profit-generating endeavor and so repayment of the loan is questionable). Non-self-liquidating loans are unappealing to private banks with limited resources, so the source for infrastructural development often must be public. To attract private capital, developing countries must adopt austerity budgets that will generate funds and present a "responsible" fiscal profile. Such measures are politically unpopular because they demand personal sacrifices. Moreover, developmental assistance with generous repayment terms, the only feasible alternative, is not available in large amounts.

Religious Divisions

Religious divisions are also a problem facing some Third World countries, especially in the Middle East, where the three great Western religions co-exist and collide.

Lebanon, for example, contains Christians and members of the two major sects of Islam—Sunni and Shia. Changes in the relative composition of these groups and demands for the reassignment of political power reflecting the changes created the basis for civil war in 1975. Outside interference by Palestinians, Israelis, and Syrians destroyed most of the remaining societal base of Lebanon, formerly the financial center of the Middle East.

Another well-publicized Third World religious conflict is between the Israelis and Palestinians. In addition, Muslims confront Christians in Ethiopia and Sudan, Hindus confront Sikhs in India, and Muslims and Hindus have fought bloody wars over Kashmir (which has a majority Muslim population and a Hindu ruler).

Environmental Degradation

The global environmental crisis not only affects North-South relations but has a chilling effect on development in the Third World as well. Environmental degradation has two major North-South aspects. From a

First World perspective, Third World activities are upsetting the delicate ecological balance and contributing to ozone depletion and the greenhouse effect. The principal villain is depletion of the equatorial rain forests, which used to form a "green band" around the earth's equator, but are increasingly being cut down. The rain forests play a major role in breaking down carbon dioxide; their destruction promotes the greenhouse effect. When added to so-called "smokestack" industries that are moving to the Third World, the contribution of Third World pollution to the greenhouse effect is approaching 50 percent or more.

Third World countries view environmental criticism as hypocritical for three reasons. First, they argue that what triggered the ecological crisis was First World pollution, especially extensive burning of fossil fuels that release carbon dioxide into the air. Second, industrial and agricultural development are necessary to raise funds to repay debt, and many in the Third World feel themselves caught between contradictory demands to repay loans and to clean up the environment. Third, many of the polluting industries in the Third World simply relocated there after leaving First World countries.

Environmental concerns that were not present when the First World developed will slow economic development in the Third World. Loans will be tied to costly antipollution equipment that raises costs but not profits, and demands to use clean but more expensive forms of energy will make life more difficult.

PATTERNS OF THIRD WORLD CONFLICT

The problems facing the Third World are difficult, enduring, interrelated, and interactive. As long as deep political divisions challenge the legitimacy of Third World regimes and states, political instability will continue to make individual countries unattractive to sources of developmental funding. Further, as long as there is endemic misery within these states, the transfer of loyalty to the state is not likely to occur. In good times, states are able to claim credit for improvements.

All of the difficulties in the Third World transcend the end of the Cold War international system. And because they have not been overcome, the instability will continue to lead to violence. The end of the Cold War competition for influence has initially affected Third World conflict only marginally. Some of the effects of the long-term involvement of the East-West competition remain. Yet neither of the former competitors is interested in expanding its commitments or creating new ones.

As a result, the artificial distortions introduced by the East-West over-lays have been removed from conflict situations. The example cited earlier holds: The deep-seated conflict between India and Pakistan is about a lot of things—communal and ethnic rivalry, rightful ownership of land, politi-cal hegemony, even the control of South Asia's valuable resource, water for irrigation—but it was never about communism versus anticommu-nism. Casting it in that light—American support for Pakistan and Soviet support for India during the Bangladesh War of 1971—deflected attention from the real problems and their solutions. Now that the reality is clear, there is the chance that both East and West will find the settlement of differences in Third World conflicts in their best interests.

However, the end of the Cold War also means that the motivation to provide assistance to the Third World is gone. Many Third World nations, especially the states of the Asian subcontinent and in the Middle East, became quite adept at playing the superpowers off against one another for both economic and military assistance. The Soviet camp was always better at supplying arms than at providing economic assistance, yet the threat to choose one side was often used to extort assistance from the other.

To the extent that East-West interest was instrumental (to prevent influence by the other side) rather than intrinsic (actual concern for the Third World), the developing countries have lost leverage. The larger and potentially more powerful Third World states can gain the attention of the North as regional powers. The smaller states, whose activities can less affect the overall system, run the risk of standing outside the margins of geopolitical concern.

Regarding the character of the conflict and violence in the Third World, political and economic misery will continue within some states to breed internal organized violence seeking to overthrow regimes and re-place them by other groups. Irredentism will also impel groups toward separatism and the formation of new states. These internal challenges will still take the forms of insurgency and counterinsurgency because they are appropriate to the physical and human conditions in many Third World countries. Other forms of internal violence will include terrorism and specialized forms of instability, such as narcotics-derived and other crimi-nally motivated violence.

Clashes between Third World states will also continue. Many of these are historical, dating back centuries or even millennia. It is possible to argue, for instance, that the Iran-Iraq War was a continuation of the battles between Mesopotamia and Persia that occurred during biblical times. The possibility of missile and chemical warfare, however, makes future clashes far more deadly and dangerous.

Internal Violence

Armed organized violence within countries of the Third World results from the crisis of governmental legitimacy as well as the inability of governments to provide adequately for their citizens. Sometimes the cause of intergroup hostilities is multinationalism; at other times, corrupt or incompetent governments are incapable of providing a decent standard of living or hope for the future. When people's expectations are frustrated and when they perceive that their actions can "rectify" the wrongs done against them, the potential for violence exists.

Internal wars tend to be fought for two main reasons. Sometimes they are fought for the control of government, where one side seeks to displace the other. The roots of such conflicts may be ideological, national or tribal, or motivated by the need to overthrow a corrupt or dictatorial leader. At other times, internal wars are fought for the purpose of seceding so as to form a new political entity. Wars fought for control of an existing state are more common; secessionary wars tend to be less common but more fervent and bloody.

What is common to both kinds of internal war is their totality of purpose. Total wars have the political purpose of physically overthrowing a government and replacing it with a preferred alternative. Moreover, total wars are rarely settled by compromise; rather, one side usually wins and the other loses. This distinction is important to our discussion of outside intervention in total wars.

Most wars for control of government are either a military coup or an insurgency. Military coups are executed by armed forces seeking to seize power from an existing civilian or military government. The military coup was particularly popular during the 1960s and early 1970s, especially in Africa. At one point, sixteen of thirty-five independent African states were ruled by military juntas that had come to power by way of coups. In Nigeria, the military coup became the "normal" means of governmental succession.

Today the military coup is no longer as popular. In a few countries, the military manages to maintain power (as in the Sudan) or an essential veto over which civilians rule (as in Pakistan). Most recently, attempted military coups have failed (as in Haiti in 1991) or the military regimes have been overthrown (as in the Ethiopian *dirgue* in 1991).

The most common form of internal war is insurgency. There is considerable disagreement about what an insurgency is exactly. It has been called various names—small war, partisan war, guerrilla war, low-intensity conflict. The term used by the U.S. government, low-intensity conflict, suggests that an insurgency is less intense than a high-intensity conflict. While it is true that most insurgencies involve fewer casualties than high-intensity conflicts (for example, world wars), the people fighting them are usually very intense about their purpose. The term is both demeaning and misleading.

The methodology of insurgent warfare is also controversial. In general, insurgencies involve irregular forces (not organized in standard European-style ways) using unorthodox tactics (hit-and-run, ambush) to gain the political loyalty of a population and destroy enemy forces. The political element of insurgent warfare—gaining the loyalty of the population—the so-called hearts and minds of men—is often more important than the military outcome.

Insurgent warfare is the preferred strategy of the militarily weak. Movements that adopt this method of warfare usually lack the military and political power to do anything else. The strategies associated with insurgent warfare thus emphasize protracted and patient organization and conduct, whereby slowly accumulating action shifts the balance of power from government to insurgency. Insurgent warfare has been described as the strategy of the "fly against the elephant."

Furthermore, there is often difficulty in overcoming an insurgency. Efforts to overthrow a government generally only arise when grievances against the government exist, which usually indicates that something is wrong. If the government is unwilling or unable to redress grievances, the insurgent group's appeal is established. The strategy and tactics of insurgent warfare are consciously designed to thwart and frustrate conventionally organized armed forces using the conventional European tactics that most Third World armies employ. Moreover, insurgencies tend to be ignored until after they gain visibility and success. Visibility only occurs when the insurgency becomes powerful enough to challenge the government openly. The longer an insurgency lasts, the stronger it gets, and the more difficult it is to defeat. In the past, U.S. involvement in countering insurgencies did not occur until late in the conflict, when the battle was essentially lost. State Department official Todd Greentree, in *The United States and the Politics of Conflict in the Developing World,* calls this phenomenon the "brushfire corollary," referring to the tendency to jump in at the last minute to put out the brushfire.

During the Cold War competition, it was not uncommon for the Soviet Union to sponsor one side, usually the insurgents, and the United States the other side, typically the government. However, these roles were reversed when President Ronald Reagan announced in 1985 his intent to support insurgent movements against Communist regimes. The policy, reflected in U.S. support of the Afghan *mujahadin* and the Nicaraguan *contras*, became known as the Reagan Doctrine.

The Cold War competition meant that disputants could count on reasonably generous assistance as long as they were willing to dress themselves in Communist or anti-Communist ideological garb. In the post–Cold War world, ideologically based assistance is unlikely to be available. If the successors to the Soviet Union become "normal" states, they will not be predisposed to the competition; in any case, they will lack the resources for the competition. Moreover, the death of the Communist model is apparent to all but the most myopic.

Although the classic insurgency theory maintains that outside assistance is unnecessary to start or sustain such a movement, it will clearly be harder for insurgencies to succeed without the East-West armaments competition. Where can potential insurgencies turn for financial assistance in the future? Two possibilities may produce new forms of internal violence. The first is the connection between insurgents and narcotics traffickers. The phenomenon is limited to those areas where drugs are produced, such as Southeast Asia (heroin) and the Andean countries of South America (cocaine). The prototype of this kind of movement may be the *Sendero Luminoso* ("Shining Path") in Peru (see Chapter 7 for a case study). Within the U.S. government, the problem has created a national security concern known as *counternarcotics*.

The other possibility for financial assistance is terrorism. Although much terrorism is sponsored by national governments (such as Libya, Syria, and Iran) and is internationally directed, there are also terrorist organizations within some states that have traditionally gotten outside assistance. The precedent suggests that these groups will expand their activities to open criminality, such as robbing banks and kidnapping. The Tupamaros of Uruguay serve as an example of a movement that has used these techniques extensively. Substantially, these actions are not much different than ordinary terrorism. They are likely to become a part of the problem identified by the U.S. government as *counterterrorism*. (For more on insurgency, see Chapter 3.)

External Violence

There is nothing new about military conflicts between nation-states in various parts of the Third World. Many regional conflicts predate the colonial period and were later muted by colonial overlordship. One example is the conflict between Muslims and Hindus on the Asian subcontinent. As the colonial veil was lifted, however, many of these long-term rivalries were reactivated in visible and violent ways. Thus, the Muslim League and the Indian Congress were able to cooperate in the effort to usher the British out of the subcontinent. Yet the new nations of India and Pakistan were fighting over irrigation water and Kashmir within months of independence, reviving a conflict that dated back to the first incursion of Muslims into the region hundreds of years before the British arrived.

The decolonizing process also created the basis for Third World conflicts in the way that independence was granted. As noted earlier in the chapter, many African and Middle Eastern state boundaries were artificially drawn, creating disputed territories that later resulted in conflict. Many Middle Easterners—notably the Iraqis—maintain that most of their regional problems are attributable to how Britain and France drew boundaries as they withdrew.

During the Cold War competition in the Third World, regional conflicts often gained an East-West overlay. Sometimes these relationships became quite complicated, as in the triangular relationship between the United States and the Soviet Union with India (courted most actively by the Soviets, particularly after 1971), Pakistan (a U.S. ally in two defense arrangements—the Central Treaty Organization and the Southeast Asian Treaty Organization), and China (a rival of India courted by both superpowers at different times).

The lingua franca of the Cold War was military and economic assistance. While the result was often arms races that many decried, the process provided some restraint because of the need for spare parts, ammunition, and the like. Thus, both superpowers and other armorers modulated armaments levels in the eight-year-long Iran-Iraq War such that neither side had enough firepower to win (or lose) decisively.

The end of the Cold War competition affects the current situation in at least two ways. First, the United States and the former Soviet Union have left old clients extremely well armed with front-line military equipment. This is most obvious in the Middle East, making more lethal the whole host of conflicts there: Arab states versus Israel, Syria versus Iraq, Iraq versus Iran. Unfortunately, active private and international arms and weapons industries in several Third World countries have freed the Third World from dependence on replacement parts and ammunition.

Furthermore, the former restraint on regional actors had been weakened by the end of the Cold War. Historically, the United States and the Soviet Union opposed regional rivals gaining decisive advantage over one another. Thus, when Syria sought in 1970 to intervene in the Jordanian civil war on behalf of the Palestinians, the Soviets were able to prevent the intervention because of the Syrians' reliance on Soviet arms. Similarly, a lack of restraint probably emboldened Saddam Hussein's invasion of Kuwait in August 1990. During the Cold War period, when Iraq was heavily dependent on Soviet military assistance, the Soviets could and probably would have vetoed the aggression.

Regional conflict is likely to be more important to the overall international system in the future for several reasons. The first is the relative absence of East-West military confrontation; in a sense, regional conflicts are the only "game in town" for the new order. Second, the withdrawal of superpower overlordship may encourage certain states and leaders to aspire to preeminent regional positions. These potential hegemons do not have to worry much about East-West competition confounding their plans for greater power and prestige. Saddam Hussein is the most obvious case in point. Similar competitions may emerge in different places, such as that between Brazil and Argentina for the preeminent position in South America.

In addition, the lethal potential of many Third World countries is increasing as their arsenals grow larger and more sophisticated. Cold War generosity combined with multinational production in places like Brazil and China to equip nearly twenty states with some type of ballistic missiles. A growing list of developing countries is obtaining chemical and biological weapons that raise the lethality of their arsenals.

There is also the problem of nuclear proliferation, which has concerned analysts for three decades. Today, five countries admit to having nuclear weapons (the United States, former Soviet Union, Britain, France, and China), two are widely acknowledged as having them but do not admit it (India and Israel), several are on the verge of nuclear capacity, if they do not already have it (South Africa and Pakistan), and twenty more could gain nuclear capability during the 1990s (including Iraq and the Koreas). The international system is unprepared for a world with so many nuclear powers. During the Cold War, elaborate theories and systems of bilateral Soviet-American nuclear deterrence were fashioned. Although it is uncertain whether those constructs can be extended to a Third World with multiple nuclear powers, deterrence is clearly more of a problem in today's evolving world order.

North-South Interactions: Positive or Negative Sum?

The wave of democratic revolutions during 1989 spawned a sense of optimism about the future of the international system. There was great hope for a democratizing globe, including the countries of the Third World. It was hoped that the new world order would mean peace.

The Third World, of course, is only selectively democratic and is by no means peaceful. Major questions for the new world order are whether the First World can or should intervene in the Third World to aid in its transformation and whether such intervention can make a significant difference.

The underlying problems in the Third World, as well as their solutions, are not new. The answers probably rest on the development that almost all Third World states seek. Development is neither an easy nor simple solution. It must occur within the cultural contexts of many diverse places. It is not enough to try to make them carbon copies of Western democracies—this lesson was learned all too vividly when the United States assisted in the radical modernization of one of the most conservative societies on earth, Shi'ite Iran. Nevertheless, Third World development and a better standard of living are universally desired.

The alternative to development is the continuation of the instability and violence that has plagued the Third World throughout its independence. Third World instability was tolerable before, because there were other, more pressing security concerns, beside which it seemed to pale by comparison. Now, Third World instability is the major source of instability in the system. The extent, character, and control of Third World conflict will thus be major elements in the new world order. The ways in which the North treats or fails to treat the underlying causes of Third World instability will contribute materially to that order.

Operation Desert Storm was the first major post–Cold War instance where a Third World conflict became a pivotal concern for the entire international system. The situation may have been *sui generis* and thus not instructive for the future operation of that system. (Arguments on both sides are covered in Chapter 7.) Certainly, it sends very mixed, even contradictory signals that have to be taken into account.

In one sense, the outcome of the Persian Gulf War between Iraq and the coalition led by the United States strongly makes the case for promoting peace in the Third World. Human suffering continued for well over a year after the war ended; the toll in human lives, though nominal for the United States, was great for Iraq.

What are the lessons of Desert Storm? The war intended to send a message to other potential Saddam Husseins that acts of aggression will not be tolerated. It was a message of deterrence, accomplished by the forceful removal of Iraq from the occupied land. However, the war also conveyed a different message, especially in the United States, that can be summed up in three words: No more Iraqs. The need to call up the U.S. Reserves was an emotional ordeal that many would find difficult to repeat. The halfhearted support of some major U.S. allies (for example, Japan and Germany), who have an even greater dependence on Persian Gulf oil, was disillusioning. The subsequent reduction of U.S. active forces raises questions about the capacity of the United States to assemble similar forces in a short period of time regardless of will and desire. Many Americans may wonder in retrospect whether they really want to be the police officers of an ungrateful world order. On the other hand, the enormous gap between American and Iraqi military capability may well deter others from running the risk of confronting the American juggernaut.

The best way to avoid future Desert Storms, of course, is by creating a peaceful world. Such a world is not upon or nearly upon us. However, how the West acts will influence the shape of Third World conflict.

First World Options

There are four broad ways that the First World can deal with the Third World in the years ahead. First, it can engage in a policy of benign neglect, leaving it to the Third World to solve its own problems. Second, it can pursue selective activism, intervening in a few select countries and ignoring the rest. Third, it may join in a concerted program to manage Third World conflict. Finally, the First World can launch a program of massive development in the Third World, as the members of the Group of Seventy-seven developing world countries have been advocating for over two decades.

The first option, *benign neglect,* involves no real effort on the part of the First World to help the Third World solve its problems. Rather, it involves passive action during times of instability unless some overwhelming interest is jeopardized. Given that there are relatively few or no events in the Third World that threaten the First World, such a policy would require a minimum effort.

Although benign neglect may offend any missionary or activist zeal present in the First World, it is not without merit. It is a relatively noncontroversial policy within most First World countries. The countries of the Third World do not have large or powerful political constituencies within most First World countries, an exception being large migrant minorities from former colonies. Except in the most exceptional of cases—natural disasters, bloody wars—the plight of the Third World does not translate into a demand for activism. Thus, the fate of Third World countries can often be ignored. The history of developmental assistance programs within the United States is a striking case in point; whenever there is pressure to cut federal budgets, foreign aid is a prime candidate because it lacks a strong political constituency.

In addition, benign neglect is the least costly policy to follow toward the Third World. In an era of constricted economic resources and surplus demands on those resources, benign neglect may amount to no more than living within our means. Certainly this is true of the successors of the Soviets and the Americans. As the West Europeans turn their attention to the development of Eastern Europe and the successor republics of the former Soviet Union, it may be true for them as well.

Activism in the Third World can be politically dangerous. Economic involvement is almost always criticized as wasteful or fruitless (or both), and if an action has any military potential, the specter of Vietnam may be raised. The easiest way to avoid criticism is to avoid involvement.

Finally, benign neglect arguably reflects the First World's vital national interests. If vital interests are places and situations warranting the application of military force (a common criterion), it is questionable whether any such interests exist aside from where petroleum is found.

The benign neglect orientation is not beyond reproach and criticism. It will win no friends in the Third World itself, since many there believe it is a First World obligation to aid their development as part of the reparation for colonialism. A policy of neglect, whether benign or not, is an open repudiation of any obligation; its effect is bound to be minimization of the flow of assistance from North to South.

Benign neglect fails to address the underlying causes of Third World instability. To say that Third World problems defy solution because they are too intractable or expensive to solve only ensures continued violence, instability, and misery in the region.

The Persian Gulf War between the United States and Iraq suggests that there are Third World situations that cannot be neglected. Therefore, a policy of at least selected activism is needed to deal with situations and conditions of this type. Selective activism has obvious merits. For example, it represents a continuity with ongoing policy. Militarily, it is an extension of the Nixon Doctrine, which says the United States will come to the direct military aid only of vital states. Economically, it reflects the policy to assist only those states most certain to succeed, hoping their success will spill over to their less prosperous neighbors. This continuity reflects a realistic assessment of the world. No single state in the new order can afford a policy of comprehensive engagement everywhere, but all Third World regions contain countries and situations that, if things went wrong, would injure First World national interests. The First World could not ignore the Persian Gulf in 1990; the variety of responses to requests to join the anti-Iraqi campaign surrounding Desert Storm indicates clearly the differential assessments about *how* important the region is and what the appropriate responses to the crisis were, which is why some states became more engaged than others.

Another advantage of selective activism is its affordability. Although it is obviously more expensive than noninvolvement, neglect is probably the most costly alternative in the long term because it would allow Third World problems to grow over time.

Finally, a multilateral approach to the Third World based on selective activism is most compatible with the collective security orientation of the new world order. The idea is that if the world community responds firmly to outbursts of violence, which are most likely to occur in the Third World, other potential usurpers of the peace will be dissuaded.

However, selective activism may have some disadvantages as well. For example, the First World has a poor track record in choosing which Third World situations to become involved in. U.S. involvement in Southeast Asia did not, for instance, improve things there. There are two main questions concerning the use of selective activism: (1) Who decides when and where such activism will occur? and (2) How effective will it be in serving the interests of the Third World?

Any multilateral policy of selective activism will demand that the First World be capable of concerted action. This presumes that the former Soviets, notably the Russians, will continue to share an interest in supporting global peace. It also assumes the various major powers, especially those most economically advantaged, will be able to cooperate in the problem-solving process. A serious cause for concern was the mixed, sometimes halfhearted response to the Iraqi invasion of Kuwait by some major states.

Another possible First World response to the Third World situation is *major power cooperation*. The Soviet-American cooperation (executed through the United Nations Security Council in the summer of 1990) in the Iraqi crisis suggests that such an approach is possible. U.S. President Bush and former Soviet President Gorbachev endorsed this principle at the Moscow summit in July 1991, and Russian President Boris Yeltsin has also suggested a broad range of cooperation since then.

At this early juncture in the evolution of the post–Cold War system, however, the eventual extent and nature of cooperation are unknown. The system envisioned by the United Nations required two conditions: (1) the United States and the former Soviet Union (now Russia) had to agree on policies of enforcement (which would require compatible views), and (2) they had to be willing to carry out the responsibilities implied in the Charter.

Neither of these conditions was assured. The emergence of the successors of the former Soviet Union as "normal" states, as Gorbachev described it, is by no means certain. Moreover, without more successful economic reform it was not likely that the successor Commonwealth of Independent States would be able to afford much activity in the Third World.

The emergence of superpower cooperation, especially if it was backed by the economic resources of the European Community and Japan, would have both positive and negative results. Positively, it would generate the resources needed to influence the shape and direction of Third World development. However, that the economically competitive First World powers could agree on the precise enforcement policies would be unlikely. In addition, such an arrangement would certainly be criticized as manipulative by the Third World.

The last possible First World approach to the Third World is *massive development*. Here the First World would execute the guidelines of the new international economic order by beginning the massive transfer—1 percent to 3 percent of GNP—of aid from North to South in order to generate rapid development in the Third World.

The massive development approach has been advocated by the Third World for over thirty years, so its acceptance would be reasonably assured. In addition, since development is key to Third World stability, it would address the heart of the problem. Moreover, massive development would likely be the most cost-effective alternative. By creating general prosperity in the Third World, the First World could eliminate or reduce its costly military intervention in Third World violence. The Third World could then become a productive part of the world economic system.

The development approach would require massive public funding (particularly for infrastructure items) from both First World sources and host countries. Given the emphasis on economic privatization that underlaid the 1980s international economic expansion, large government expenditures for this purpose would likely be opposed on economic grounds. In practical terms, moreover, a sufficient amount of money would probably not be politically available for such a program. Competing domestic interests in all First World countries would effectively preclude the transfer of massive public funds to the Third World.

The various First World states have different interests in the Third World as well as in individual developing states, so their reactions are likely to be mixed. Massive activity anywhere from the states of the former Soviet Union, for instance, is unlikely. And while the United States faces fiscal restraints, its position as the only remaining military and economic superpower makes it difficult for it to remain aloof. The European states will be influenced by the unique factors arising from their colonial pasts and their participation in continentwide European development. Wealthy Japan remains politically nonassertive, in some ways because of its imperialist past.

The result is likely to be the absence of any unified First World approach to the Third World situation. Individual First World states are more likely to adopt different strategies as circumstances change.

CONCLUSION

The international system is moving from a Cold War to some other system, but the place of the Third World in that system is uncertain. Third World problems have not been changed as a result of the end of the Cold War; nothing resembling the Eastern European revolutions has occurred in Third World countries to bring them promise and hope for the future.

The Third World sat on the periphery of the Cold War system. Its contributions to the system were marginal; it served as a place from which natural resources could be obtained as well as a place where the Cold War could be fought without the threat of nuclear destruction at home. The cavernous material and cultural differences between the First and Third Worlds could be and were ignored or cast in Western terms. Solipsism was okay.

A major question about the new world order is how it will address the Third World situation. The telecommunications revolution has removed any last vestiges of ignorance of what is being missed by the South; people in the developing world see the general prosperity very clearly, and they want to participate. The inability to hide what was going on in Communist regimes in Eastern Europe contributed to their downfall. The mass media helped to make people in the East aware of how their situation differed from that of Westerners. The same is increasingly true of people in the Third World today.

Solving the problems of Eastern Europe will be relatively easy when compared to the Third World. Eastern Europe has a trained and educated work force. This is not true of most Third World countries. Yet the problem here is not only educating the majority of the population but also avoiding the "brain drain" where the educated of the Third World migrate to the First World.

Difficult problems face the Third World. Those problems are not likely to be solved easily or quickly; their solutions will be so hard to attain that despair may result. In the past, there has been inadequate incentive in the North to do anything more than despair. It is uncertain whether there will now be enough reason to address the difficult problems of the developing world.

For the situation to improve in the Third World, it must move from its current position at the periphery of the world system toward the center. In addition, for meaningful change to occur, it must be in the self-interest of First World states to assist in the process.

Do First World countries share an interest in transforming the Third World? The NICs model, from which both the First World and Pacific Rim countries profited, offers some hope. In addition, some incentive may come from the desire to prevent the violence that is likely to remain in the Third World under the new international system. Until conditions in the Third World improve, there is little hope that the violence within and between Third World countries will end.

CHAPTER 3

The Venerable Foe: Insurgency

Insurgent warfare, which takes many forms and has various names, can be traced back over three thousand years to the admonitions and instructions on war of the Chinese military strategist Sun Tzu. It originated as armed groups encountering larger and stronger opponents chose to take evasive action rather than direct military action with an inevitable disastrous outcome.

What we now call *insurgent warfare* is the culmination of what many militarily inferior forces have learned to do to succeed against stronger foes. It is a method of war that gradually inverts the traditional strengths of large armed forces from an advantage to a disadvantage. As many observers have noted, it is "warfare on the cheap."

Despite its frequency throughout human history, insurgent warfare is largely misunderstood today. This is especially true in the United States and among the leaders of the U.S. military. For example, the ongoing debate over whether the war in Vietnam was conventional (the official view of General William Westmoreland and many U.S. Army apologists) or insurgent points to the confusion that hampers American efforts to deal with insurgent warfare.

In the contemporary debate, insurgency has many names, none entirely satisfactory. In official Washington, D.C., for instance, insurgent conflicts have recently been referred to as *low-intensity conflicts* (*LICs*). The U.S. government official responsible for understanding and countering insurgency is called the Assistant Secretary of Defense (ASD) for Special Operations and Low-Intensity Conflict (SOLIC). This combination of terms is confusing—while *special operations* refers to specialized and unorthodox tasks (such as freeing hostages), *low-intensity conflict* may not necessarily entail special operations. The U.S.-preferred term (low-intensity conflict), devised to distinguish Third World insurgencies from "high-intensity" events like strategic nuclear war or war in Central Europe, connotes that they are somehow less significant. Others prefer different terms, including *guerrilla warfare, small war,* or *partisan war.*

The debate over what to call insurgency only confuses our understanding of what it really is. Some confusion arises regarding the military
means and political ends for which insurgent warfare is fought. In terms
of means, insurgency refers to how forces are used strategically and
tactically in front of an enemy. As a strategy, it attempts to wear down
and weaken a militarily superior foe over time. Its major goal, attrition,
is accomplished by prolonging war and exhausting a less dedicated foe.
Tactically, insurgency usually involves irregular, part-time, often nonuni-
formed forces who employ such tactics as ambush, hit-and-run, and
avoidance of contact where superiority at the point of engagement does
not guarantee victory.

Insurgent warfare can serve a number of political ends when military
weakness makes the success of a conventional approach unlikely and when
ideal physical and political conditions exist. One major traditional use of
insurgency has been to repel powerful foreign aggressors. The French and
the Americans were not the first victims of what Vietnamese General Vo
Nguyen Giap called "people's war"; the same approach had been employed to rid Southeast Asia of Kublai Khan and his Mongol hordes in the
thirteenth century. Similarly, as Roger Hilsman demonstrates in his brilliant autobiographical work *American Guerrilla* (1990), the United States
assisted these kinds of movements against the Japanese occupation of
Burma during World War II; and the Apache Chief Cochise would have
been comfortable with the term *insurgent warfare* in his campaign to repel
the "invading" U.S. Cavalry in Arizona.

Insurgent warfare tactics are also used to promote internal war, especially revolutionary war aimed at overthrowing a government. During the
Cold War period, insurgent warfare was commonly used in this way. In most
of these cases, it occurred under the banner of the "War of National Liberation" popularized by Soviet Premier Nikita Khrushchev or was associated
with techniques developed by Mao Tse-tung during his campaigns against
the Japanese and Kuomintang (Nationalist Chinese of Chiang Kai-Shek).

The result has been a tendency to equate insurgent warfare with Communist or Marxist political purposes. The inference is unwarranted, for
insurgent warfare can be fought for any political end. The *contras* in
Nicaragua and the *mujahadin* in Afghanistan fought insurgent wars. Much
of the early fighting in the American Revolution can also be described as
insurgency. Modern insurgents would be comfortable, for instance, with
the campaigns of Ethan Allen and the Green Mountains Boys in New
England or of Francis (the "Swamp Fox") Marion or Nathanael Greene in
the Carolinas during the Revolution.

This is an important distinction. Insurgencies have long occurred in
the Third World and will continue to do so. The conditions for

insurgency—weak and unpopular governments viewed as roadblocks to future progress—form the political basis of dissent. Moreover, much of the Third World is physically remote, mountainous, and lushly vegetated (for example, jungle habitats). Insurgency tends to work best in these kinds of physical conditions because rugged terrain makes pursuit by government forces difficult. In contrast, insurgencies have not fared well in areas of the Third World that lack these physical conditions (such as northern Africa and much of the Middle East).

Increasingly, though, the connection between insurgent means and Marxist ends is weakening. Although it is likely that isolated Marxist insurgencies will occur (such as among the *Sendero Luminoso* in Peru and the New People's Army in the Philippines), the unwillingness of the former Soviets to nurture such movements will make them less popular in the future. Political opposition groups will still be drawn to insurgency, but the political banners they will support and their material and ideological sponsors are uncertain.

To understand insurgency, we need to look at the kinds of societies in which it is most likely to emerge. In addition, the history of insurgency is important in terms of the contributions of its prominent proponents. Of particular importance here is the Maoist approach of mobile-guerrilla warfare, which creates special problems for conventional armed forces. Finally, we must examine the unique politico-military balance of insurgency as well as the special problems the United States has faced in dealing with it. Understanding insurgency is a prerequisite to understanding the problems facing counterinsurgency, the focus of Chapter 4.

THE ROOTS OF INSURGENCY: UNDERLYING CAUSES

The incentive to engage in insurgent warfare exists when societal misery prevails. In the modern world, those factors, from political illegitimacy to economic deprivation to ethnic and intercommunal hatred, are largely concentrated in the Third World. The number of developing states in which these conditions exist is, of course, greater than the number of states experiencing insurgent warfare because some societies are more prone than others to engage in organized violence. Generally, revolution is least likely to occur in the poorest nations or the most highly developed ones. Rather, as Crane Brinton points out in *The Anatomy of Revolution* (1965), revolutionary violence is most likely to emerge in societies experiencing some growth and prosperity but where significant groups find themselves outside that prosperity. Moreover, when this occurs in a weak society (one in which a substantial portion of the population is indifferent or hostile to the government), the result may be recourse to some form of insurgent warfare.

The first step in understanding insurgency is knowing where insurgencies typically occur and who usually participates in them. Many analyses of insurgency, especially those focusing on the military aspects of insurgency and counterinsurgency, mistakenly treat it as a mechanical exercise. This perspective ignores the human element that drives people to engage in insurgency. Like all military acts, insurgency is a political action begun by people to achieve certain political goals. When the goals are to overthrow a government and replace it with one more compatible with the insurgents' interests, the purposes of the insurgency tend to be extraordinarily important to those involved and so they pursue them with a fierce tenacity. This important element of insurgency is lost in analyses that neglect the issue of underlying causes.

Revolution-Prone Societies

Not all nation-states are equally vulnerable to insurgency. Clearly, there must be some form of grievance against the state around which an aggrieved segment of the population can be rallied toward insurgency. During the Cold War, there were usually Soviet-bloc *agents provocateurs* available to foment and nurture grievances into full-blown opposition movements, but these only worked when grievances already existed. In the post–Cold War world, this "help" will be less readily available, making the job of organizing insurgency more difficult.

Insurgency, then, will likely be harder in the post–Cold War world, though it will not disappear. Wherever there is perceived inequity regarding the human condition, someone will ask "Why me?" The question will be raised more frequently in the increasingly transparent world of modern telecommunications and the spreading worldwide demand for political freedom. The seed of insurgency will remain as long as human misery persists.

In a study conducted in 1970 called *Why Men Rebel,* political scientist Ted Robert Gurr coined a useful term for describing the societies most vulnerable to revolutionary activity: *relative deprivation* refers to the perceived discrepancy between value expectations and value expectancies in a society. That is, the inclination to revolt is most likely to be present when people perceive an inequity in the wretchedness of their condition—when they receive less (their expectations) than they feel they deserve (their expectancies).

This process has four steps. The first is the simple recognition of deprivation. As suggested, in an isolated social setting where the human condition is uniformly wretched, one may recognize he has little, but fail to think that unusual. The first step amounts to an individual or group saying, "We lack something."

The second step is the realization that the condition is not universal: others have whatever we lack. This is common in Third World societies where most resources are controlled by a small elite. Capital outflow and development have accentuated this internal maldistribution, thereby heightening the likelihood of this stage of the relative deprivation process.

In the third step there is the realization that the deprivation is not only inequitable but also unfair. This realization is tantamount to questioning the justice of the existing order and deciding whether it is right to remain loyal to it. Raising such questions suggests two things. First, people and groups receive benefits by virtue of their position—class, ethnicity, or some other base—rather than on some egalitarian scale, particularly in multinational Third World societies. Second, that the justice of the order can be questioned suggests that the process is most likely to proceed in weak societies whose political order lacks legitimacy. Again, this is characteristic of many Third World societies.

The final stage in the relative deprivation process involves recognizing the efficacy of political action to change the situation. "We can do something about this condition." In many developing societies, the potential avenues for peaceful participation in the governmental process are restricted. Often, the groups responsible for creating the inequities also rule, and their goal is to maintain their positions and privileges. They are thus unlikely to sympathize with those who seek to change the inequity.

If the political system does not offer peaceful means to relieve relative deprivation, people are faced with a difficult choice. They can accept their condition and continue to be frustrated by it, or they can go outside the system to try to improve it. If enough people seek the latter alternative, the result can be violent opposition.

The relative deprivation process does not usually occur in the poorest societies, where absolute deprivation is greatest, because they are unlikely to go beyond the first or second stage. People in poor societies not only receive very little from the government (low value capabilities) but they also expect very little (low value expectancies). The process is most likely to occur in societies where some developmental activity has created a gap between what people feel they rightfully deserve and what they believe they will receive.

Gurr (1970) describes three forms of relative deprivation. In the first type, called decremental relative deprivation, peoples' expectations remain fairly constant but the ability of society to meet those expectations decreases. Some contemporary examples include the Nicaraguans' reaction to U.S.-created scarcities under the Sandinistas, leading to their ouster in the 1990 elections as living standards declined; and the current economic situation in the Philippines under the successor of President Corazon Aquino.

In the second kind of relative deprivation, referred to as aspirational, people's expectations rise dramatically while the society's ability to satisfy them remains static or fails to keep up with the growth of demands. This is the classic revolution of rising expectations phenomenon in which exposure to the world situation demonstrates how much one is missing and thereby inflates the desire for more. Exposure to modern telecommunications can only exacerbate this perception. Eastern Europeans, for example, saw images of the riches of the West on German and French television as their material condition improved little. In the Third World, the struggle over black political rights in South Africa has received a lot of media attention, but less remedial actions than many blacks demand.

In the third form of relative deprivation, called progressive, people's expectations rise as society's ability to satisfy those expectations actually declines. It is the most volatile form of relative deprivation because it maximizes the gap between what people want and what they receive. The former Soviet Union provides a striking example of progressive deprivation—the early promise of *glasnost* suggested that political rights and economic prosperity would be expanded, but the economic result was quite the opposite. This type of deprivation is found in Third World countries that are highly dependent on petroleum revenues (such as Mexico) because fluctuations in these revenues affect government services.

The kinds of situations that encourage the emergence of revolutionary movements are thus widely present in the Third World, especially in those countries that have experienced a limited amount of prosperity. The antidote to relative deprivation is a society and policy that provide for the general welfare equitably. As long as that is lacking in Third World societies, they will remain weak and the potential for insurgency will continue to develop.

Revolutionary Leaders and Followers

Just as different societies show varying levels of vulnerability to revolutionary violence, so too do different groups and individuals. Revolution is largely a middle-class phenomenon. The leadership usually comes from the upper-middle and middle classes and the followers from the lower-middle and lower classes. The societal pyramid in Figure 3.1 illustrates why this occurs in Third World societies. At the pinnacle is a small but powerful elite that controls the political and economic activity of the society. Positioned beneath the elite is a larger but still small middle-class made up primarily of government workers, teachers, most of the military, and small businesspeople. At the base is the lower class or peasantry, which constitutes the mass of Third World society. This group is historically composed of a predominantly rural population engaged in subsistence agriculture, but increasingly includes the underemployed and unemployed urban masses.

The middle class is most prone to perceive relative deprivation in the Third World. In contrast, the elite is least likely to become involved in revolutionary activities because it controls the system from which it benefits. The elite is conservative in that it seeks to conserve a pattern of societal relationships. Moreover, its willingness or resistance to share power helps determine the revolutionary potential of a society.

Although the peasantry suffers the most absolute deprivation, this group has traditionally been nonrevolutionary. Prior to the growth of the mass media, especially television, the lower class was unlikely to get past the first or second stage of the relative deprivation process in realizing that inequity exists. Even today, the peasantry as well as more worldly urban dwellers generally lack the education and sophistication to recognize the efficacy of political action.

In contrast, the middle class is in a position not only to recognize that inequity exists but also, by virtue of their education (teachers), vantage points (civil servants, the military), and habitation (shopkeepers operating

Figure 3.1   Societal Pyramid

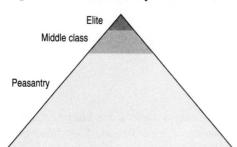

in urban centers), to perceive that the system creates the inequity. In revolution-prone societies, the middle class has restricted upward mobility. While there are some opportunities for a rise in status, these are limited. If the system operates to reinforce these limitations rather than broadening the opportunity to rise in status, relative deprivation may result. Whatever the basis of the limitation—tribal, social, or economic—perceiving it as unfair and in need of change is most important.

In terms of leadership, those in the educated upper-middle class are most likely to recognize inequity and seek to change it. For example, many leaders of the American Revolution—Alexander Hamilton, Samuel Adams, and Paul Revere—had been successful merchants hit especially hard by British attempts to tax the colonies. Some twentieth-century examples include Mao Tse-tung (a teacher), Indonesia's Achmed Sukarno (an engineer), Ho Chi Minh (the son of a teacher), Fidel Castro (a lawyer), Che Guevara (a physician), and Peru's Shining Path leader Abimael Guzman (a philosophy professor). What these people shared was frustration caused by limited opportunities for upward mobility. Sukarno, for instance, was a trained engineer who was prevented from rising above the status of draftsman within the Dutch colonial system. Similarly, Che Guevara was an unsuccessful doctor whose last medical posting was in a Central American leper colony—the only position he could find.

Revolutionary leaders, then, share a common belief—that they are being constricted not by their own limitations but by an unjust order. It matters little whether their perceptions are accurate. Rather, what matters is that they reach the decision that only the violent overthrow of the system will bring about appropriate societal change. Whether violence ensues largely depends on the society's ability to accommodate the demands for change or to suppress the discontent. Of course, an accommodating system is unlikely to face sustained or substantial violence. When an insurgency emerges against a government that resists change, however, this indicates that the insurgent group of leaders has progressed through the stages of the relative deprivation process and has attracted enough followers to sustain itself. This process almost always contains elements of allegiance and coercion, but its existence indicates that something is wrong in the society against which revolution is directed.

The Appeal of Insurgent Warfare

In the contemporary world, revolutionary activity aimed at overthrowing governments is largely confined to the Third World. It is here that weak societies combine with physically weak or coercive states to trigger relative deprivation within the middle class. In contrast, in most postrevolutionary First World states, the middle class has expanded to the point that it effectively controls the political system.

In most areas where revolutionary groups arise, some form of insurgent warfare is usually the overwhelming choice of the revolutionary movements. The most popular model—variants of Maoist mobile-guerrilla warfare—offers certain advantages to the potential insurgent.

The first advantage is that its approach is appropriate to the developing world both geopolitically and physically. In most Third World countries, the government possesses an overwhelming monopoly on power but has problems projecting that power throughout the country because of certain physical land conditions. Countries located along the equator are generally mountainous, hot, and heavily overgrown; as a result, they have underdeveloped transportation and communications systems. The Middle East and northern Africa are exceptions to this physical description. As such, equatorial conditions provide sanctuaries where revolutionary movements can repair to avoid extinction, organize, and begin the process of converting the population to their cause.

These physical characteristics contribute to the second advantage of the strategy; they maximize the likelihood that a movement will survive, gradually expand, and eventually succeed. Insurgent warfare is consciously designed for a group initially weaker than its adversary. During the Cold War, most Third World governments received generous amounts of arms from Cold War suitors, thereby giving them greater military power than any potential insurgent groups.

The third advantage of the insurgency strategy includes an emphasis on human rather than material resources and the focus on redressing political wrongs. Particularly in its earliest stages, insurgency has a high political content, necessitated by its initial military weakness. The first step in conducting an insurgency, then, involves creating a support base in the population by way of extensive political conversion. Helping the public to see the benefits of a more humane form of governance is clearly the best way to accomplish this purpose. Some recourse to terrorism and other forms of coercion may be tactically effective in the short term, but conversion is a more solid base for support.

Fourth, insurgency theory provides a framework for gradual success through patient adherence to the strategy. The body of the theory is the blueprint for revolution; for example, North Vietnamese General Vo Nguyen Giap's *People's War, People's Army* describes itself as a "political handbook" for Third World revolutions. Although not all insurgencies following his plan have been successful, their track record is positive enough to be attractive to potential insurgents.

The fifth advantage of insurgencies is that they are difficult to defeat after they become established. An insurgent movement in its early stages is more easily defeated because it is small, militarily and politically weak, and hence vulnerable. As it nurtures support in the population, however, counterinsurgency becomes progressively more difficult and frustrating.

The sixth and final advantage of insurgency is that outside interference by another state is so difficult. Insurgencies are internal affairs about government control, so any outside interference is usually resented by the population. In addition, the insurgents benefit because they can accuse the government of being the "stooge" of outside imperialists. This is especially true of Third World situations involving racially distinct— particularly Caucasian—forces, who are likely to be viewed as attempting to reimpose outside rule.

THE "POOR MAN'S WAR": A HISTORICAL PERSPECTIVE

It is easy to understand why insurgency has long been universally popular: Throughout much of history, militarily weak populations have faced more powerful, organized enemies who sought to impose their will on them. Insurgency is one successful way that various groups have used to solve this problem over time.

In the modern era, insurgency is associated with Communist movements in the Third World, especially the military instruction developed by Mao Tse-tung in the 1920s through the 1940s, and later modified by others (such as Giap and Guevara). But many of the basic principles of insurgency were recorded by Sun Tzu in China over three thousand years ago. Mao later updated and modified them to accommodate the needs of the Chinese revolution.

Sun Tzu

Little is known about Sun Tzu, the father of modern insurgency. He lived in China about one thousand years before the birth of Christ, a time of considerable dynastic wars in China. Sun Tzu served as a military advisor to several warlords of the realm. His military advice is recorded in *The Art of War* (1963), which became popular in the West after Mao borrowed from it with great success.

Sun Tzu was the first to use what is now called the "indirect approach" to war. The leading twentieth-century partisan of the approach, Sir Basil Liddell Hart, acknowledges the lineage in his introduction to *The Art of War*. The most basic principle of Sun Tzu's approach was to avoid massive contact with the enemy except in circumstances of overwhelming advantage. That is, if one's own force is the equal or inferior to the opposing force, maneuvering and retreating to avoid contact is preferable to risking defeat.

At the heart of the Sun Tzu approach are maneuverability and an emphasis on the tactics of division and conquest. In *The Art of War,* for example, Sun Tzu gives this general advice to armies: "When the enemy advances, we retreat; when the enemy halts, we harass; when the enemy seeks to avoid battle, we attack; when the enemy retreats, we pursue." His strategy also stresses the importance of having superior knowledge of the enemy and its strategy. This knowledge, he argues, makes acts of deception more effective: "All warfare is based on deception. . . . To subdue the enemy without fighting is the acme of skill. Thus, what is of supreme importance is to attack the enemy's strategy."

However, Sun Tzu's strategy does not address the relationship between the political purpose of war and its military means, other than to say that generals who avoided interference from the "sovereign" were more likely to prevail than those who could not. Modern insurgency theory has a significant political aspect as well as a set of political instructions for insurgent groups. Although Sun Tzu does not address this directly in *The Art of War,* he does suggest that the foresighted military commander will treat his soldiers "with benevolence, justice and righteousness, and repose confidence in them" so "to formulate victorious policies."

The Art of War is a slender volume composed largely of what we now call doctrine—the best ways to accomplish ends based on experience. Its direct contribution is to provide a theoretical base for a strategy of movement and evasion as well as to justify certain military techniques such as hit-and-run and ambush. Sun Tzu's ideas were later incorporated in the contemporary strategy devised by Mao Tse-tung that represents the type of insurgent warfare most commonly practiced today.

Mao Tse-tung

Mao Tse-tung's contribution to insurgent warfare was twofold. First, he adapted Sun Tzu's strategy to the conditions facing twentieth-century China: internal turmoil and a massive invasion by Japan. In the process, he perfected a style of insurgent warfare known as mobile-guerrilla war. Second, Mao added the notion of the politics of mass mobilization and the inextricable relationship between the political support base of insurgency (the population) and the military conflict. An insurgency that successfully weds a strong political support base with an appropriate military strategy based in the indirect approach is difficult—if not impossible—to defeat.

In his *Selected Works* (1967)—a five-volume collection of his many speeches—Mao Tse-tung is explicit about the need to develop and nurture a tight bond between the people and the insurgency. He admonishes, for instance, the importance of appealing to the masses: "Our central task is to mobilize the masses to take part in the revolutionary war. . . . We must lead the peasants' struggle for land and distribute the land to them, heighten their labor enthusiasm and increase agricultural production, safeguard the interests of the workers." If the conditions of the masses are not constantly addressed, then "fighting loses its meaning."

Insurgent war thus becomes a struggle for people's loyalty. Its bottom line is, to use the phrase coined by Lyndon Baines Johnson, "the battle for the hearts and minds of men." Mao asserts that the contest for loyalty is ultimately more important than the military struggle: "Weapons are an important factor in war, but not the decisive factor; it is people, not things, that are decisive. The contest of strength is not only a contest of economic and military power, but also a contest of human power and morale. Military and economic power [are] necessarily wielded by people." According to Mao, political and military elements are intertwined: "Political power grows out of the barrel of a gun" and "the Army is the chief component of the political power of a state" are notable quotations. Military force is thus of great importance in bringing about the victory of an insurgency.

Moreover, the relationship between the insurgents and the people extends beyond the initial base of organization and operation. As the insurgency widens, its appeal is based on its treatment and conversion of the masses. The purpose is to provide a bond with the people that is stronger than the government's appeal. Thus, according to Mao, the insurgent army "must build good relations with the masses, be concerned with them and help them overcome their difficulties." This relationship is both inherent (liberation from tyranny) and instrumental (aids the revolution): "The principle of unity between the army and the people . . . means maintaining a discipline *that forbids the slightest violation of the people's interests,* [by] conducting propaganda among the masses, organizing and arming them, lightening their economic barriers, and suppressing the traitors and collaborators" (emphasis added). This quotation is fundamental to understanding Maoist revolutionary doctrine. The political dimension of insurgency is the basis of its success. Indeed, an insurgency will stand or fall to the extent that it is able to convert the masses of the population to its side. Sometimes conversion contains elements of coercion intended to shrink political opposition or to lessen the flow of intelligence about the insurgency to the government. However, the emphasis of conversion is to provide a better alternative. Of course, the quality of the government makes the insurgents' job easier or more difficult.

The style of warfare advocated by Mao Tse-tung, then, is derived from Sun Tzu. It emphasizes and compensates for the initial weakness of insurgents, but allows a gradual conversion to more conventional fighting as the insurgency strengthens and the government weakens. In a speech focusing on the campaign against Japan, Mao described the following ten "principles of operation":

1. To attack dispersed, isolated forces first; to attack concentrated, strong enemy forces later.
2. To take small and medium cities first; to take big cities later.
3. To make the wiping out of the enemy's effective strength our main objective, rather than the holding or seizing of a place.
4. To concentrate an absolutely superior force to encircle the enemy force. . . . To avoid battles of attrition in which we lose more than we gain or only break even.
5. To fight no battle unprepared. To fight no battle if we are not sure of victory.
6. To give full play to our style of fighting . . . continuous warfare.
7. To wipe out the enemy through mobile warfare.
8. With regard to attacking cities, resolutely to seize all weakly defended enemy points and cities. To seize at opportune moments all moderately defended enemy points and cities if circumstances permit. As for strongly defended fortified enemy points and cities, to wait until conditions are ripe and then take them.
9. To replenish our strength with all the arms and most of the personnel captured from the enemy.
10. To make good use of the intervals between campaigns to rest, train, and consolidate our troops.

Mao's is clearly a patient, long-term strategy. As a battle for people's loyalties, of which military aspects are only one part, it is an extremely difficult approach to defeat with conventional Western doctrines and forces. It is attractive to many Third World insurgents because most government forces there are trained and equipped by Western governments.

Vo Nguyen Giap

Mao Tse-tung's insurgency strategy was later adapted by the North Vietnamese General Vo Nguyen Giap in his successive campaigns against the reimposition of French colonial rule (1946–54) and the massive U.S. intervention on the side of the Republic of Vietnam (1965–73). Originally, Giap was a history professor with no formal military background. He rose to prominence by devising the successful siege of Dien Bien Phu in 1954, which caused France to leave Vietnam. He later adapted what he called

Table 3.1 Stages and Forms of the People's War

Stage	Form
Contention	Guerrilla warfare
Equilibrium	Mobile warfare
General counteroffensive	Regular warfare

the "people's war" to his campaign in order to force the Americans out of Southeast Asia.

The people's war is a variation of the more general form of guerrilla-mobile warfare. It is a strategy consisting of three stages, in terms of the form of fighting. In particular, it presupposes a military capability and base that precede engagement; for Giap, this meant a Viet Minh underground from World War II to contest the returning French, and an organized North Vietnamese Army (NVA) and insurgent underground, the Viet Cong, to confront the Americans.

The three stages of the people's war model are shown in Table 3.1. An insurgency begins with the guerrilla warfare tactics of Sun Tzu. As Giap graphically suggests in *People's War, People's Army* (1962), the guerrilla triumphs by "avoiding the enemy when he [the guerrilla] is the weaker, now scattering, now regrouping one's forces, now wearing out, not exterminating the enemy, determined to fight him everywhere . . . thus undermining his spirit and exhausting his forces." Strategically, the purpose is to exhaust and frustrate an enemy with superior forces and firepower. Giap emphasizes that, during this phase, the guerrillas "should not be exhausted by trying to keep or occupy land."

In the second stage of the people's war model, mobile warfare, the character of the fighting changes. Gradually, larger, more conventional forces are committed in situations where they are overwhelmingly superior at the point of engagement, or they revert to guerrilla evasiveness when they are weaker. The purpose of this stage is to shift the balance of power to the insurgents. When the balance shifts decisively to the insurgents, then the general counteroffensive begins, engaging standard conventional units to apply the *coup de main* and overthrow the government. When necessary, the strategy also allows for freedom of movement through the various stages (for example, if the general offensive proves premature, one can revert back to mobile warfare).

Prior to the American intervention in Vietnam beginning in 1965, the North Vietnamese and their Viet Cong allies had moved progressively through the guerrilla and mobile warfare stages to the point that the general counteroffensive was poised to bring down the government. The U.S. intervention (and encountering major American units in places such as the Ia Drang Valley) caused the North Vietnamese to revert back to mobile warfare, including the guerrilla tactics used by conventional units that were intended to frustrate large American operations. The 1968 Tet Offensive was the North Vietnamese's last attempt during the American phase of the Vietnam War to move on to the final stage. After its failure, the North Vietnamese reverted back to the second and first stages. It was not until after the Americans left Vietnam that Giap and his colleagues moved through all stages of the strategy, with the successful general counteroffensive against Saigon occurring in 1975.

Che Guevara

The person most closely associated with insurgent warfare in the Western Hemisphere was Ernesto "Che" Guevara (1928–67). An Argentine medical doctor, Guevara migrated to Central America, where he joined Fidel Castro prior to his return to Cuba. Guevara rose through the ranks of the Cuban movement, at one point becoming the number two man within the revolution. When the Cuban revolution succeeded, he sought to spread the movement throughout Central America and South America.

Guevara was principally known for distorting the principles of insurgent warfare, which ultimately led to his death in the Bolivian mountains in 1967 in an unsuccessful attempt to foment revolution among Bolivian tin mine workers. On one level, he was a devoted Maoist practitioner, accepting the tactical military advice of Sun Tzu and adopting his own thorough, even romantic ideas about the insurgent. In *Guerrilla Warfare* (1961), for instance, Guevara argues that the guerrilla "must have a moral conduct that shows him to be a true priest of the reform to which he aspires. To the stoicism imposed by the difficult conditions of warfare should be added an austerity born of rigid self-control that will prevent a single excess, whatever the circumstances. The guerrilla soldier must be an ascetic." While Mao probably would have agreed with most of this description, Guevara differed in his views on how to gain the allegiance of the people he was seeking to liberate. For Mao, this was a slow, arduous task that assured the population's support and protected the insurgents. Guevara sought to leapfrog that phase and jumpstart the revolution.

Guevara called his insurgents the *foco*. The idea was that a small, dedicated band of revolutionaries could enter a country and engage in hostile acts against government forces and facilities. Their success, in turn, would produce converts to the cause. The Maoist principle—that political conversion must precede military action—is inverted in Guevara's strategy, where military success is viewed as leading to political support.

However, Guevara's strategy was unsuccessful in Bolivia in 1967. Guevara and his forces (mostly Argentines) entered the Bolivian mining region, where the Indian miners had recently ended a long strike against the government. The Indians considered the Argentines undesirable intruders; moreover, their grievances with the government had largely been resolved. Thus, the Indians aided the government effort to track down and capture the invaders and execute Guevara.

MOBILE-GUERRILLA WARFARE

Mobile-guerrilla warfare is a politico-military strategy for conducting insurgent warfare that evolved over time. Its political base and strength arise from the conscious effort to enlist an alienated or indifferent population into the movement by providing a better system of governance. Suppression of dissidents and government supporters may be an integral part of the action. Its military base is the gradual conversion of a military situation of inferiority into one of superiority.

Political conversion provides the human (recruits) and material (food and clothing) infrastructures for the insurgency. Military success reinforces the political attraction of the movement. When correctly balanced and complete, the insurgency is extremely difficult to counter. The best time to defeat the insurgency is during its initial stages (before the insurgent base is firm) or if the insurgents violate their own principles (as did Guevara in Bolivia and the *contras* in Nicaragua). Actually, the *contras* never succeeded in establishing any significant base of support within the country from which they could operate.

Mobile-guerrilla warfare cannot be equated with any particular political group or ideology. The precondition for insurgency is a government that has alienated its population or left it indifferent. If an insurgent group can offer a better alternative, it has a chance to succeed by applying the model. In the future, the potential for pro-democratic insurgencies against remaining Communist and non-Communist dictatorships certainly exists.

In the mobile-guerrilla model of warfare, depicted in Table 3.2, each phase is distinct in terms of purpose and conduct. Movement through the stages presumes success at an earlier stage. At the same time, if circumstances demand, an insurgency should be flexible enough to allow backward movement as well.

Table 3.2   Mobile-Guerrilla Warfare Model

Stage[a]	Forces Used (Conventional or Guerrilla)	Activity	Objective
1. Organizational (Contention)	Build both, avoid fighting	Recruitment, protection	Base foundation, survival
2. Guerrilla (Equilibrium)	Use guerrillas, train conventionally	Guerrilla war to attrite enemy	Shift balance to insurgents
3. Conventional (General counteroffensive)	Integrate, use conventional forces	Destroy the enemy	Win power

[a]The designations of the stages are the author's; Giap's categories appear in parentheses.

The Organizational Stage

The organizational stage begins when a potential insurgent group decides that political change will require the use of organized violence. At this point, however, the movement is usually small, weak, and vulnerable. The insurgency is easily defeated if the authorities can identify and attack it at this early stage.

The first tasks of the insurgents are to develop a politically appealing action program and to find a place that is physically and politically distant from the government where the program will have appeal. At this point, the purpose is to persuade the population that the insurgents' program is superior to the government's and thus is worthy of public support. This is best accomplished by offering positive incentives to the population, such as by providing superior services, or through propaganda techniques.

In the organizational stage, an insurgency has three primary goals. The first is to find a primary safe place where the insurgents can operate successfully without danger of government interference. Ideally, the sanctuary should be within the target country because this will be closer to the population and will extend the insurgency's appeal. If the government has sufficient armed forces or intelligence capability or both, the insurgency may have to seek external sanctuary in neighboring countries. To succeed under this circumstance, it must gain control of widening parts of the target country. However, the failure to establish an internal sanctuary indicates that the insurgency lacks popular support.

The second goal in the organizational stage is to form a material support base for the insurgency by providing it with material necessities (food, clothing, and shelter) and a recruitment base for developing the guerrilla and conventional armed forces. Despite the common misperception, mobile-guerrilla warfare does not involve only irregular, guerrilla fighters. Mao, in particular, emphasized the development of a standard, conventional army for the ultimate task of seizing power. He often compared the relationship between the conventional and guerrilla forces to that of the left and right hands—each reinforces the other.

The third goal is to find sources of armaments and, hopefully, funds. Mao maintained that an insurgent movement should be self-sufficient, arming itself by stealing from the government or by picking up arms abandoned by defeated government forces. In some isolated cases, that may still be possible—the New People's Army in the Philippines is largely self-sufficient. Given the enormous armaments levels of many governments, however, an outside source of money and arms is certainly helpful to offset the government's initial advantage.

Obtaining arms and funding may be a major problem for future insurgents. During the Cold War, insurgent groups could appeal to one of the superpowers—usually the Soviet Union—for assistance in return for some ideological fealty. Now that the Cold War competition has ended, so has the source of assistance. Future insurgents will have to develop alternative funding strategies, such as Shining Path's financing of their efforts with "narcodollars" provided by Colombian cocaine traffickers.

In the organizational phase, the military arm of the insurgency is weak. Thus, two major goals of the insurgency are to develop forces to protect itself and to prepare for movement into the second stage of the revolution (engagement). During this stage, military contact is avoided except in isolated instances designed, for instance, to entice government forces to overreact to a provocation, further alienating them from the population. At the same time, the guerrillas may occasionally be used to screen and protect the conventional forces, whose training begins during this phase.

The first stage of the insurgent model is critical to success. For the insurgents, it represents the point of their greatest vulnerability. Later, if they gain the support of the population or a major part of it, they are extremely difficult to root out and destroy. During the first stage, the government has the greatest opportunity to destroy a movement. If the government succeeds, it is testament to the lack of alienation in the population to support insurgency; if the government fails, that fact is evidence of grievances in the population.

If in the first stage the insurgents faithfully follow the dictates of

Maoist strategy and provide a superior alternative to the people, they will be difficult to defeat. The battle at this time is over popular loyalty; it is a political battle which, if lost, cannot easily be recouped through military means.

The Guerrilla Stage

The guerrilla stage involves organized fighting initiated by the insurgents. It is called the *guerrilla stage* for two reasons. First, the guerrilla forces developed during the organizational stage are now the main fighting forces, whereas the conventional forces are not employed until later. Second, during this stage the primary tactics are those of the guerrilla described by Sun Tzu and developed by Mao and Giap.

At the start of the guerrilla stage, the insurgents remain militarily weaker than the government, making large-scale confrontations too dangerous. Thus, the Sun Tzu-Maoist doctrine—to fight only when the guerrillas have enormous advantages at the point of contact—becomes a matter of survival. If success is not assured, the guerrilla will avoid contact, retreating and melting into the friendly environment of the first stage.

The purposes of combat during the second stage are to weaken the government and gradually widen the insurgents' areas of operation and strength. This requires considerable patience on the part of the insurgents, particularly in the early stages when they are weak and find few situations that meet their criteria of engagement. If followed faithfully, however, two salutary effects accrue.

First, the morale of the government forces gradually decreases. Government forces come to realize that forays into the countryside are likely to end in one of two ways, neither happy. The government forces may never encounter the enemy forces, in which case the action proves futile. If contact is made, it is likely to be on the terms of the insurgents in the form of an ambush or some other encounter, and the result is defeat. Realizing over time that one either fights and loses or does nothing, morale is gradually sapped, the government forces become demoralized, weapons are abandoned on the field, and government forces either desert or defect to the insurgents.

The second effect is to create the image of the insurgents as winners. If the results of combat are uniform success for the insurgents, gradually more and more people outside as well as inside the liberated zones will view the insurgency as a winner and be attracted to it.

The process, which is paralleled by expanding political action, is a gradual change in the balance of power from the government to the insurgents. As the government loses more and more troops, they encounter more difficulty replacing deserters and converts other than by conscription, which only further alienates the population.

The major characteristic of the guerrilla stage is its protracted nature. At its onset, the degree of military and political activity is likely to be slight, even virtually indetectable outside the country. The rate of increase in the tempo of operations will depend on the success or failure of government counteraction. Following the Maoist doctrine, however, the guerrillas must remain patient and wait for the right opportunities.

From the outside, the problem is that insurgencies often do not appear to become dangerous until they are nearly successful. In the organizational stage, insurgent movements with a long-term prospect of success are largely opaque to both the government and outsiders because the target population shields the insurgents. The early stages of the guerrilla phase, involving only isolated attacks in remote rural areas, likewise receive little publicity.

The danger is that there will not be an adequate response until it is too late. Politically, insurgencies breed and thrive in the presence of perceived injustice; the cure is reform, which governments typically resist in the early phases. Militarily, the large unit tactics taught by Westerners to government armies are likewise unlikely to be effective because guerrillas simply move out of the way of such units to avoid engagement.

The Conventional Stage

When the balance turns decisively against the government, the insurgents turn to the conventional stage—administering the final military blow that crushes the government's forces and puts the insurgents into power. In rural-based conflicts, such as in China and Vietnam before U.S. intervention, that decisive point was reached when the government forces were trapped in the main urban centers and the insurgents controlled the countryside as well as transportation and communications between government-held cities.

In the classic Maoist formulation, the conventional forces in training since the organizational stage administer the final blow. The guerrilla forces are then integrated into the main body of the army to crush what is left of the government's ability to resist.

Conventional forces are critical at this point. A force that is solely guerrilla may lack the firepower and human resources to deliver the final blow. During the Vietnam War, for instance, the North Vietnamese Army (NVA) played this role; although it acted as a guerrilla force tactically at times, its weight was brought to bear in 1964 and 1965 to help produce the final overthrow of the Republic of Vietnam (RVN), and it probably would have succeeded in the absence of American intervention. As the Americans were leaving in 1972, North Vietnam shifted to stage three again, but U.S. airpower and South Vietnamese ground forces were capable of stopping them. In 1975, the NVA attacked again, and an exhausted army of the Republic of Vietnam (ARVN), lacking U.S. support, ammunition, and even fuel for its vehicles, crumbled.

One last point should be made. Insurgents are capable of miscalculation (as the North Vietnamese were). For that reason, the decision to revert from stage three back to stage two is always available. It is arguable, for instance, that this is what happened in Vietnam in 1968, after the U.S.-ARVN counteroffensive (following the Tet Offensive) shattered the NVA and destroyed the Viet Cong as a fighting force. Under these circumstances, the insurgents simply reverted back to guerrilla fighting to provide a screen while a new conventional army was being organized.

INSURGENCY AS CONVENTIONAL WAR INVERTED

Insurgent warfare was developed by people incapable of defeating conventional military forces by conventional means. It therefore developed as a way to invert the priorities, strategies, and tactics of traditional warfare. Insurgents seek to neutralize standard military forces; large army formations are sidestepped, concentrations of firepower are avoided by dispersal or tunnelling, sophisticated reconnaissance is stymied by hiding under jungle foliage. In addition, insurgency adds the explicit political dimension of the contest for people's loyalties to the more traditional military activities of armed forces.

Fighting insurgents with conventional techniques is frustrating. Because guerrillas do not stand and fight in the traditional way, we tend to confuse and denigrate what they do and how they do it. The comment by a U.S. Army general during the Vietnam War that "any well-trained soldier can defeat a guerrilla" is a quintessential statement of misunderstanding. We must recognize that the insurgents' agenda is different and that defeating them means defeating their strategy.

In addition, there are four defining aspects of insurgency: (1) the conditions leading to the success of an insurgency; (2) the problem of the "center of gravity" in an insurgency; (3) the problem of asymmetry of objectives between insurgents and those who oppose them, notably outsiders; and (4) how to measure the success of an insurgency or its opposition.

Conditions for Insurgent Success

For an insurgency to begin, there must be hostility toward the government among those most prone to form an insurgent movement. In addition, a large portion of the population must be indifferent toward the government in order for conversion to the insurgent cause to occur. Insurgencies seldom flourish in areas characterized by popular government support.

If an insurgency is going to do more than exist, certain other conditions are necessary. Insurgencies usually do best in relatively primitive countries, where the combination of geography and primitive transportation and communications networks makes it difficult for the government to control the entire country. From the viewpoint of the insurgents, they need a sanctuary where they can be immune from destruction, especially during the highly vulnerable organizational stage.

In the prototypical guerrilla-mobile war, the Chinese Communist forces of Mao Tse-tung were nearly decimated in the 1920s before their doctrine was perfected. To avoid annihilation, they traveled the mythic Long March to the Hunan Mountains, where they were effectively shielded from attack and could recuperate, regroup, and recruit the beginnings of the force that would eventually sweep through China. When the French returned to Indochina, Ho Chi Minh, Vo Nguyen Giap, and the Viet Minh were able to escape to the mountainous north of Vietnam, where they were immune to effective French attack. When he returned to Cuba in 1956, Fidel Castro and the eleven surviving members of his band headed for the rugged Sierra Maestra Mountains, where government forces were unable or unwilling to root them out. More recently, the Afghan *mujahadin* used the sanctuary of rugged mountain terrain to protect themselves from the government.

Technically, the sanctuary can be either inside or outside the country in which the insurgency is focused. An external safe haven can provide physical respite from government troops (for training and the like). Eventually, however, successful insurgencies must establish a secure base of operations within the country. The failure to do so admits the insurgency lacks popular appeal, without which it cannot succeed. The Achilles heel of the U.S.-supported *contra* movement in Nicaragua was their inability to establish an in-country sanctuary.

The final condition of success has to do with access to adequate armaments. Pure Maoist doctrine argues that an external source is unnecessary because the armaments requirements of the insurgent are modest (limited mainly to hand-held and hand-carried weaponry that is easy to transport and conceal). Operating in remote, rugged terrain where roads are primitive or nonexistent, insurgents do not need and have no reason to possess the heavy armament of conventional warfare. Indeed, to the extent such equipment might limit the mobility of the insurgents, it may be counterproductive. Moreover, having to turn to outside sources of arms may weaken the appeal of the insurgency. As the U.S. Army's basic document on insurgency (FM 100-20) points out, dependence on outside support "implies the inability to sustain oneself."

"War on the cheap" is also "warfare for the primitive." It would be hard—if not impossible—for someone to set up an insurgency in a modern, developed country. Assuming one could find enough people of like mind to begin, where would one go to organize in such a way as not to be instantly exposed? Extremist groups in the United States (such as the "survivalists") would love to hide in the woods to organize whatever activity they would like to undertake. Instead they become the focus of feature stories for local and network television reports, are harassed and, to the extent they engage in extralegal behavior, prosecuted. Insurgency thrives in a situation of anonymity and protection; if these circumstances are denied or unavailable, it does not thrive.

Centers of Gravity

The secret to winning wars is to determine what it is about the enemy that is absolutely necessary for its continued prosecution of hostilities— the center of gravity—and then destroy it.

In twentieth-century conventional war, the center of gravity usually has something to do with the industrial capacity of a country, the so-called "industrial web" of production necessary to continue hostilities (such as steel to build weapons or fuel to power the war machine). In some cases, the center of gravity is the other nation's capital or its top political or military leadership.

In insurgent warfare, the center of gravity for both sides is the same: the political loyalty of the population. Since most insurgent wars are internal wars fought for the control of a country, each side has the same population as its center of gravity, and the purpose of both the political and military activity of the war is to influence the perceptions and loyalties of the civilian population.

In conventional war, centers of gravity are discrete. Normally in a war between countries, one can assume that the populations of the combatant countries are loyal; if one wants to weaken that loyalty through political or military acts directed against the enemy, one can do so without attacking one's own population. The situation is more complicated, however, when both sides share the same center of gravity. Both sides seek to convert the same population and depend on the same body of people for their support. Ultimately, the issue comes down to which side makes the more effective appeal. This creates at least two differences between insurgent and other types of warfare.

First, the relationship between military and political action is much more intimate and direct in insurgent warfare. The purpose of all wars is to achieve certain political objectives, but in conventional war one rarely measures individual actions specifically in terms of a political purpose. In insurgency, each military act must be measured in terms of whether it will increase or decrease the support of the insurgents or the government. Often, acts that make little military sense will be undertaken for their political impact. The Tet Offensive of 1968 in Vietnam is an example. Militarily, the offensive was a disaster for the NVA and Viet Cong, who suffered such enormous losses during the American and South Vietnamese counteroffensive that they were unable to mount another major offensive for four years. Politically, however, the Tet Offensive was a success because it attacked successfully the American center of gravity—public support for the war—and thus engaged the process of U.S. withdrawal from Southeast Asia.

The second problem is how to attack and weaken the strength of the opponent without undercutting one's own support. Since supporters of both sides are intermingled in the population, this may be physically difficult to accomplish. Moreover, acts of brutality are against one's own people (though of a different political persuasion), so repressive acts may alienate the neutral portions of the population that both sides must court. In military analogy, this is the problem of building schools during the day (positive appeals to the people) and then bombing them at night because they are used by the enemy. Moreover, both sides, but especially the insurgents, try to create situations to which the government forces will overreact to the point of atrocity and thereby alienate the public. These problems do not surface in conventional war, where there are distinct centers of gravity that can be attacked without undermining one's own political support.

Asymmetry of Objectives

Contending sides in wars enter hostilities with some political objective toward peace—what Sir Basil Liddell Hart called "the better state of the peace." These objectives can be total or limited. Totality involves overthrowing and destroying the other side, whereas limited objectives are anything less than the government's overthrow or the insurgents' elimination.

Insurgencies are typically total wars because their outcome involves either the insurgents' overthrow of the government or the government's defeat of the insurgency. Unfortunately, this symmetry and intensity is not so obvious to the outsider, especially if it views the conflict as low-intensity and thus not very fervent.

Part of the confusion about insurgencies in general arises because Third World insurgencies do not look like total wars. The military pace and intensity of these wars, especially in their early stages, are typically small and not terribly bloody. But this is because the means available to both sides are not grand, and thus the combat seems less than total.

This causes two problems. First, these are wars of total means for the combatants, in the sense that they employ all of the military means they possess. Compared to the lethal weapons employed in Desert Storm, a war between forces equipped with rifles may not seem that intensive, but that does not detract from its desperation to the participants. Second, the lack of grand military scale may also obscure the importance of the outcome to both sides.

This is important: Insurgent wars are normally wars of total political purpose for both sides. One characteristic of such wars is that they are hardly ever resolved by negotiation unless both sides exhaust themselves short of decision. Negotiation presumes the ability to compromise, and control of government is not divisible, particularly between groups who have been fighting and killing one another for a long period of time. The problem of asymmetry occurs when a third party seeks to intervene in such a war, normally as a counterinsurgent. Once again, two problems arise. First, the intervening party usually enters the fray for a limited purpose, such as restoring some status quo ante. By definition, a limited objective is less important than a total purpose to the person who holds it. The party with limited purposes is almost certain to be less determined and more unwilling to sacrifice. Second, an outsider with a limited objective does not require a total victory to achieve their objective. They are more likely to seek a negotiated settlement that is unacceptable to either internal party. The situation in Vietnam illustrated this dynamic: To the North Vietnamese, the goal of unifying the country was total and encompassing; to the United States, maintaining an independent South Vietnam was a limited and ultimately less important goal.

Measuring Progress

Although it is simple to measure the ultimate success or failure of an insurgency, measuring its success along the way is more difficult, especially during the first and second stages of mobile-guerrilla warfare when decisive fighting rarely occurs. The success of conventional warfare is traditionally measured in terms of the territory occupied or liberated and the numbers of enemy killed and weapons destroyed. None of these measures of success can be applied to insurgency, however. To insurgents, issues like territorial control are irrelevant; when faced with the choice of defending territory and risking defeat or abandoning territory to avoid defeat, the guerrilla will always choose the latter alternative. The battle is for the hearts and minds of men, and is not served by lost military encounters.

Furthermore, insurgencies tend to win by avoiding defeat, whereas the government can only succeed by defeating and destroying the insurgency. Insurgencies win by not losing; government forces win by winning. All theories of insurgency based on protracted warfare start from the assumption that it is the insurgents' mission to wear down the enemy by defeating its morale and will to resist.

The greatest problem is making interim judgments about the success of an insurgency. During the Vietnam War, for example, "body counts" of the dead failed to convey the real situation. If somehow one could poll the population regularly—an impossibility in a primitive country at war—the results might be instructive. The only indicator of success is how long the insurgency goes on, though it too is imperfect because some insurgencies continue for long periods of time without taking any decisive action.

CONCLUSION

Most Americans neither emphathize with nor understand insurgency. In part, we may be too far from our own insurgent past to indentify with what is going on in the Third World. Insurgencies occur in faraway places remote from the American consciousness, so they lack immediacy. Also, insurgency and counterinsurgency have never been militarily important to Americans.

American history books fail to emphasize that the United States was born as the result of a conflict characterized in part as insurgent. Although it may offend some to describe the American patriots who fought the Revolution as Maoists, there is some truth to the assertion. That the American Revolution was partly fought as an insurgency is not surprising. It pitted a militarily inferior foe against an opponent with overwhelming conventional forces. When the Revolution began in 1775, there was no American army, only a group of loosely organized militias that came and went as the spirit moved them at the siege of Boston. George Washington worked to transform these irregular forces, who had learned techniques such as ambush and fighting from behind natural barriers from the Indians, into a conventional army to confront the British. The process was long, arduous, and bloody.

Washington was unable to challenge the British army directly with success; when the main bodies of the armies confronted one another, as at Brandywine, New York, or Monmouth, the Continentals usually were unsuccessful. Unconventional methods simply made more sense. The major exception was at Saratoga, but the army that the British General "Gentleman" Johnny Burgoyne put into the field had been weakened by guerrilla-style harassment along the route from Canada and was outnumbered.

The physical circumstances also militated for insurgency. The colonies were large—in fact, too large to be physically controlled—and the terrain was mountainous and heavily forested, especially in New England and the southern colonies. Guerrilla tactics, such as those adopted by the Green Mountain Boys and Francis Marion, were simply correct for the circumstance.

Although Washington certainly did not act from a sense of Maoist doctrine, he won the war by moving to something akin to the third stage of mobile-guerrilla warfare. Finally possessing a numerically superior force, he laid siege to the British at the climactic engagement at Yorktown that "stood the world on its head."

Of course, the American Revolution was not a true mobile-guerrilla contest, but it did share some aspects of it. The Revolution was the only American war in which Americans engaged in techniques of guerrilla warfare. Similarly, Native Americans, notably the Apaches in Arizona, used guerrilla warfare techniques during the period in which they were subdued. Moreover, Americans acted as leaders and advisors of guerrillas in opposing the Japanese in Asia during World War II.

Insurgencies tend to occur in unfamiliar locales far from American shores. In particular, they occur in Third World countries with equatorial climates, rugged mountains, harsh weather, and unfamiliar flora and fauna. These are often areas with which the average American has no experience, knowledge, understanding, or empathy. Moreover, by the time an insurgency generates sufficient publicity to attract attention, it is usually in the advanced stages.

Another problem tied to Americans' difficulty in dealing with insurgency is that the warfare is militarily alien. Historically, the U.S. experience in dealing with insurgents has been less than exemplary. Whether it involved rooting the Seminoles out of the Florida swamps in the 1820s, battling the Filipino insurgency between 1899 and 1902, or chasing Pancho Villa around New Mexico, Arizona, and northern Mexico, insurgency is a form of warfare with which the American military has never been very comfortable or successful.

Mastering insurgency is superfluous to Americans in any direct sense. Since we have a broadly legitimate political system that does not require violence to change, there is little reason for Americans to learn insurgency to solve their own problems. It is the strategy of primitive political systems suffering from primitive physical conditions; the United States is hardly fertile ground for the strategy.

In addition, insurgent warfare inverts the "American way of war." The American military style, as it has evolved from the campaigns of Ulysses S. Grant and William T. Sherman during the American Civil War, features the application of massed force against an opponent. It was devised by Grant as he pursued Robert E. Lee around Virginia during the bloody but climactic campaign in 1864 and 1865 and honed by Sherman, who destroyed the buffalo herds to starve out the Plains Indians. The American military style reached its zenith in the world wars, the vestiges of which were evident in the massive air campaign against Saddam Hussein in the early days of the Persian Gulf War.

The American model is total war conducted by a large, powerful nation. It is a style of war with which the American military is comfortable; preparing for a massive, climactic World War III in Europe during the Cold War was the epitome of the American way of war.

Insurgent warfare is not only unlike American-style war but is designed to counteract the American style as well. The American military does not like insurgency because of its lack of understanding of and success at it. At the same time, the American military prides itself in its basic apoliticism that occasionally appears as antipoliticism. Any dynamic that injects a political element into an otherwise "pure" military endeavor taints the enterprise. Insurgency not only injects an explicitly political element into war but often subordinates the military element to the political as well.

For Americans, the problem has not been how to adapt insurgent techniques into the military repertoire (except in instances involving aid to groups like the *contras*). Rather, the United States historically has been more likely to support the beleaguered government against which an insurgency is being mounted or contemplated. This is the problem of counterinsurgency, our focus in Chapter 4.

CHAPTER 4

The Intractable Nemesis: Counterinsurgency

During the Cold War, the United States more frequently opposed insurgent wars than it aided or assisted them. *Counterinsurgency,* either by advising a friendly government about how to defeat an insurgent movement or by physically committing American forces, has been a controversial part of the U.S. military experience. Part of the controversy lies in the alien nature of insurgency-counterinsurgency within American military doctrine as well as in our historical difficulty in dealing militarily with these kinds of situations. But there is more to the controversy.

American postwar involvement in insurgent or counterinsurgent situations can only be understood in the context of the Cold War competition in the Third World. As the countries of the former European colonial empires achieved independence, they became the subject of competition for influence and, in some cases, for allegiance between East and West. The race was to see how much of the map would be painted blue (pro-Western) and how much red (pro-Soviet).

New Third World countries were vulnerable to the Cold War competition, and some even longed for it. In most cases, the group that first came to rule in Third World countries lacked several commodities needed to aid their attainment of legitimacy and thereby successful nation-building. They were poor and underdeveloped economically. The resources that could create prosperity and build a strong, legitimate state were unavailable. Moreover, most governments were poorly prepared to run a political system. The officials were undereducated, and it was only rarely that colonial policy sought to prepare countries for self-governance until the last moment before independence. As a result, the new governments often showed ineptitude, incompetence, and, even worse, corruption and venality. Finally, the politics of these new multinational states was often the politics of nationality against nationality—a struggle to gain control so that one group could rule at the expense of the others. As a result, some groups were almost always discontented, ready to throw their support behind some dissident group that offered a better deal.

The instability within Third World countries usually favored the Soviets. When independence was granted to most colonies in the 1940s through the 1960s, they adopted the appearance of the Western democratic systems of their former masters. In practice, though, their inexperience often resulted in a slide toward nondemocratic rule (usually toward the Right rather than the Left). To those oppressed by such systems, the Soviet and Chinese models were appealing.

One aspect of the Soviet appeal in the Third World was that it was directed at those who lacked power. Marxism was a revolutionary doctrine that offered the hope of a utopia for the oppressed. The downfall of that utopia is clear today, but it was not so obvious in the 1960s. Moreover, the Communists offered practical guidance, in the form of Maoist strategy, that could be adapted to local conditions (as Giap did in Vietnam).

Most importantly, however, support of "wars of national liberation" was part of both Soviet and Chinese policy. If an insurgent movement was willing to espouse Marxist ideology and possibly to send some of its leaders to China or the Soviet Union for training and indoctrination, there was a good chance of gaining material support. In some cases, the profession of Marxist sentiment was sincere. In others, it was not, and so it could not be translated into Soviet influence.

The Cold War competition cast internal wars in East-West geopolitical terms that were centered on the consequences for the United States of an insurgency succeeding in overthrowing an anti-Communist government. Although the question was relevant, asking it as a first question often substituted for asking what was wrong in the first place and what, if anything, the West—or the United States—could do about it. American interest and involvement in insurgency situations has ebbed and flowed in the long term, a reflection of U.S. foreign policy generally. The activist view was most strongly associated with the Kennedy administration. John F. Kennedy was the first U.S. president to take an active interest in insurgency and counterinsurgency—in what were often called "brushfire wars" at the time, the analogy being to the flareup of brushfires in the American West and the need to put them out. Believing the ideological Cold War competition to be encompassing, Kennedy insisted the United States enhance the very small forces available for that purpose. Special Forces, the so-called Green Berets, became the showcase of his military effort and the object of some intense internal insurgent warfare within the armed forces, especially the U.S. Army. The Vietnam experience soured the American public on this level of activism. The only president since Kennedy to advocate such a strident level of activism was George Bush.

The other side of the controversy was the belief the United States should not actively involve itself in Third World situations. In this view, direct involvement would overtax American resources and draw the United States into situations that would put its vital interests at risk. Thus, prudence dictates providing assistance to beleaguered Third World governments in terms of weapons, training, and economic and humanitarian aid, but not in terms of U.S. forces. This was the position of President Richard M. Nixon and is known as the Nixon Doctrine.

In the post–Cold War world, the patina of East-West competition has been removed from calculations about insurgencies. The question of appropriate U.S. involvement remains vital, however, because the failure to address the underlying sources of Third World instability means insurgencies will continue, if without the ideological underpinning. If the world system values minimizing instability and violence, then counterinsurgency techniques will be necessary if development fails to stifle the urges toward insurgency. Without the Cold War overlay, then, counterinsurgency can be viewed in terms of its own merits, rather than through the lenses of the Cold War.

In this chapter, we examine the dynamics of countering insurgency, particularly the problems created for an outside power participating in counterinsurgency. Our focus first is on the problems that face the counterinsurgent based on the perceptions that gave rise to insurgency. Next, we examine the political and military dimensions of mounting counterinsurgency, as well as the great difficulties of coordinating the two efforts. Finally, we look at the critical problems of timing outside involvement and how the United States organizes itself for the effort.

THE BASIC DIFFICULTY: "THERE IS A PROBLEM HERE"

The need to consider counterinsurgency presupposes that there is an ongoing military movement intent on overthrowing the regime in power. Insurgencies do not arise in a vacuum; they begin when some portion of a population is alienated from the state or government and takes up arms. In other words, deep political grievances form the foundation of insurgency; when such grievances are absent, insurgencies do not arise or die quickly (as Che Guevara learned in his abortive revolution in the Bolivian Andes).

Thus, when there is enough opposition to the government to justify a counterinsurgency effort, this suggests that there is something wrong with the government in power. People do not form revolutionary movements to overthrow duly elected governments that perform their duties conscientiously and within the public trust. Insurgency is a serious and dangerous activity and one that people do not enter into lightly. Therefore, a country with an ongoing insurgent movement has a government that is not functioning properly in some way. To assess the problem, one must begin by looking at what gave rise to the insurgency; to do otherwise runs the risk of mounting an irrelevant and likely unsuccessful campaign.

Successful counterinsurgency is more difficult than insurgency for two reasons. First, the problem for a government facing an insurgency is that it is alienated from the population. This may well translate into poor intelligence, which leaves it unaware of the forming insurgency. Yet, if a government fails to snuff out insurgents when they are weak, the problem rapidly escalates. According to the former French revolutionary and associate of Che Guevara, Regis DeBray, destroying the embryonic insurgency is "the golden rule of counterinsurgency."

The second reason counterinsurgency is more difficult than insurgency is that its requirements for success are greater. For the government to be truly triumphal, it must destroy the insurgency; as long as the insurgency exists, the authority of the government is compromised. That authority is not undeniable until the insurgency no longer lives; militarily and politically, the government must win to win. In contrast, an insurgency need not be victorious to enjoy success. As long as the insurgency continues to exist, it challenges the government's authority (its main purpose). And the longer it survives, the more the government's authority is eroded. It is this gradual, patient campaign of attrition that is the insurgents' strategic principle. Time is on the side of insurgency; it only has to avoid losing to win. The alternative, protracted but indecisive insurgencies (such as in El Salvador), are unsatisfying and draining to all, but especially to the government.

The problem of counterinsurgency is perceived differently by the government being challenged than it is by outsiders considering intervention. From the government's viewpoint, the solution to the problem is likely to be seen as primarily a military exercise. To the outsider, however, the weight of political discord is likely to be most important. As a result, there develops tension and disagreement between the government and those who seek to assist it, which explains in part the greater difficulty in counterinsurgency.

The Government's Perspective

The government's view of defeating an insurgency is distorted by the interrelated facts that the insurgency is directed against it and its policies. Unless the government is so totally venal and cynical that it is consciously suppressing the people for its own narrow and selfish gains, then it will be initially nonplussed by the existence of a concerted effort to destroy it. Those who run the system will naturally view the insurgents as the villains and see their suppression as just.

In most Third World countries that experience insurgency, the root of the problem is that the government rules for the benefit of one group and at the expense of others. In some cases, privilege and benefit are class-based, where an elite maintains itself in power to exploit the masses for its own material gain. In El Salvador, for example, a handful of wealthy families control most of the productive land, squeeze the profits from that land, and refuse to transfer land to the largely landless peasantry. Here the appeal of the Marxist insurgency, which opposed the government for over a decade, was to redistribute land, and it was a powerful appeal.

In other parts of the world, the basis of exploitation differs. In Africa, for instance, it is normally tribal, such as when one tribe rules at the expense of its rivals. In Nigeria, for instance, the Islamic Hausa-Fulani and Christian Ibo tribes have battled for control and whoever is in power rules at the other's expense. The long struggle between Watutsi and Bahutu, which resulted in the splitting of former Rwanda-Burundi into separate states, is another example.

Religious suppression can also be the catalyst. Islamic-Christian inter-communal disagreement fueled the Eritrean campaigns against Ethiopia and underlays the continuing violence in the Sudan. Divisions among Hindus, Muslims, and Sikhs plague the Asian subcontinent, and inter-communal violence fuels chaos in Lebanon and the feuds between the Palestinians and Israelis.

As long as multinationalism and economic disparity mark the Third World, there will remain the potential for insurgency and hence the need to fashion counterinsurgent plans. Indeed, if the gap between rich and poor within Third World societies continues to widen, this potential will increase. The problem is how to deal with it.

There are two basic ways to undercut an insurgency; how they are combined largely determines the likely success or failure of a counterin-surgency. The first is political: the battle for the hearts and minds of men. The tools for waging the battle include reform of the grievances that gave rise to the insurgency, honest governance conducted by freely chosen officials, and a visible commitment to improving the lot of those who are the targets of the insurgents' appeal. This approach attacks the center of gravity by asserting a legitimate claim to govern.

Although the political strategy may seem so obvious that any govern-ment would adopt it as its primary focus, this is not always the case. There are impediments to implementing the strategy. For example, the government may not want to do so. In many Third World countries, governance is the prize by which privilege and wealth are extracted from society. To do what is necessary to assert legitimacy requires that the government and its supporters forfeit some of their privileges, which they may not be interested in doing. Rather, it is usually more appealing to hold on for as long as possible and then to abscond with the riches. The elite within El Salvador has been accused of such a strategy, as was the former Duvalier dictatorship in Haiti.

Another factor that hinders a government's willingness to address grievances is that the insurgency will attempt to impede the government's attempts to assert legitimacy. The political battle is about which side is considered legitimate, and the insurgents are going to try to make their own positive case. When that fails, they are likely to engage in actions like terrorism to discredit the regime; the more they are forced to do so, the weaker their position becomes.

The other alternative for defeating an insurgency is through military force. The government is likely to find this approach attractive, if it can be made to work. If the government can defeat the insurgency on the battlefield, the insurgents lose. In this case, questions of redressing insurgent grievances are avoided. The beleaguered government is thus likely to emphasize the military part of the counterinsurgency, especially if the insurgency has some success.

The problem with the military approach is that it can only be mounted against a passive insurgency that does not understand its own strategy. Insurgent warfare is, after all, designed to thwart the achievement of decisive success by government forces. Moreover, the government's forces are usually Western-trained and schooled in Western strategies and tactics, which are inappropriate to fighting insurgencies. Finally, a protracted military campaign is long and exhausting; when it is not accompanied by a clear attempt to improve the people's lot, recruiting and maintaining the forces become even more difficult for the government. This was the case in the Republic of Vietnam during the latter stages of its attempt to maintain an independent South Vietnam.

In reality, of course, a counterinsurgency incorporates both political and military elements into its attempts. There is no benefit to engaging in civic actions if the insurgents are free to roam about and destroy those efforts. At the same time, though, it makes little sense to liberate the countryside and expect the public's gratitude if the underlying conditions that created the problem are left unattended.

Finding the proper mix to deal with an insurgency is a difficult task, particularly against a strong insurgency. If the insurgents are inept, the task may be manageable. But when the insurgency is well organized and emerges from the organizational stage, its appeal is extremely difficult to counteract. In this case, the temptation arises to enlist the assistance of an outside party, which creates a whole different set of problems and dynamics.

The Potential Intervenor's Perspective

During the Cold War, the ideological persuasion of insurgents and counterinsurgents provided the primary litmus test for interest in intervening in internal wars. In most cases, these wars matched an insurgent band espousing some variation of Marxism and employing a form of Maoist strategy against an anti-Communist but not necessarily democratic government that had a military officer corps trained in and forces supplied by the West. In these circumstances, involvement was based on geopolitical concerns. The primary issue was how an adverse outcome in a given war would affect the global or regional interests of the United States (or whoever else was contemplating involvement). The deadly affairs within a state became little more than an extension of the global Cold War.

The Cold War overlay distorted the Western view of insurgencies. Because of the Maoist roots of military doctrine and the Soviet readiness to assist insurgent groups, insurgency and communism became nearly synonymous. The answer to the question "What is wrong here?" became "The Communists are taking over." Sometimes, this was an accurate answer; at other times, it was not.

The Communist–anti-Communist mask oversimplified many Third World situations. The real cause of insurgency usually had little to do with East-West rivalries; rather, it was tied to the legitimate claim to rule. One side may have portrayed itself in ideological terms so as to attract support, while the other side may have appealed to the opposite end of the ideological spectrum, but that did not mean that the real issues were about Cold War concerns.

The Cold War overlay distorted the analysis of real reasons in several different ways. For example, it tended to divert attention from the root causes of insurgency, which are almost always internal. Extrapolating the internal struggle for power and legitimacy into a faraway extension of the Cold War made it easy to avoid answering "What is wrong here?" The presumption was that insurgencies were foreign-bred cancers that could be excised with the surgeon's scalpel, rather than homegrown maladies caused by the malfeasance or ineptitude of those one was considering supporting.

Another Cold War distortion came in the inaccurate depictions of both the government and the insurgents. Insurgencies usually respond to some perceived oppression, but potential supporters can hardly believe they are contemplating aiding oppression. In order to warrant support, the government must be portrayed as heroic and the insurgency as wicked. There is danger in widespread belief in false images, and especially in assuming that the combatants will perform in stereotyped ways.

During the Vietnam War, for instance, the American perception boiled down, in large measure, to the depiction of the leader of the Vietnamese independence movement, Ho Chi Minh. Ho had collaborated with the American Office of Strategic Services (the OSS, predecessor of the Central Intelligence Agency) during World War II against the Japanese occupation of then French Indochina. At the war's end, Ho prepared to declare the independence of his nation, as promised by President Franklin Roosevelt in the Atlantic Charter in 1940. To that end, Americans and Vietnamese celebrated Ho's declaration, a document lifted almost entirely from the American Declaration of Independence and Abraham Lincoln's Gettysburg Address.

Yet Ho presented a problem. Although he was acknowledged initially as the leader of Vietnamese nationalism, he was also a Communist. His ideological preference was no secret; he had been a founding member of the French Communist party after World War I and had spent a considerable time in Moscow during the interwar period. The problem was how to depict him—as a nationalist (good) or a Communist (bad).

Ultimately, the image of Ho as Communist prevailed, and the United States cast its lot with his anti-Communist opponent in South Vietnam, President Ngo Dinh Diem. As the United States displaced France as the principal outside opponent of Vietnamese communism-nationalism, the fact that the struggle was over the hearts and minds of the Vietnamese people was lost in the shuffle. Diem and his successors were portrayed as heroic and Ho Chi Minh and his followers as evil. By acting solipsistically, Americans created a vision not shared by the Vietnamese. Reality was the victim.

Distorting the seriousness of the problem created by a successful insurgency has yet another consequence: the tendency to overestimate the likely success of intervening on behalf of the counterinsurgents. This tendency manifests itself in two different ways. First, there is the tendency to presume that intervention can effectively tip the balance to the government, when the opposite is more likely the case. Foreigners can rarely have a positive impact on the contest for the political loyalty of the people. In fact, foreign presence is often used by the opposition to accuse the government of dependence on the "neocolonialists." For example, the Shining Path rebels of Peru reportedly want U.S. intervention in the coca-growing Upper Huallaga valley as a way to consolidate their control over the local population. Moreover, the need to import foreigners to improve the government's performance is an open admission of the government's weakness, another advantage of the insurgents.

Second, there is a tendency to overestimate the amount of leverage possible over beleaguered governments. These governments generally have been engaging in unpopular practices and have resisted reforming those practices, or the insurgency would not persist. The outsider normally recognizes the problem and counsels its solution, but such advice generally is neither welcomed nor embraced. Moreover, there is a perverse internal dynamic by which the supported government comes to believe that the longer it receives assistance, the less leverage the assistance giver has; that is, the larger the investment becomes, the more difficult it is to cut one's losses. Thus, assistance decreases rather than increases influence.

This dynamic was also evident during the American experience in Vietnam, and specifically with Diem. As the U.S. investment increased over time, Diem thought he could safely ignore American insistence on political, economic, and especially land reform. He concluded that American threats to withhold assistance, which would have had the effect of promoting the prospects of Ho Chi Minh, were hollow.

The upshot is the very real danger that outsiders will simply not understand what they are getting themselves involved in. Westerners are well removed from their own revolutionary experiences and may lack empathy for the Third World struggle for legitimacy. Moreover, insurgencies occur in distant, unfamiliar places that are hard for Americans to relate to. The tendency is to make the situation familiar by relating it to their own experience and universe. The result can be frustration when things do not happen the way they are expected to occur. That frustration is epitomized by a statement attributed to an American soldier summarizing his Vietnam experience: "We were there to help but the Vietnamese are so stupid they can't understand that a great people want to help a weak people."

THE POLITICAL DIMENSION: CENTERS OF GRAVITY AND HEARTS AND MINDS

The contest for political loyalty is different for the insurgents than it is for the counterinsurgents. The insurgents enter the competition as unknowns, at least in terms of their performance. That they exist means that the government's performance contains exploitable weaknesses. In attempting to win the people's loyalty, the insurgents must accelerate the discreditation of the government. Since most people in any system are politically apathetic, this means politically energizing the masses to blame the government for their problems. For the politically active who are outside the system, their role is convincing the people that the insurgency offers the most effective way to relieve their frustration. They must politically activate the masses and co-opt the politically active middle class.

The government and its potential supporters face a different problem regarding the center of gravity. To some extent, a perception of illegitimacy already exists among some part of the population; it needs to be restored to legitmacy for the government to succeed. The government's performance is a known quantity; if it is to prevail, it must first recognize itself as part of the problem. Confronting that reality, it must then determine the necessary actions to win back the loyalty of the population and decide whether it is willing or able to commit itself to those actions. If the insurgents are at all competent, of course, they will seek to frustrate such governmental efforts by attempting to cause the government to commit acts that will further alienate its center of gravity.

The contest for the hearts and minds of men, which requires a complex combination of military and political actions, and is one in which both sides have the same objective: gaining legitimacy. The problem is how to attack and excise the other's support without undercutting one's own. The dynamics of the problem can be seen by looking at the competition from three vantage points: (1) the tension between reform and repression, (2) the ability to attack the enemy's support base without destroying one's own, and (3) the frustration of outside powers seeking to aid beleaguered governments.

Reform versus Repression

When confronted by insurgents engaging in violence against the state, the first reaction by the government is to treat the problem in primarily military fashion. Insurgency-prone Third World governments often react this way initially because they are nonrepresentative and rule coercively within an alliance between the political elite and the military.

No insurgency can be defeated without destroying its military force; the problem is accomplishing that task. Given insurgent strategy, direct military assault is problematically effective; insurgents, after all, avoid engagement with superior military forces. If the government views the problem as exclusively military and responds with conventional strategies, it is likely to be frustrated. All too often, governments have taken their frustrations out on the people whose support they must regain, making matters worse.

Insurgency is a political and military phenomenon, so it follows that counterinsurgency must also have a political dimension. It may be possible to capture the center of gravity by force, but the long-term solution to who will govern is a matter of who can turn authority into legitimacy— acceptance of rule by the population. This critical element of the battle for popular loyalty is won or lost in people's minds; it is a political act only achievable through political action.

In Third World countries, the political action of the government must involve two types of reform. One is political reform, the provision of fair and equitable political treatment of the population by honest, well-meaning officials. Too often, these characteristics are missing; officials are corrupt or inefficient, have reached their positions through favor or nepotism rather than qualification, and are clearly using their positions for their own personal benefit rather than for the general good. Political rectitude can go a long way toward undercutting opposition appeal.

The other kind of reform is economic and social. In Third World countries where resources are scarce, maldistribution of wealth only makes matters worse. If people believe the source of their misery is a political system manipulated by an elite group intent on maintaining its privilege at the expense of others, relative deprivation can translate into insurgency.

The need for reform is usually more apparent from the outside than from within the government. A great frustration for nations seeking to assist governments resisting insurgencies is that, although they can see the problems and their solutions, the government either does not recognize or refuses to deal with the problem. The resistance may have two bases. The first is that the government may simply disagree with the assessment. Almost all governments have the support of some constituency and believe servicing that constituency is in the public interest. Thus, succumbing to populist demands—especially if presented in Marxist rhetoric—may be viewed as the wrong way to solve the problem posed by insurgency. The second and more insidious possibility is that the government sees military repression as the best way to avoid unwanted reform. For example, if land reform is the demand of the insurgents and the government's support base is concentrated in the large landholders whose property would have to be redistributed, the government may decide that the solution is worse than the problem and attempt military destruction of the insurgency instead.

Fortunately, not all Third World governments are resistant to change. Reform-minded and civically responsible leaders have come to power in some Latin American countries, such as Mexico, Brazil, and Argentina, where the prospects of insurgency are ebbing. However, the real test will be for Peru's new President Alberto Fujimori, who is attempting reform in the face of an active insurgency (the *Sendero Luminoso*).

Attacking without Destroying the Center of Gravity

The basic politico-military problem for any government confronted with an insurgency is how to destroy the insurgency without also destroying the government's own support base. If the insurgency lacks popular support, as in Che Guevara's *foco* in Bolivia or the Malayan insurgency of the late 1940s, the government's task is relatively manageable. A problem exists when the insurgency has enough support in the population to be able to blend in with and be protected by it.

The potential success of the insurgent or government is well illustrated by the following analogy. Suppose that an insurgent band, rushing down a country road, is being pursued by government soldiers. The insurgents reach a fork in the road, where a peasant is standing, and they take the road to the right. Shortly thereafter the pursuing government forces reach the fork and ask the peasant which way the insurgents went. If the peasant points the soldiers to the road to the right, where the insurgents actually went, the battle for the hearts and minds has not been lost and the government stands a chance. But if the peasant points to the road to the left, the hearts and minds competition has probably been lost.

Let us take the analogy one step further. What if the government patrol does not know if it can trust the peasant? If the insurgency is at all well developed, the peasant may be an insurgent or a sympathizer. In this case, the patrol may seek accurate information through intimidation, possibly taking the peasant captive and threatening execution if the truth is not revealed. But what has been accomplished? If the peasant is executed, this may only reinforce criticisms of government brutality. The peasant thus becomes a martyr to the revolution. If the peasant instead reveals the truth, he may wonder in retrospect why his own government did not trust his loyalty.

The analogy paints the counterinsurgent problem in stark terms, though some may take exception to the depictions of the insurgents as good and the government as evil. But this has been done to demonstrate a point. If the insurgents are venal, corrupt, and brutal, they may have some transitory successes, but their defeat is highly likely. The problem is for the government—when insurgents have been loyal to insurgency philosophy and when the government has not served the people well. In this case, the problem may be so frustrating that the government acts in ways that actually aid the transfer of political loyalty to the insurgents.

One such case is detailed in a 1989 report issued by the U.S. Army and the U.S. Air Force Center for Low-Intensity Conflict. The report, titled *Counterinsurgency in the Philippines: Problems and Prospects*, describes four problems: (1) the insurgents provide the only social services in parts of the country; (2) the traditional elite, which runs the country, opposes reform; (3) about 90 percent of the arable land is controlled by 10 percent of the population; and (4) there is widespread corruption and ineptitude at local government levels as well as a pattern of human rights abuse. To make matters worse, the government traditionally neglects the countryside—the stronghold of the insurgents—and has no discernible national counterinsurgency strategy. The government report concludes that the prospects of success for the Aquino government against the New People's Army (NPA) are reasonably good to defeat the insurgency. One wonders how.

The Outsider's Frustration

When a Third World state comes under the siege of an ideologically distasteful insurgency, it is natural for an outside state with close ties to the regime to want to help its friend. Doing so, however, is dangerous because the outcome is likely to be adversely affected by the assistance. There is even an inverse relationship between the amount of assistance (and public visibility) to a beleaguered state and the positive effect of that assistance, especially when the aid includes armed intervention.

An intervenor's potential frustration has several distinct sources. One is the problem of leverage mentioned earlier. Beleaguered governments are unlikely to appreciate advice from an outsider that would cause them to relinquish some of their power. On the one hand, resistance to political demands for reform in areas like wealth redistribution is probably opposed for reasons of principle or self-interest. To abandon a position in the face of outside pressure is personally compromising. On the other hand, there is what Todd Greentree calls the "counterinsurgency contradiction"—the tendency to react to insurgency with acts of political and military repression rather than with greater democratization. The contradiction, of course, is that repression only further alienates the government's center of gravity and thus may assist the insurgency. It is also easier for outsiders to give advice than it is for the country being physically besieged; this, in turn, creates further frustration between the advising outsider and the government receiving the advice.

Furthermore, the government may not be in a position to enact the reforms that the outsider counsels. Government ineptitude is usually a cause of insurgency. There are probably government officials, benefiting from the ongoing system, who resist change. This was former Soviet President Gorbachev's experience with the middle-level party officials (*nomenklatura*) during his reform attempts. Moreover, there is an absence of resources to implement reform in the Third World.

Greentree points to another source of frustration called the "democratic contradiction." For the United States to sustain a commitment to a beleaguered government, it must be demonstrated that the particular government it seeks to assist is worth saving. While the initial motive for American interest may be geopolitical, that is not enough. Unless the American people and their elected representatives in Congress are convinced that those being assisted are worthy of it—that they are committed to democratic ideals—then support will likely be withheld. The people involved in Third World conflicts often do not meet Americans' self-images of rectitude. Culturally and physically different from Americans, their worthiness is not always self-evident. Part of the Reagan administration's difficulty in sustaining support for the Nicaraguan *contras* was that many Americans had trouble distinguishing the moral superiority of the rebels over the ruling Sandinistas. In addition, the assistance is not always appreciated by the Third World government or people receiving it. Vietnam veterans, for example, received little or no thanks for their efforts. Thus, the absence of gratitude almost always undercuts support.

Another frustration is that ultimately the outside involvement cannot be decisive. At the political level, an outsider cannot win the battle for popular support or loyalty—only the contesting indigenous parties can do that. If the government is unsuccessful in the political struggle, there is little the United States can do except offer sound advice. If the Third World government cannot or will not follow that advice, the United States cannot serve as a substitute in the nation-building process. In fact, the attempt to intervene usually further alienates the people from the government by making them appear to be lackeys for the Americans.

The same is true at the military level. People in Third World countries resent the presence of outside military forces, especially those that look like the European colonialists they evicted. The distinguished analyst of counterinsurgency, Sir Robert Thompson, who headed the British campaign in Malaya, argues that "reliance on a military solution will always fail particularly when sought by foreign troops."

Since 1945, there has not been a single instance of a successful intervention in an insurgency with substantial support (such as in the second or third stage of a mobile-guerrilla campaign) by a racially distinct outside intervening nation. It can be argued that the qualification, in terms of stage of development, makes the assertion a virtual tautology; in reply, intervention is rarely ever contemplated until an insurgency is advanced enough to be prominent and troublesome.

THE MILITARY DIMENSION: SHOOTING THE SYMPTOMS AND THE BRUSHFIRE COROLLARY

The intensely political elements of insurgency and counterinsurgency affect the way military action is undertaken to defeat an insurgent group. Military conduct in insurgency is different than in conventional war because of the insurgent style of warfare, the different military criteria for success of the insurgency and the counterinsurgency, and the intrinsic and intimate relationship between military actions and their political consequences. These form a series of disadvantages for the counterinsurgents. In addition, the counterinsurgents face the problem of attacking militarily the vital center of the insurgency, not just its symptoms. And outsiders face the problem of the timeliness of their intervention (the brushfire corollary).

The Counterinsurgent's Disadvantages

Conventional military strategies and tactics developed for European combat are generally ineffective against an opponent employing mobile-guerrilla methods. Conventional methods emphasize firepower, superior masses of soldiers and equipment, and large campaigns that sweep territory, gain control of land, and inflict punishment on the enemy. It is warfare characterized by armies organized in large formations (brigade, batallion, even corps) and an outcome that is supposed to be militarily decisive (the destruction of the enemy's forces).

In contrast, insurgents seek to obviate these conventional preferences. Since insurgents lack substantial numbers of soldiers, heavy equipment, and lethal technologies, they seek instead to avoid encounters in which those factors could be decisive. Their methods involve small units (platoons or companies) using mobility and tactical flexibility to maneuver to their best advantage in ambushes and attacks against isolated conventional detachments.

Guerrilla-mobile style fighting is rarely decisive in defeating a militarily superior conventional force, which is why the strategy requires developing a counterpart conventional force for the final blow. The military purpose of insurgents is to annoy and weaken the enemy, not to destroy it.

Insurgents' success comes when they demoralize their opponent to the point that the enemy becomes easy prey for the conventional army.

Attempting to counteract insurgent warfare with conventional means is largely an act of frustration, as the long U.S. experience in Vietnam showed. Insurgents can only be defeated by adopting their own methods (such as using small unit tactics and air cavalry on helicopters to trap and ambush insurgent formations). The problem is, as the Bacevich et al. study of El Salvador pointed out in 1989, that style of warfare is much less dramatic than large unit maneuvers with artillery crashing and tanks columns moving out of base, and hence less attractive to many Third World military leaders.

The United States learned this lesson during the Vietnam War. In the early stages of the war, it managed to encounter and defeat main North Vietnamese conventional forces that had infiltrated South Vietnam for stage three of the mobile-guerrilla war (in such places as the Ia Drang Valley in 1965). Large unit tactics worked in this circumstance. However, when the North Vietnamese and Viet Cong reverted to the guerrilla stage, large unit sweeps (called "search and destroy") were ineffective. The United States then had to develop small unit techniques appropriate to countering guerrillas. It now attempts to pass those techniques along to those it assists.

Styles of warfare clash partly because insurgent and counterinsurgent success criteria differ. Insurgent success is measured by avoiding defeat. As long as the insurgent force continues to exist, the government cannot claim victory. Moreover, the longer the insurgency endures, the more legitimacy it is likely to accumulate. Thus, the insurgency wins—or has the potential to win—as long as it avoids losing. That realization dictates husbanding forces rather than putting them in harm's way when they might be destroyed.

The government's problem, however, is more demanding. To be successful, it must physically defeat and destroy the insurgency, including its military forces, as well as regain popular support. Because the insurgency remains a threat to the government as long as it physically exists, the government's objective can be attained in only one way—the total defeat of the insurgents' forces.

Another disadvantage of the counterinsurgents is recognizing and exploiting the intimate link between the political and military aspects of insurgent warfare. The root of this problem is that the insurgents set the basic rules of engagement of the contest. Their approach is highly political, to the point that military matters are routinely subordinated to political considerations. It is easy for the insurgents to think this way, for their "doctrine" tells them it is correct. Furthermore, most insurgents are amateur soldiers unburdened by notions of the separation between the military and political aspects of what they do.

Military professionalism may thus serve as a disadvantage at this level. If a Third World country's military leadership was trained by the West, then it is also likely trained in the virtue of apoliticism that Western military establishments—notably the American—value. In conventional war, the direct and immediate political consequences of military acts rarely intrude at the operational level. In insurgent warfare, though, political impacts must routinely be taken into account. For those steeped in traditional warfare, this is a difficult adjustment, and some resist making it. This is one reason conventional military people dislike insurgent warfare; another is that they are not very good at it.

Shooting Symptoms

Counterinsurgent success requires that the insurgency's military forces either be annihilated or weakened to the point that the insurgency loses its cohesion as a political and military entity. To accomplish this requisite, the insurgents must somehow be physically isolated from the population and dealt with in a military sense.

The classic example of counterinsurgent success was the British action in Malaya in the late 1940s. The British succeeded in isolating the insurgents in one physical locale. The insurgents, mostly ethnic Chinese, were physically distinct from the Malay population and disliked by the majority, who thus did not protect them.

Most counterinsurgencies, however, are not so successful. In the worst case, the insurgents are an integral part of the national population and have at least a large enough support base to receive protection. Thus, the problem of extracting insurgents from the population without alienating the public becomes difficult.

Neither purely military nor purely political actions alone will accomplish the counterinsurgents' goal. A purely military agenda—one that seeks to destroy the enemy forces—may terrorize the population into abandoning the insurgency if it is wildly successful, but insurgent strategy minimizes that likelihood. As a result, it is likely that a purely military approach will do little more than attack the symptoms of the insurgency (alienated citizens) while ignoring the causes of the problem. At the same time, a purely political approach neglects the fact that the insurgents are likely to take counteraction in order to thwart government attempts at winning the battle for popular support.

The political and military dimensions of counterinsurgency, then, must work in concert. Ultimately, for the government to be successful, it must change conditions in the country so that the people abandon the insurgency and embrace the government. Political acts aimed at the people's betterment must be a primary part of counterinsurgent strategy. At the same time, the military situation must be such that the government can physically compete for popular support. The military campaign becomes the sword and shield behind which political action occurs.

There are several ways that the military can act to do more than just attack symptoms. For example, it can avoid making the situation worse. A conventional military force is often not well attuned to the delicate task of protecting a population from its enemies. The role of shielding the public is more that of police officer than it is of soldier; wielding the sword against an identifiable military opponent, however, comes more naturally to a conventional soldier than it does to the police officer's truncheon.

In an insurgency, anyone and everyone may be the enemy. Because insurgents typically do not wear military insignia or uniforms, they are often indistinguishable from the rest of the population. Their ability to appear as any other citizen is their camouflage; insurgents recognize this advantage and seek to exploit it.

Another alternative available to the military is to liberate and then secure physical areas against insurgent incursion. The first task is not difficult if one avoids hotbeds of insurgent support. Because insurgency theory denigrates the importance of holding territory, insurgents are likely to relinquish it. The more difficult task is maintaining control once it is established. There are simply not enough soldiers and constables physically to hold any sizable amount of the land or population and deny them to the opposition. Although insurgents do not value territorial possession other than their own sanctuaries, they do oppose being denied access to the population because this interferes with their ability to recruit others to join the cause, which is viewed as a sign of weakness. Moreover, when the government's military acts as a shield to protect the people, behind which civic actions are being undertaken to improve the people's lot, the insurgents must seek to disrupt such activity so as to avoid losing the battle for public support.

One way to provide a public shield despite a scarcity of troops is some form of the *strategic hamlets approach*. Imported to Vietnam from Malaya, the approach involves the following steps: (1) selecting a manageable number of villages, (2) liberating these villages, (3) providing them with physical protection from attack, (4) beginning civic action programs to better the lot of the villagers, and (5) training villagers as militia so that they can participate in the security of the region. Once the initial area is secured, it can gradually be increased in size.

Finally, the government may choose to assist in the civic action program. This task is primarily that of civilian officials who possess the political skills to organize programs that can benefit the populace. Although not a strict military task, it can utilize the military's skill in certain aspects of nation-building (for example, building roads and bridges).

The process of going beyond "going up the hill and shooting the guerrillas," as the Bacevich study puts it, is very slow, arduous, and complicated. It requires skills and temperament well beyond the usual requisites of soldiering. Having to weigh carefully the political consequences of military actions is not only difficult to accomplish but is also alien to much of the military mind. Moreover, the task is even more difficult for outsiders, who typically lack a full understanding of local conditions, circumstances, and culture, and thereby underestimate the difficulty of countering a well-entrenched insurgency.

The Brushfire Corollary

The *brushfire corollary,* a term coined by Greentree, refers to the process by which an outside nation (notably the United States) reaches the decision to involve itself on the side of a counterinsurgency. The corollary is based on two principal assumptions: (1) that U.S. involvement can be justified only when the Third World conflict is highly public, and (2) that the application of American resources will solve the problem. That is, when such conflicts flare up, it is assumed that they can be extinguished much like a brushfire.

Unfortunately, both assumptions of the brushfire corollary are flawed. For example, by waiting until a Third World insurgency becomes an overt affair, the United States inevitably starts out at a disadvantage. The best time to counteract an insurgency is before it gains strength, and the best way to do so is to encourage the government to engage in the kinds of reforms that will prevent an insurgency from forming at all. The United States would have had a better chance of working with the Salvadorean government on land reform if it had intervened in the 1950s or 1960s; by 1980, however, its task was much more difficult because the insurgents were well established. Early reforms, including "buying off" the few families who owned the vast majority of the arable land, would have been far less expensive in the 1960s than was the military aid program of the 1980s and later.

Insurgencies do not become obvious problems until they are well established (in the second or third stage of the mobile-guerrilla strategy). At this point, they are very difficult to defeat under any circumstances because they have already won the battle for political loyalty. Although U.S. intervention may temporarily shift the tactical balance in favor of the counterinsurgents, as it did in Vietnam, it cannot alter the political balance. Indeed, the invervention may even aid the insurgents' cause, for they can make claims of neocolonialism and of a government too weak to stand on its own.

The brushfire corollary is also flawed because it tends to depict the problem as less difficult than it actually is. It suggests, for instance, that "putting out the fire" is essentially a technical job of applying the right amount of fire suppressant (the more that is applied, the faster the fire goes out). But the analogy only applies to a military organization that specializes in masses of firepower and technological solutions or to a political system and culture that lack great patience and dislike long wars.

Colonel A. J. Bacevich and his associates reached much the same conclusion about the American assistance program to El Salvador. In the initial phase of U.S. involvement there, the guerrillas were about to seize control of the government, making the use of conventional, large military units necessary to prevent defeat. When the guerrillas retreated back to stage two of the mobile-guerrilla warfare model, however, it became difficult for the government forces to adjust their tactics to the small-unit level as well as to shift their emphasis toward winning popular allegiance.

As we have seen then, the brushfire analogy is highly misleading. If outside involvement in an insurgent war is postponed until after the insurgents are close to winning, the counterinsurgency, if it can be accomplished at all, will be long and difficult. Moreover, Americans' notable lack of patience with long wars prejudices their conduct in them, as Loren Baritz argues in his cultural analysis of the Vietnam War, *Backfire: A History of How American Culture Led Us into Vietnam and Made Us Fight the Way We Did* (1985). According to Baritz, "the American way of life and war meant that we could not succeed [in Vietnam] as counterinsurgents. . . . Our managerial sophistication and technological superiority resulted in our trained incompetence in guerrilla warfare" (p. 322).

Overcoming the flaws of the brushfire corollary will be important in future conflicts. If Americans have learned that counterinsurgent efforts are more complex than the corollary suggests, there is a danger of unlearning the lesson. The U.S. campaigns in Grenada (1983) and Panama (1989) were swift and decisive; similarly, the overwhelming technological superiority of U.S. firepower was applied with great effect against Iraq in 1991. But none of these conflicts was an insurgency. Thus, it is dangerous to assume that the same outcome can be expected in Third World insurgent war.

THE AMERICAN APPROACH TO COUNTERINSURGENCY

Although the United States has employed military force almost exclusively in the Third World since 1945, insurgency and counterinsurgency have never had a high place in the hierarchy of American military values and preferences. This is especially true of the uniformed services, particularly the U.S. Army, where the overwhelming emphasis for planning, training, and preparation has been on the European front in anticipation of a third world war.

This is not entirely surprising. The East-West confrontation stood atop of the list of national priorities, and the failure to deter a Soviet invasion of Western Europe would have had the direst impact on American national interests. During the Cold War, avoiding war with the Soviets was clearly the U.S. priority.

The American military's emphasis on conventional war in Europe and on strategic nuclear weapons and strategy came at the expense of human and monetary investment in Third World contingencies. All of the U.S. military services have had insurgency as part of their charter—the Army's Special Forces, for instance—but they have typically underfunded it because of the lack of respect for it within the professional military. This may no longer be acceptable in the post–Cold War world. As conventional forces decrease as a result of the end of the Cold War, the focus of international security concerns may turn to the conflict-ridden Third World. Most future Third World situations will not resemble the Desert Storm operation, which militarily was a European war fought in the sand, and as such was an aberration, not a precedent for the future.

To determine why the United States is not particularly well equipped to deal with insurgency-counterinsurgency situations, we need to look at its traditional military attitudes about low-intensity conflicts as well as how the government generally organizes itself for these situations.

Military Resistance to Counterinsurgency Capability

Although top U.S. officials do not admit it openly, the disdain that the U.S. Army holds for involvement in Third World conflicts is well known. A limited capability has existed since 1952, when the Special Forces were formed largely for fifth column activities and commando functions in Eastern Europe in the event war occurred. Support for Special Forces has ebbed and flowed; during the early days of Vietnam, the "Green Berets" enjoyed considerable glamour, but it faded when their role in assassinating Vietnamese officials became known. In addition, units such as the Army's

Delta Force, the Navy's SEALS, and the Air Force's Special Operations Forces have come into being with specialized missions. The Army, in particular, has lacked enthusiasm about these kinds of forces for several reasons.

First, Special Forces appear to be elite forces, and the U.S. Army has a long tradition of opposing units that think of themselves as special or superior. In fact, the units designated for special duty are often different in ways that could be considered elite. They perform in foreign, often exotic places, so they must have language and cultural training that the average soldier does not require or possess. Since Third World contingencies are often idiosyncratic, these forces must possess considerable problem-solving abilities and intellectual dexterity not required of the average soldier, who is expected to perform only in highly structured, predictable ways. The special operations forces are thus unlike other soldiers and, as a result, they are viewed with some suspicion by the "regular" army.

Second, properly conducted counterinsurgency is low-technology warfare, whereas the U.S. Army is a high-technology organization. Most militarily effective techniques for counterinsurgency use the same kinds of weapons that the insurgents employ, rather than the highly lethal and sophisticated weaponry developed for war in Europe and used so effectively in Iraq and Kuwait. Vietnam demonstrated that high-technology weaponry is not necessarily decisive when fighting guerrillas in jungles.

Third, countering insurgencies has a highly political content, which is more difficult for the military to handle. In conventional war, the object is to subdue (not to convert) the opponent; thus, the political effects on the enemy are largely irrelevant. When the object of attack is the same as the target of political conversion, then more political concern is necessary.

Fourth, the attitude of the U.S. Army is that involvement in Third World conflicts is not as important as other problems and hence requires less effort. Again, this is drawn from the historical military commitment to an independent Western Europe—the most vital U.S. interest after protecting the homeland. Third World problems are considered less important. That ordering of interests does not change as the Cold War recedes; what changes are the sources of threats to American interests. Europe, in other words, is still most important; it just is not likely to need the same level of defense.

Fifth, the requisites of counterinsurgency clash with the long-standing doctrine of the U.S. Army. The body of that doctrine is contained in *Field Manual (FM) 100-5*, which describes warfare as heavily "conventional" and geared to the clash of large, heavily equipped armies in places such as Europe. The speedy maneuvering of large amounts of highly mobile, lethal weaponry over broad spaces is the key to victory, as demonstrated in Desert Storm. Although the U.S. Army has a doctrinal statement dealing with insurgency-style activities (*FM 100-20*), it carries less weight than the conventional version.

Sixth, and possibly most importantly, the insurgency contingency has consistently been forced on the U.S. Army by civilians. The first excursion included the operations of the Office of Strategic Services (OSS) in Asia during World War II, and the most dramatic public pronouncement was John F. Kennedy's instruction to prepare for Third World brushfire wars. Thus, insurgency and counterinsurgency have never come from inside the Army itself; rather, they have consistently been orphans in the system.

The U.S. Government and Counterinsurgency

The U.S. Army has dealt with the imposed Third World mission by isolating those who carry it out in a separate career path distant from the mainstream of Army careerism. Centered physically and symbolically around the John F. Kennedy Center at Fort Bragg, North Carolina, involvement in the activities surrounding insurgency-counterinsurgency and other special operations (such as hostage liberation and counterterrorism) is an institutional entity in and of itself with which the normal Army concerns itself as little as possible.

The record of the U.S. government is not much better. During the mid-1980s, there was much concern about the reform of two basic deficiencies in governmental performance: (1) the lack of a clear and coherent Third World policy (because of confusion among senior officials about the phenomenon and their resistance to institutionalizing it) and (2) the absence of adequate coordination in the decision-making process of the executive branch (which is responsible for making and executing policy). The extent of the institutional confusion caused Congress to initiate two legislative actions that would focus attention on Third World contingencies. First, it established the position of Assistant Secretary of Defense for Special Operations and Low-Intensity Conflict (SOLIC) within the Department of Defense. Second, it created a deliberate body to coordinate policy (the so-called LIC Board), and suggested (through a "sense of Congress") a full-time position on the National Security Council (NSC) staff to coordinate these matters. The executive branch has resisted both organizational initiatives.

The Assistant Secretary for SOLIC, part of the organizational reform begun by the Goldwater-Nichols Defense Reorganization Act of 1986 and culminating in the Cohen-Nunn Act of the same year, was personally opposed by then Secretary of Defense Caspar Weinberger. He viewed the act as an intrusion on executive prerogative, another example of congressional micromanagement. Weinberger delayed nominating anyone for the position for over a year, then nominated a person known to be unacceptable to Congress. When an acceptable candidate was put forward, the individual was confronted by a bureaucratic web designed to decrease his efficiency.

The NSC position has met a similar fate. In this case, the Bush administration objected to the congressional precedent of designating particular positions on the NSC staff. President Bush considered this his personal responsibility. As a result, the SOLIC duties are assigned to an individual with primary responsibilities elsewhere, thereby diluting the level of concern with the problem.

The most difficult problem is the lack of interagency coordination of policy and action. The insurgency-counterinsurgency problem does not fit into the organizational responsibility of any single agency. Its political aspects reside with agencies such as the State Department or the U.S. Agency for International Development, its military elements fall within the Defense Department, and our understanding of the situation in any given insurgency clearly involves the Central Intelligence Agency. These overlapping jurisdictions mean that there is a need for interagency coordination of both policy and actions. The Bush administration moved in this direction by appointing the permanent LIC Board specified in Cohen-Nunn at the NSC level to develop policies and to oversee and advise on particular cases, but it has met infrequently and inconclusively.

CONCLUSION

In the emerging international system, in which Third World economic and political problems will continue to abound, more insurgencies will occur and the question of counterinsurgency will arise. The temptation for the United States to become involved will not be ideologically prejudiced, as it was during the Cold War, except possibly in support of pro-democratic insurgents or counterinsurgents. Nonetheless, insurgent groups that oppose U.S. interests and allies will inevitably arise. The question will then focus on the wisdom of becoming involved.

Counterinsurgency is difficult, and the American track record in identifying, assisting, and winning such conflicts has been less than perfect. By distilling some of the points already made into a series of six questions, however, we can better guess whether U.S. involvement will be efficacious.

What Is Wrong?

The existence of an insurgency indicates that, within the target country, at least some portion of the population believes there is a problem serious enough to attack. Insurgencies are not organized against well-run democracies. A first consideration must be the worthiness of the candidate government for support, including an assessment of what the government has done to cause the insurgency and whether it is willing to do what is necessary to reform (the democratic contradiction).

How Do You Come Down on the "Side of the Angels"?

Because Third World situations are often complex and ambivalent—with good and bad, right and wrong, painted in shades of gray—it may not be easy to determine who the "angels" are in any given situation. During the Cold War, the defining characteristic of rectitude was anticommunism. That criterion occasionally left the United States siding with decidedly sleazy characters whose sole redeeming quality was professed anticommunism, but even that will not be a guide in the post–Cold War period. This is important, because ultimately whether support for a counterinsurgency can be sustained will depend on whether the American people support the involvement. Americans place considerable emphasis on the appearance of moral superiority, and where they find it lacking, their support is likely to dwindle. The failure to sustain support for the Nicaraguan *contras* largely resulted from the inability to portray them successfully as "angels."

Does Your Side Have a Reasonable Chance of Winning?

This question has political and military dimensions, both of which are conditioned by the brushfire corollary. Politically, the question concerns the political retrievability of the situation: Has the government lost so much support that it cannot regain the loyalty of the people? Is the government willing to undertake the reforms that will give it a chance? If the situation has deteriorated to the point that outside intervention is being contemplated, is the battle already lost?

The military situation is likely to be bleak. As the brushfire corollary suggests, U.S. intervention is usually not solicited until after an insurgency is in the second or third stage of the mobile-guerrilla strategy. By then, the military balance is often tipped decisively toward the insurgency. The question is whether the government maintains the military means or will to prevail, especially since outside involvement has limited, even inverse effects.

Do You Realize the Limitations on Your Ability to Affect the Outcome?

Outside intervention in a civil war is always problematic because insurgencies can only be solved internally. Moreover, involvement in Third World conflicts always raises the charge of neocolonialism by the side against which the intervention occurs.

The level of involvement and the ability to influence the outcome are often inversely related. The more public the intervention and the more obvious the degree to which the government depends on the assistance, the more resentment is likely to be created in the population. The insurgents' propaganda will be fueled by that dependence. Also, the amount of assistance and degree of influence over the government may also be inverse, as the government realizes the extent that outsider investment makes it harder to cut the government off even if it ignores good advice, as Diem concluded in Vietnam. The notion that doing more accomplishes less is difficult to accept, especially when things are not going well. Unfortunately, outside activism may simply make the insurgency problem worse—the so-called intervenor's contradiction.

Do You Have a Viable Politico-Military Strategy?

The government to whose aid the outsider is coming must not have a viable strategy or it would not need help. The battle for the hearts and minds of people, which can only be waged successfully by the host government, must not be going well. Does the United States have a strategy for attacking the vital center of gravity that can be implemented by the government? Is there a formula for mixing the political and military aspects of counterinsurgency that can be given to the government? And if so, is the government capable of carrying it out?

A related question from the Vietnam War is whether there are adequate and accurate means of determining progress in a counterinsurgency. Given that territorial exchange is a poor depiction and that the "body count" approach failed in Southeast Asia, knowing who is winning and losing may be a difficult task, especially for the outsider (who has only a limited grasp of the cultural and social dynamics that could better indicate success).

What Will the American People Say about Involvement?

Ultimately, the most important and most difficult question is whether the American public approves of the intervention. Most Americans lack a detailed understanding of Third World countries. Moreover, relatively few vital interests are at stake for the United States anywhere in the Third World. The United States has historically lacked a coherent policy toward the Third World, so that there is no guide for becoming involved. Rather, U.S. policy has vacillated between activism and passivity, especially in the wake of major military involvements such as the Persian Gulf War.

The U.S. government's disarray on the subject makes developing an American consensus all the more difficult. One major reason for a lack of a coherent national policy is that the government itself has no clear idea of what the policy should be. It is a truism about Third World conflicts that each is unique and thus has to be considered on its own merits. Given the potential number of such situations in the future, it is not clear that this "ad hocracy" approach will yield consistent public support.

CHAPTER 5

The New Challenges: Counternarcotics, Counterterrorism, and Peacekeeping

During the 1980s, the United States engaged in a massive buildup of conventional and strategic nuclear armaments. Born in the late Carter administration and accelerated and expanded by former President Ronald Reagan, the purpose of the buildup was to counteract a growing Soviet advantage in nearly all categories of arms. Following the Vietnam War, the United States had cut back drastically on defense spending. The American people, deeply disillusioned by the outcome of that war, were in no mood to think about or to spend money on defense. Meanwhile, the Soviets continued a relentless arms-procurement process, spending upwards of one-quarter of their gross national product (GNP) on defense. In retrospect, that drive helped accelerate the overall economic decline and demise of the Soviet Union. At the time, however, it appeared ominous to the United States. The frustration behind the comparative U.S. decline in armaments was summed up by President Carter's Defense Secretary Harold Brown in Congressional testimony: "When we build, they build. When we don't build, they build."

Gradually, though, the American public's mood about defense spending changed. Ronald Reagan, running on much the same program that failed to seize the Republican nomination from former President Gerald Ford in 1976, was elected president in 1980. An important part of Reagan's appeal was his call to reverse the "unilateral disarmament" of the Carter years and thus restore America's military might. The Reagan administration hoped that a buildup of U.S. arms would convince the Soviets that they could not compete successfully in an armed conflict and thus that they should abandon the attempt at comprehensive military competition.

Analysts disagree about whether it was the Reagan armaments program that ultimately persuaded the Soviets to end the Cold War. Since the war remained cold and no one formally surrendered, there were no victors who could capture the loser's archives and discover why the Soviets decided that the Cold War no longer served their purposes. All we know for certain now is that they abandoned the competition and the reversal of it is no longer possible.

The end of the Cold War had immediate military consequences for both the United States and the former Soviet Union. While the Warsaw Pact and NATO had armed themselves heavily to deter or fight a conventional or nuclear war in Europe, now there was no one with whom to fight the war. The redundancy of the two countries' arsenals was formally recognized by the Conventional Forces in Europe (CFE) agreement, signed in Paris in November 1990 as part of the Conference on Security and Cooperation in Europe (CSCE) summit meeting. The formal dissolution of the Warsaw Pact in April 1991 signaled the end of the formal hostility between the two halves of Europe. Recent Russian-American proposals suggest nuclear arsenals will be reduced significantly as well.

The outcome of change in the former Soviet Union remains uncertain, especially the ultimate shape of the political entities that supersede the old union (a series of totally independent states or the Commonwealth). The failed coup of 1991 indicated the irreversibility of change in the post–Cold War situation, but stabilization of the internal order in the former union is not in sight.

Most analysts agree that whatever occurs in the former Soviet Union will not affect the fact that the Cold War is over. A series of democratized states would clearly be more welcome in the post–Cold War world than a bitter, fractionalized system. While the threat of maintained nuclear arms is frightening, the dissolution of the Warsaw Pact makes a revived conventional threat to Europe seem farfetched and the suicidal consequences of a nuclear attack hard to envisage. The major question about the members of the former Soviet Union is whether they will end up economically in the First or Third World.

Thus, the great number of weapons that remains in the former Soviet Union as well as questions about who now control them are the new threats. Clearly, the Reagan armaments buildup served the United States well in the massive bombing and ground campaigns against Iraq during the Persian Gulf War. Within only one month, more ordnance had been dropped on Kuwait and Iraq than in all of World War II. Those who had staked the national security on sophisticated, precision weapons were vindicated by the apparently spectacular effects that those weapons produced in a war that on television looked much like a video game.

In the post–Gulf War, post–Cold War environment, then, the old military missions, together with their arsenals and troop structures, are harder to justify. The armed forces recognized that they would be reduced in numbers as a result of the Cold War. (According to the Pentagon they would be "downsized" or "experience negative growth.") Desert Storm simply delayed the inevitable.

The end of the Cold War requires the rethinking of defense missions. These were previously defined in terms of "spectrums of conflict," for which American forces had to be prepared. Although the missions were called by various names, in content they were essentially the same. For example, the primary mission was strategic nuclear war with the Soviet Union, known as high-intensity conflict (HIC) during the Reagan years. Given the political consequences of such a war, deterrence was the highest national priority. Moreover, since the former Soviet Union knew that such a war would lead to its own destruction, HIC was the least likely conflict in which the United States might be involved.

Following the strategic nuclear contingency in importance was the possibility of a conventional war between NATO and the Warsaw Pact, known as a middle-intensity conflict (MIC). This type of conflict would be more intense than any previous war in human military experience. Since a war in Europe always had the potential of escalating to strategic nuclear war, it would probably fall somewhere between HIC and MIC. If the Persian Gulf War with Iraq had been more intense and competitive, it probably would have qualified as a middle-intensity conflict.

Three points are relevant about these contingencies in the post–Cold War world. The first and most obvious is that they are now highly unlikely (if not impossible). The former Soviet states still possess their nuclear arsenals, and the START agreement does not materially affect their capability. At the same time, it is hardly likely that such an attack would be launched. Similarly, a Soviet invasion of Western Europe would now have to be launched from Russia proper and fight itself across the boundaries of a hostile Eastern Europe.

Second, the forces, weapons, doctrines, and tactics developed for the contingencies have limited transferability elsewhere. For example, strategic rockets with thermonuclear warheads may deter attacks by similar weapons, but they have little other demonstrated utility (whether they had an effect in dissuading Saddam Hussein from using chemical weapons during the Persian Gulf War is explored in Chapter 7). Although the Gulf War provided some vindication for the weapons, forces, and tactics developed for Europe, there are not likely to be future circumstances in which they would be as obviously useful.

Finally, these kinds of contingencies are ones with which the U.S. military is comfortable. While most military people recognize that the old ways of war no longer apply today, they still tend to revert to the old thinking in operational discussions.

Thus, the spectrum of conflict is moving in the direction of Third World contingencies, previously considered low-intensity conflicts (LICs). Although the U.S. Army may find these conflicts more difficult to handle (for the reasons discussed in Chapter 4), the U.S. military in general will have to embrace very different mission possibilities in order to maintain its relevance in the post–Cold War environment.

DIFFERENT PROBLEMS, DIFFERENT SOLUTIONS

In addition to insurgency and counterinsurgency, peacetime contingency operations are the new missions of the post–Cold War world. The U.S. Army refers to these operations as the "peacetime competition" end of the operational spectrum. They include *counternarcotics* (the military's contribution to President Bush's "war on drugs"), *counterterrorism* (for dealing with worldwide terrorist activities aimed at American citizens and interests), and *peacekeeping* operations (for enforcing ceasefires and armistices between formerly warring parties). Each of these three missions is relatively new to the U.S. military. Although the United States has maintained specialized capabilities (for example, Special Operations Forces, or SOF) to deal with some of these problems, the units have always had a low public profile (called "black" operations because either their existence or activities were kept secret). Today, however, they are well-known integral parts of the military.

The three missions—counternarcotics, counterterrorism, and peacekeeping—are similar in many ways. For instance, they are all intended to deal with North-South, Third World problems. The counternarcotics mission aims to tackle the North-South problem of "hard" narcotics being consumed in the First World (particularly in the United States) but grown and processed in the Third World. South American countries are the major growers (Peru and Bolivia) and processors (Colombia) of the coca plants that become cocaine, which is sold on the streets of American cities. Southeast Asia is the producer of the poppies that become opium and heroin. Synthetic drugs, such as crystal methamphetamine ("ice"), were developed and are imported from the Far East (Taiwan, the Philippines, Korea). Part of the solution to the drug epidemic in America, then, requires disrupting the flow of drugs from South to North.

The counterterrorism and peacekeeping missions are similar in several respects. Most terrorist activity emanates from the Third World, especially from the volatile Middle East. Terrorism resembles insurgency in that a sense of desperation drives people and groups to their acts of terror. As long as disparity in condition exists in the Third World, there will remain a seedbed for terrorism and a need to counter it. Similarly, the peacekeeping forces that seek to enforce ceasefires typically have been stationed inside or between the borders separating Third World countries. Most peacekeeping operations in the past involved relatively small, neutral countries; however, if the new system moves closer to United Nations provisions on collective security, it is possible that U.S. forces may be used more often than they have been in the past. (The most prominent example was of the stationing of American peacekeepers in the Sinai Peninsula in 1980 to supervise the return of Sinai to Egypt as part of the Camp David accords.)

In addition, all three missions are considerably different than the conventional military missions. As a result, conventional approaches, forces, doctrines, and tactics are often inappropriate or ineffective in dealing with the problems of narcotics, terrorism, and maintaining peace. Thus, the large-unit, high technology, high firepower, and lethal warfare that the U.S. military establishment favors is not relevant to the missions it must now undertake. The new missions require a more subtle and sophisticated approach with which the American military is largely unfamiliar.

Analysts disagree, for example, about whether the U.S. military plays any significant role in the effort to stop the flow of illicit drugs into the United States. The eradication of the sources of illegal drugs and the destruction of their processing facilities would require a physical American military presence, but this would also alienate the citizens of the target countries. In 1990, when then-Commander of the U.S. Southern Command General Max Thurmond proposed a massive military strike against the growers and processors of illegal drugs, the affected South American governments politely but firmly said "no thanks." Moreover, despite the use of highly sophisticated electronic means of detection, the interdiction of incoming drug shipments has not been successful.

Countering terrorism is similar in ways to countering the flow of narcotics. The solution to defeating a terrorist act is the ability to identify and punish the instigators; if terrorists know that this will be their fate, they may be deterred. Because counterterrorism is a delicate, subtle, and personal type of warfare, it is part of the U.S. military's special operations. For example, the use of the battleship USS New Jersey to pummel the Lebanese hills in 1983 after the terrorist bombing of U.S. Marine barracks was an ineffective attempt at counterterrorism because it did not specifically target the terrorists even if it did cause some to quit the area, which was, in fact, a part of the mission. In contrast, the 1986 bombing of Libyan dictator Muammar Qaddafi's compound sent a much clearer message of the price of the terrorist bombing of a West German discotheque; that the mission failed to assassinate Qaddafi was its only operational shortcoming.

Peacekeeping is a passive activity that consists of interposing peacekeepers between antagonists so that to attack they would have to do so against the peacekeepers first. This means the peacekeepers must forfeit the initiative and act only to defend themselves physically. It is not clear whether peacekeepers, as opposed to aggressive fighters, reside within the American military.

Although counternarcotics, counterterrorism, and peacekeeping are similar in many ways, they also differ. For example, the skills necessary to interdict speedboats or airplanes carrying narcotics cannot be applied to hostage situations involving terrorist organizations or to overseeing a ceasefire. Each mission requires certain unique skills to implement each of these doctrines, and tactics for which conventional norms offer only scant instruction.

Part of the military establishment's resistance to the missions is due to its lack of familiarity with them. A U.S. Army general, for instance, probably knows little about the psychology of terrorists. Also, the missions require special forces, which are often opposed by the armed forces. (All the sources of opposition to insurgency and counterinsurgency discussed in Chapter 4 apply to these missions as well.)

Another source of military resistance to the new missions are the assumptions that they are not real military activities, that the military's solutions may be inappropriate or ineffective, and that failure may tarnish the military's image. Although high-ranking military officers do not admit it freely, the initial reaction of the military to its proposed involvement in the war on drugs was great reluctance.

Finally, each mission was imposed by civilian authority rather than being proposed by the military, thus leaving the military with little sense of personal "parenthood" for the mission. The most obvious case in point is the war on drugs. As recently as 1988, the military argued that it was not appropriate to this task. However, its attitude changed after President Bush announced that the war on drugs would become a centerpiece of his presidency and that the drug campaign could become a source of funding. The U.S. Coast Guard, for instance, found that it could acquire new cutters that it had been previously denied by participating in the drug war, and the Air Force found that certain categories of aerial reconnaissance capability were easier to justify if made a part of the narcotics interdiction program.

COUNTERNARCOTICS: "FIGHTING" THE WAR ON DRUGS

When President Bush entered office in January 1989, he inherited the blight of illegal drugs in American society. Upwards of eight million Americans are addicted to cocaine, and another twenty-five million are recreational users of crack cocaine or other illegal substances. The drug "business" is a $100-billion-a-year (nontaxed) enterprise. The use of drugs is tied to violent crime in urban areas—in part because the propensity to violence is a side effect of using drugs like cocaine and in part because addicts commit crimes to get the money they need to buy drugs. The drug epidemic is also tied to the spread of AIDS, in that addicts transmit the disease through contaminated hypodermic needles and to their unborn infants through the bloodstream. After adding the amount of time lost from work as a result of drug use, the total estimated cost of drug addiction in the United States approaches $200 billion a year.

The Bush administration, inheriting the "Just Say No to Drugs" program from the Reagan administration, sought to enhance and enlarge the effort. To that end, Bush declared a "war on drugs." He named Ronald Reagan's Secretary of Education, William S. Bennett, as a special assistant to direct an interdepartmental office to deal with the problem. New resources were promised to finance the war.

Declaring a war on drugs had two immediate consequences: it made the drug problem a more public and international (North-South) issue, and it drew the military into the effort. Most illegal drugs (with the exceptions of marijuana and some synthetic drugs) come to the United States from Third World countries. A comprehensive U.S. approach to stopping the flow of drugs required expanding the effort to deal with the source through cooperative programs. In early 1990, President Bush traveled to Cartagena, Colombia, for a "drug summit" with the heads of government of the affected Andean states; the purpose was to increase their anti-drug efforts, a process repeated at a second summit in San Antonio in February 1992.

In addition, the military was brought into the war on drugs. But due to its earlier difficulties in dealing with similar efforts, it lacked adequate sophisticated equipment, personnel, money, and even firepower to deal with the drug cartels. Even so, U.S. armed forces, particularly in light of the end of the Cold War, were viewed as having a role in this war as in any other. Yet the military role in the war on drugs has been and continues to be controversial, especially in terms of the effectiveness with which it can or cannot deal with the drug problem. To understand the basis of this controversy, however, we first need to look at the structure of the drug problem.

Structure of the Drug Problem

President Bush entered office amid general agreement that the drug epidemic was a widespread problem with dire consequences and that finding a solution was a top priority. Moreover, drugs were viewed as related to social and economic ills resulting from the breakdown of the family unit and the destruction of cities as social entities, thereby overburdening the U.S. judicial and penal systems. Although alleviating the drug problem would not by itself solve these other problems, it was generally agreed that they could not be dealt with effectively until after the war on drugs was fought.

There was less agreement on how to solve the drug problem, however. Some Americans argued, for instance, that the eradication of drugs would lead to the same problems that occurred after the prohibition of alcohol in the 1920s. They advocated the legalization and decriminalization of drug use in the United States in order to relieve the criminal justice system of the burden of enforcing drug-related sanctions and to weaken the criminal element by making drugs available through legitimate outlets. In addition, legalization could be regulated so that there was some control over who could and could not gain access to narcotics. Moreover, legalized drugs could be highly taxed in the way that other unhealthy substances (such as tobacco and alcohol) are to produce the funds needed for drug treatment programs as well as for educational programs to discourage drug use.

However, the legalization of drugs is not supported by the majority of the American public and was explicitly rejected by the Bush administration. Before resigning in 1990, Bennett argued that legalization would only increase drug use by removing the inhibition that many Americans have against breaking the law. Furthermore, the consequences of drug addiction, the administration argued, made legalization immoral and thus unacceptable.

The more popular approach to solving the drug problem through the elimination of illegal drugs was also characterized by disagreement on how to go about it. Some argued that the supply of drugs could be attacked in three ways: through (1) the destruction of drugs at their source of production (source eradication), (2) the interdiction of illegal drugs entering the country, and (3) vigorous enforcement of antinarcotics laws within the United States. Others emphasized the need to attack the demand for drugs—by educating the American public about the dangers of drug use and by treating drug addicts. The first proposed solution, which has a supply-side emphasis, is international (Third World) in nature and implies the use of military force. The second proposed solution, based on criminal prosecution, public education, and drug treatment, is primarily domestic in nature.

Source Eradication. This approach to the drug problem involves identifying the sources of illegal drugs, destroying their crops (from which drugs are extracted), and attacking and destroying their drug-producing facilities. In the case of cocaine, this means destroying the coca leaf crop that grows in the high Andean mountain valleys of Bolivia and Peru, as well as attacking the processing facilities controlled by the major Colombian drug cartels in the rugged Colombian countryside. In the case of heroin, it means attacking crops primarily grown in Southeast Asia and Turkey.

The source eradication method, however, is plagued by four basic problems related to the inability to regulate the production of cocaine. The first problem is who should do the destroying. The obvious candidates—the law enforcement or military forces of Peru, Colombia, or Bolivia—disagree on ends and means. In some cases, they profit from the coca trade. As a result, there have been instances when the police have warned the coca growers of impending eradication sweeps by the military, and vice versa.

In addition, the enforcement of eradication can be extremely dangerous. The coca growers in Peru are protected from enforcement agencies by the Shining Path guerrillas, who act brutally against anyone who cooperates with enforcement efforts. Similarly, Colombian drug dealers invested some of their huge profits in recruiting and equipping their own rival armies, effectively declaring war on those who seek to enforce the law.

Proposals for U.S. involvement in eradication efforts are usually rejected by drug-growing countries on the basis that it would infringe on their sovereignty, undercut their support, and thereby elevate the popularity of opposition groups (such as Shining Path). Another problem is the ongoing rivalry between the U.S. military and the Drug Enforcement Agency (DEA).

Second, the source eradication approach is also problematic in terms of its potential effect on coca growers, mostly peasants who long ago relocated to areas like the Upper Huallaga River valley of Peru to escape the poverty of Peruvian cities. They have been growing coca for centuries, and it yields a significantly higher profit than any other crop. Thus, depriving the coca growers of their income may only alienate them from the government and drive them into the arms of the Shining Path insurgents. One solution is crop substitution. In 1990, the Fujimori government of Peru announced a program involving land transfer and subsidies for coca growers to cultivate alternative crops. However, the program has been hindered by a general distrust of the government in Lima and a lack of sources of funding for the subsidies (the United States is a primary candidate). The danger that the subsidies may even sustain the coca-growing culture is also a consideration.

The third problem with source eradication is topographical in nature. The Andes Mountains, where the coca culture flourishes, are physically characterized by treacherous terrain, which makes military operations difficult to execute. One way to overcome this difficulty is through the aerial spraying of defoliants, but still the rugged terrain and jungle vegetation hinder efforts to identify and treat coca fields. Moreover, an approach by land is limited to only one usable road leading into the Upper Huallaga Valley.

The fourth and final problem is that the eradication approach presents a potential threat to the ecosystem. In response to eradication efforts, some coca growers simply increased the amount of land under cultivation. In Peru, this has caused a deforestation problem that the Fujimori government identifies as a priority concern. At the same time, chemical pollution has two sources—coca growers who use chemical fertilizers to stimulate growth in the poor soils of the region, and the government, which sprays the coca crop with toxic defoliants. The result is pollution of the soil and groundwater. As an ultimate irony, one recent response by growers has been to grow opium-producing poppies instead of coca, because it can be more easily concealed and yields higher profits.

Interdiction. If coca and the other raw materials of the drug trade cannot be eliminated successfully through the source eradication approach, one possible alternative is *interdiction*—attempting to prevent illegal drugs from entering the United States. This includes interdiction of incoming supplies of drugs by land, sea, and air, each of which creates special problems. Given the geography and economics of drug smuggling, this approach is difficult to execute. It also implies the use of military forces.

Interdiction by land primarily involves cutting off the supply of cocaine and other drugs being carried across the Mexican border or smuggled through airports and the like. One major difficulty is the 2,000-mile-long border that separates Mexico and the United States. The border is so isolated at spots that effective patrol is arguably impossible. Joint American and Mexican government cooperative efforts to staunch the flow have met with only limited success. It has been suggested that the U.S. Army, as it returns from overseas patrol, could shoulder part of this duty.

The flow of drugs transported by sea is also extremely difficult to control. The Florida coastline—the target of much seaborne drug traffic—is over 1,000 miles long and has numerous inlets and waterways in which boats carrying drugs can hide. Moreover, drug traffickers often use high-speed boats that elude detection and capture. Fidel Castro's Cuba has been accused of shielding drug-laden boats before they make the short dash from Cuba to the Florida Keys or peninsula. Much of this interdiction activity is undertaken by the U.S. Coast Guard, which, as an agency of the Department of the Treasury, is only a semi-military force.

Interdiction by air also has special problems. Most airborne drugs entering the United States come in on small private aircraft that land at remote airfields in the southeastern United States or that air-drop their cargos at designated places. It is difficult to distinguish drug-carrying aircraft from legitimate air traffic. Proposals to improve detection include using U.S. Air Force Airborne Warning and Control System (AWACS) aircraft and establishing a "picket line" of aerostats—tethered balloons with radar—along the southern shoreline. Yet interception has its own difficulties, such as the "rules of engagement" of suspected violators. Under what circumstances, for instance, would military aircraft be permitted to force down or shoot down suspect aircraft? Given the uncertainties of this kind of operation, it would only be a matter of time until an innocent civilian aircraft would be engaged with loss of life.

Interdiction efforts are also frustrated by the economics of drug smuggling. The profit margins of drug trafficking are so great—upwards of 90 percent on crack cocaine—that the smugglers still make a huge profit even if a significant part of their contraband is intercepted (and the interdiction rate rarely exceeds 10 to 20 percent). In turn, the tremendous profit generated by the drug trade allows the traffickers to purchase sophisticated jet aircraft and high-speed boats and to replace them with ease when seized or destroyed. Moreover, the smugglers can afford to arm themselves with equipment that often exceeds that of the enforcement agencies.

In addition, interdiction is only effective against drugs imported into the United States. Even if all the cocaine and heroin could be destroyed before they reached the American mainland, it would not mean the end of the drug problem. Marijuana, for instance, is grown in so many areas of the United States that serious efforts to eradicate it are seldom undertaken. And artificially manufactured drugs, such as crystal methamphetamine, are made from chemicals legally available to anyone in the country. Although "ice" production is associated with the Far East (especially Korea and the Philippines), there is nothing physically to prevent the growth of an indigenous "industry" in the United States.

Public Education and Drug Treatment Programs. Another possible approach to the war on drugs involves attacking the demand for drugs. This includes educating the public about the dangers of drug use; enforcing narcotics laws so as to reduce the availability of drugs and to deter usage among those inhibited by illegal activity; and making treatment and rehabilitation programs available to drug addicts.

There is a North-South dimension to the domestic demand-oriented drug effort. In its dialogue with Third World suppliers, the United States emphasizes supply-oriented actions as the source of the drug problem. Third World countries counter that the real problem is tied to the inability of the United States to reduce the demand for illegal drugs. They argue that cocaine use is not a problem in Peru (where coca leaves are grown), whereas Americans consume upwards of 60 percent of the world's illegal drugs. At an extreme, the Shining Path insurgents of Peru justify their association with narcotics traffickers on the grounds that illicit drug use is helping to bring "Yankee imperialists" to their knees by undermining American society.

The supply-versus-demand debate between the U.S. government and the Andean states continues to hinder the war on drugs. The drug-producing countries often accuse the United States of not being serious about dealing with the cocaine epidemic. They cite as an example the mild treatment of former Washington, D.C., Mayor Marion Barry after his prosecution on cocaine possession charges. The ultimate outcome of the charges made against former Panamanian strongman Manuel Noriega may also provide evidence to Third World countries of the extent of American resolve in the war on drugs.

Given the dangerous effects of using narcotics, one might assume that *public education* efforts would be relatively easy to accomplish with success. Unfortunately, though, it is difficult to reach the people most vulnerable to drug use through educational efforts. While those in the upper and middle classes (most are occasional or recreational drug users) are relatively easy to target, hard-core users, who represent the real problem, are difficult to reach through educational methods. Many of the hard-core addicts, on whose usage much of the drug market thrives, tend to be relatively poorly educated minorities living in poor urban areas who are difficult to target through educational appeals.

Another possible way to reduce the demand for drugs is through *strict law enforcement*. This approach has two presumed effects. First, by arresting drug addicts and especially drug dealers, they are removed from the mainstream of society. Second, strict enforcement may deter recreational users who fear arrest and public prosecution. Unfortunately, though, the deterrent is less effective on ghetto dwellers, who may fear the stigma less. Moreover, enforcement efforts are seriously hampered by an overburdened legal system that cannot provide quick and certain justice.

Through the *drug treatment* approach, recovered addicts cease to be drug consumers. However, most U.S. cities lack the treatment facilities needed to target the large numbers of hard-core users. (Some argue that this is a result of concentrating too many resources on interdiction.) In addition, the recovery rate for crack cocaine addicts, for example, is very low (even the most successful programs report a recovery rate of only one in five).

The Use of Military Force in the Drug War

Although the U.S. military was initially reluctant about its participation in the anti-drug effort (for reasons noted earlier in the chapter), the application of military force may be relevant to the supply side of source eradication and interdiction. General Colin Powell, chairman of the Joint Chiefs of Staff, said in his testimony before the Subcommittee on Defense of the House Appropriations Committee in 1991 that a "high-priority national security mission of our armed forces [is the effort to] stem the production and transit of illegal drugs and their entry into the United States." The problem, of course, is how to accomplish that mission. Sending U.S. forces into the coca-growing valleys of Bolivia and Peru or the processing regions of Colombia (a possibility raised in 1990 as part of the Andean Initiative) was specifically rejected by all the governments involved as an unjustified infringement on national sovereignty.

If American forces cannot be used directly in eradication, perhaps small Special Forces units can be used to train and equip Peruvian or Bolivian forces to engage in eradication or to advise and equip Colombian forces to attack jungle processing laboratories. American Special Operations forces have been dispatched to Peru and Bolivia to train native forces for this effort. Other efforts focus on crop substitution, a nation-building activity in which military forces are only useful in shielding the peasant growers from narcotics traffickers and insurgents. This method is similar to the strategic hamlets approach to counterinsurgency.

There are also limits on the use of military force in interdiction. Sophisticated military technologies like surveillance can be useful in the air and sea interception of incoming drugs, but they are not as effective in patrolling activity along the Mexican border.

Military involvement in interdiction raises two difficult problems. First, the geographical factors of drug smuggling and the enormous economic incentive to penetrate the United States at any cost may make the task too difficult unless there is a virtual suspension of the civil rights regarding search and seizure of people entering or leaving the country. Second, although under the principle of *posse comitatus* the military can be deputized as part of the "posse" of drug enforcement, the traditional separation of military and police functions is preferred by the military.

The military's overall commitment to the drug war, then, may be more symbolic than substantive. Drugs are a societal problem requiring the mobilization of societal resources across a wide range of government functions. In view of this, the military can play only a limited role in the war on drugs.

COUNTERTERRORISM: THE FRUSTRATION
OF ENDS AND MEANS

Terrorism is one of the most emotional and controversial areas of national security. Many terrorist acts—the bombing of airplanes in flight, random shootings, hostage taking, executions—are understandably revolting and incomprehensible to the average person.

The vast majority of terrorist acts occur in the Third World against other Third World peoples. Only occasionally do these acts spill over into the First World, and then usually because of a connection with some Third World problem. According to Neil Livingstone (1986), an expert on terrorism, the average American is statistically more likely to be killed by lightning than by a terrorist act. Even so, Americans have been kidnapped by terrorists and American planes have been blown up by terrorists, so the fear of terrorism is not without cause.

Dealing with terrorism is made more difficult by the widespread disagreement over what terrorism is, what causes it, and what it seeks to accomplish. The disagreement is often culturally based—Westerners associate terrorism with fanatic groups engaged in criminal acts, whereas elsewhere terrorist tactics occupy a position of some respect if undertaken for proper causes. Hence, the saying that "one man's terrorist is another man's freedom fighter" engenders sharp disagreement, depending on the audience.

The Problem of Terrorism

It is extremely difficult to define exactly what does and does not constitute terrorism. Because it is a highly emotive and partisan subject, students of terrorism tend either to defend it or be repelled by it. Given this difficulty, it is useful to categorize terrorism in terms of six descriptive characteristics, recognizing, however, that no set of descriptions will satisfy all observers.

First, terrorism involves the use of *criminal acts to achieve political ends*. Of course, the term *criminal acts*—defined on the basis of the legal codes of the society against which terrorist acts are aimed—points to the controversy over terrorism. The opponent of terrorism criticizes terrorist acts involving the indiscriminate murder of innocent persons (for example, airline bombings), but the terrorists respond that their acts reflect a state of war and that their ends are defined in terms of political purposes that justify organized violence. It is in this context that the slogan "one man's terrorist is another man's freedom fighter" gained its notoriety. From the viewpoint of terrorists, their political purpose justifies their actions (they are "freedom fighters"); from the viewpoint of the recipient society, however, terrorist criminality cannot be justified as extralegal political activity. This distinction points to the debate about how to conceptualize counterterrorism. Should it be treated as criminality, in which case it becomes a legal problem? Or should it be treated as war, in which case the rules of warfare apply?

The second defining characteristic of terrorism is its *indiscriminate nature*. Acts of terror are politically motivated; they seek to gain the compliance of a target population to a political position that the terrorist group advocates. The method involves terrorizing the population, making it fearful of continued acts of terror and thereby causing the population to accede to the terrorists' demands. The mechanism for instilling that fear is the indiscriminancy of terrorist actions. The people at whom terror is directed must be made to live in a state of fear, never knowing when the next lethal attack will occur. Thus, terror must be used randomly. Particularly when terrorism is directed at democratic systems, the whole population, which must convince its elected representatives to accede to terrorist demands, is the target. This is clearly the underlying rationale, for instance, behind the Irish Republican Army's (IRA) attacks against London. The problem is that terrorist acts, not unlike strategic bombardment against civilians during conventional war, may actually increase the resolve of target populations rather than demoralize them.

This leads us to the third characteristic (and weakness) of terrorism: that its acts and campaigns are normally aimed at *influencing government actions rather than gaining control of governments*. The typical purpose of the terrorist is to force governments to change policies; thus, a terrorist campaign may be aimed at the release of "political prisoners" (usually members of their own or sympathetic groups) or at a political policy deemed unfair (a Palestinian homeland). If one happens to be sympathetic to the particular cause, then the action gains legitimacy; if not, the action is considered illegitimate.

The modesty of goals that terrorists typically espouse reflects a fourth characteristic: Terrorism is a *tactic of the weak*. The goals that terrorists pursue tend to be minority positions where the policy outcome cannot be achieved through normal political processes. Moreover, the dynamics of terrorist activity require a high degree of secrecy if the randomness of action and surprise is to be maintained. Secrecy is best achieved by terrorist movements that are reasonably small and impenetrable by outside forces. Weakness in appeal and weakness in numbers reinforce one another. The situation is analogous to forming an insurgency in a Third World country. Just as insurgents begin as a small and weak group, so do terrorists. The insurgent gradually gains strength by engaging in successful acts against government forces; the terrorist hopes to gain strength through successfully terrorizing the target population. However, the analogy breaks down after this point. Counterterrorists are generally better organized than the government facing an insurgency, making progress beyond the equivalent of the first stage of insurgency difficult.

The fifth characteristic of terrorism is *sponsorship*. With the exception of very small radical groups, most terrorism is sponsored by some outside force, which trains, equips, and funds particular terrorist groups. The most common form of sponsorship is by states, where individual national governments sanction and underwrite terrorist activities. The most highly publicized examples are in the Middle East, where Syria, Libya, Iran, and Iraq typically head the U.S. government's list of terrorist states because of their support of various Palestinian and Shiite movements directed against Israel and conservative Arab states. The former Soviet Union had long been a sponsor of terrorist groups. The United States' attempted assassination of Muammar Qadaffi in 1986 is defined by some analysts as an act of state-sponsored terrorism because it intended to convince the Libyan leader to cease his sponsorship of terrorist acts.

Not all terrorism has direct government sponsorship, however. The IRA's actions are not tied to the Republic of Ireland or any other national government. Rather, the IRA receives most of its material and other support from private sources dedicated to an all-Catholic Ireland. In most of these cases, however, there is inadequate support for private efforts. Thus, the most challenging and dangerous terrorist movements have state sponsorship.

The final characteristic of terrorism is its *causes*. There are two broad arguments about what causes a terrorist movement to develop. Those more sympathetic to terrorism argue that certain social, economic, and political conditions produce terrorists. That is, a sufficiently wretched way of life leads to despair and hopelessness and thus serves as a breeding ground for terrorists, who have little to lose and much to gain potentially through their sacrifice. This explanation is used by many to describe why the Palestinian refugee camps in Israel have been potent sources of terrorist recruitment.

Other analysts argue that terrorism develops because of its appeal to people of certain cultures, religions, even political ideologies. This argument is based on the assumption that certain groups of people place less value on human life generally and are thus able to conduct the violent physical acts of terrorism. It is often argued, for instance, that Americans were at a disadvantage in the Vietnam War because of their culturally based inability to engage in the acts of terror used by the enemy to terrorize the population.

Support for the two explanations of the causes of terrorism has deep North-South connotations. Much of the Third World sympathizes with the first explanation—that wretched conditions lead to terrorism—because its solution would involve development and a North-to-South transfer of wealth. In the North, cultural differences are more often emphasized as the cause of terrorism. Western culture considers many terrorist actions repulsive, thereby justifying the eradication of terrorists. Third Worlders, in turn, view this attitude as akin to "shooting the symptoms" in counterinsurgency. It is no surprise, then, that terrorism continues to be a controversial subject.

The Problem of Counterterrorism

There is also much disagreement about how to deal with terrorism. At one level, there is the rhetorical problem of what counterterrorism means. Many analysts make a distinction between antiterrorist and counterterrorist activities. *Antiterrorism* refers to defensive measures taken to decrease the vulnerability of society to terrorist attacks, such as increased security at airports or monitoring the whereabouts of known terrorist groups through international police cooperation. *Counterterrorism* refers to active, offensive actions intended to suppress terrorist activities by denying terrorists the ability to engage in such acts, including physical acts of violence against terrorist organizations and individual terrorists.

Intuitively, counterterror is more attractive than antiterror. For one thing, it gets at the "heart" of the problem by attacking its source—the individual terrorist and the supporting organization. Successful counterterrorism also acts as a deterrent for potential terrorists. Moreover, it allows the government to seize the initiative; in contrast, the antiterrorism approach involves waiting passively for the terrorist to attack.

Despite the potential advantages of counterterrorism, its usage remains controversial for at least three reasons. First, counterterrorism is very difficult to execute, and even when done effectively it may cause the government to act in ways that the public may find morally and culturally unacceptable. Second, there is disagreement over whether a legal or military approach should be taken. Finally, counterterrorism is not the function of any one government agency, which creates a jurisdictional tangle that hinders the development of effective counterinsurgency policy.

The difficulty of engaging in counterterrorism has at least six interactive aspects. First, terrorist groups are *clandestine organizations* headquartered in unfriendly countries where U.S. intelligence assets may be deficient (as in Syria and Iraq). When counterterrorism involves taking the action to the opposition, a first requisite is identifying and penetrating the organization. Terrorist groups often cooperate across national boundaries and operate under different guises, further complicating the identification process. This difficulty was evident in the American hostage problem in Lebanon; the most difficult problem was finding them.

Second, there is the problem of *initiative*. Although counterterrorism is intended to take the initiative away from the terrorist, the terrorist's effectiveness comes from attacking at unexpected times in places impossible to target. Given the clandestine nature of terrorist organizations, it is much easier to reconstruct a terrorist plot in retrospect than it is to anticipate it in advance.

Third, there is the related problem of the *idiosyncracy of terrorist acts.* The only common denominator among such terrorists acts as an airline hijacking or bombing, a truck bombing in a crowded urban area, the kidnapping of a corporate executive, or the assassination of a local governmental official is that they are hideous and heinous. However, each terrorist act is very different in terms of anticipating when or if it will occur. Thus, antiterrorist activity may prevent one terrorist act but have no effect on another.

A fourth difficulty is that terrorists are often accorded *government protection* by the countries in which they operate. At a minimum, then, the counterterrorist must overcome not only the terrorists but also the host government.

The fifth problem involves identifying the *center of gravity* of the terrorist organization—who and what to attack. Successful terrorists, like competent insurgents, seek to imbed themselves in the population so as to make their identification more difficult as well as to make it harder for others to attack them without alienating the population. One example is the 1983 bombing of the Lebanese countryside and the Bekaa Valley by the *USS Iowa,* which was intended to force terrorists away from American positions in the area. While the attacks undoubtedly punished a number of terrorists, they also caused the suffering or death of many innocent civilians.

Sixth, many of the most effective counterterrorist acts suffer from *cultural offensiveness* to most Americans. Practitioners generally agree that punishing terrorists and deterring future terrorist acts require that counterterrorism be selective and personal so as to identify and punish the actual perpetrators. Effective action may cover a range of actions, up to and including the assassination of known terrorists. The U.S. government is prohibited from abetting or committing assassinations, a reflection of American cultural values.

Another underlying problem of counterterrorism is developing frameworks within which to conduct the campaign. One alternative is to treat terrorism as a legal problem. If terrorism is considered a criminal activity, then countering terrorists must be done within the same framework as other legal and judicial proceedings (including rules of evidence, legal and civil rights, search and seizure, and acceptable means of arrest and trial). Given the clandestine nature of terrorism, however, the legal approach makes effective counterterrorism very difficult.

Another alternative is to treat terrorism as a military problem. The rationale for this approach derives from the assertion that terrorists have declared war on society and have committed what they themselves depict as acts of war. If this position is adopted, the rules of engagement change; mostly, juridical requirements are relaxed and militarily effective actions can be undertaken.

The counterterrorism community would prefer to treat the problem as military in nature. A good deal more is known about who commits terrorist acts than is publicly acknowledged, but the special operations forces trained as counterterrorists find their hands tied because their evidence does not meet the standards of a courtroom. In the United States, terrorism is treated as a legal problem. The results are that terrorists can proclaim themselves at war and act accordingly, but society treats their acts as criminal behavior and thereby affords terrorists legal protection. The difficulty of the U.S. government in successfully extraditing from Libya the accused bombers of Pan American Flight 103 points to the frustration of the legalistic approach.

Another major problem in dealing with terrorism is a lack of sufficient government organization. This problem has three distinct aspects. First, the government's assets in the counterterror field are not only limited but also scattered throughout the system. We do not know how many forces are available because many of them are so-called "black" operations, meaning that the forces and their budgets are classified. This is necessary because effective counterterror requires the same anonymity and secrecy as does terror itself. The most public government organization with this kind of capability is the U.S. Army's Delta Force; however, it is small (a force of about six hundred) and is responsible for a range of other special operations tasks in addition to counterterror.

Second, the various tasks associated with counterterrorism are spread among various government agencies, making a coordinated campaign difficult to organize. For example, the State Department is designated as the lead agency for all international terrorist acts; the Justice Department has jurisdiction over domestic terrorism, a responsibility it assigns to subagencies such as the Federal Bureau of Investigation (FBI) and the Immigration and Naturalization Service (INS); the Federal Aviation Agency (FAA) is responsible for airline hijacking; the Central Intelligence Agency (CIA) collects foreign intelligence on terrorist activity; and the Department of Defense is responsible for defending its own personnel from terrorists and for assisting other agencies in this regard.

Finally, counterterrorism is ineffective because it lacks immediacy and urgency. The American public opposes terrorism in principle, but in practice very few Americans are affected by terrorist activities. Those who are usually reside in overseas areas (such as Beirut) where terrorism is most likely to occur. Furthermore, during Operation Desert Storm, Saddam Hussein did not unleash terrorists to attack the United States directly as Americans feared.

PEACEKEEPING AND PEACEMAKING: WHO, WHERE, AND WHY?

One major result of the end of the Cold War has been a revival of interest in the United Nations as a participant in creating and regulating peace. This change—tied to the ability of the United States and the former Soviet Union to cooperate within the U.N. Security Council—was evident in the 1990 resolutions justifying the successful military action against Iraq. The revived interest extends to the major mechanism for U.N. action in the Cold War period—peacekeeping.

As peacekeeping evolved after the first U.N.-sponsored peacekeeping force was interposed between Israel and Egypt following the 1956 Suez War—the United Nations Emergency Force (UNEF)—it became an activity that largely excluded superpower participation. The reason was that one or the other was frequently sponsor of a contending party being separated, and thus clearly partisan. As a result, neither nation could participate as a neutral (which peacekeeping requires); in the emerging system where they are not opposed, their role may expand.

There is an important distinction between peacemaking and peacekeeping. *Peacemaking* refers to the creation of a ceasefire and disengagement between two parties (countries or groups within countries) engaged in hostilities. The purpose of the peacemaker is to separate the combatants, by force if necessary. This action requires forces that have some offensive capability and that are willing to engage in combat to create peace. Peacemaking is logically prefatory to peacekeeping.

Peacekeeping, is more passive and can only occur after the fighting has stopped and the combatants have disengaged, as U.N. peacekeepers learned in Bosnia-Herzegovina in 1992. It is the job of the peacekeeper to keep the former warring parties separated while a more permanent basis for peace is negotiated.

Peacekeeping Forces

The methods of peacekeeping forces today were set by the original UNEF operation, including the characteristics of peacekeeping forces and the assumptions under which they operate.

U.N. peacekeeping forces have developed four basic characteristics over time. First, they have generally been drawn from the nonaligned countries or smaller members of the Cold War alliances. This has been done to avoid partisanship, which was a problem in the early part of the U.N. operation in the Congo (Zaire) between 1960 and 1964. Some countries, such as Canada, Norway, and Morocco, have specially designated and trained units committed to U.N. peacekeeping. Second, training includes instruction that peacekeepers can use their weapons only for personal self-defense (as in an attempt to breach the peacekeeping line separating forces). Third, the basis on which peacekeeping forces operate is to interpose themselves physically between the combatants. So situated, the idea is to make it physically impossible for the combatants to attack one another without first crossing and attacking the U.N. lines.

Fourth, peacekeeping missions have historically been financed on an ad hoc basis by the major powers, notably the United States and Great Britain. Unfortunately, the financing system does not guarantee a consistent availability of funds. During the Reagan years, the United States refused some payments for peacekeeping because it disagreed with certain actions of the peacekeepers. The result was a financial crunch for the organization and ill will between the United States and the United Nations. The Bush administration later agreed to pay back the debts.

Experience has taught a set of basic assumptions that underlies any peacekeeping operation. First, peacekeeping forces will only be put in place with the consent of both (or all) contending parties, and will not act as peacemakers. The original UNEF demonstrated the wisdom of this principle and the consequences of its failure. When the force was first created along the Egyptian-Israeli border in Sinai, both sides agreed to having it there, though the Israelis did not agree to stationing peacekeeping forces on their territory. As long as mutual consent was effective, UNEF kept the enemies apart. When the Egyptians withdrew their support in 1967 and demanded the withdrawal of the peacekeeping force, the inhibition was gone and the Six Day War of 1967 ensued.

Second, peacekeeping forces require ongoing and strong support of the Security Council, especially from its permanent members. In the past, sponsorship of one or both contending parties by one or the other super-power made this a limiting factor; the emerging cooperation between Russia and the U.S. will likely expand the future of peacekeeping in the new international system and could assist in peacemaking, as was needed in Bosnia-Herzegovina.

Third, the peacekeeping force must have a clear and practicable mandate. The forces must know what is expected of them, and their mission must be one they are capable of performing. There must be an adequate number of competent forces available from the contributory nations. Finally, there is the underlying assumption of peacekeeping that force can be used only as a last resort.

Peacekeeping forces, then, must have a different orientation and level of discipline than average forces, because of the constraints and frustrations under which they operate. In most cases, their presence is resented by those who view them as a barrier to achieving their own goals. Occasionally, that resentment will result in violence.

Three basic issues, each of which will become more important if the role of peacekeeping is to include the major powers, continue to surround peacekeeping issues. The first issue has to do with the peacekeeping chain of command. The U.N. Charter provides for a military chain of command through the Military Staff Committee, which calls for rotating command among the five permanent members of the Security Council. That provision has never been invoked due to past superpower inability to cooperate militarily. As a result, the command of individual operations has been decided instead on a case-by-case basis, as was the case in forming the coalition for Operation Desert Storm.

The second issue is the composition of peacekeeping forces. Although the United Nations has a number of reliable and effective peacekeeping-participant states, many more will be required if peacekeeping becomes a larger enterprise in the future. In the past, expanded participation was hampered by Cold War affiliations. However, as military alliances and their underlying antagonisms disappear in the new post–Cold War world, an increase in peacekeeping-participant states becomes more likely.

The third and final issue is the financing of U.N. activities. The United Nations does not have a "taxing" power to levy binding assessments for operations beyond the basic financing of the organization. Instead, it relies on its wealthiest members for financing. When a member disenchanted with some U.N. action uses its unhappiness to justify withholding funds, the organization's effectiveness is restricted.

The United States as Peacekeeper

Except for its limited role in monitoring peace in the Sinai as a result of the Camp David accords, the United States has no real history as a peacekeeper. Official government documents (such as the *Annual Report* of the Secretary of Defense) claim that peacekeeping is an expanding priority, but it is unclear what this means operationally.

To adopt the new and unfamiliar mission of peacekeeping, the United States will have to resolve three important problems: (1) the unavailability of appropriate peacekeeping forces, (2) the uncertainties about funding (particularly in light of projected defense cutbacks now beginning to occur), and (3) whether non-American peacekeeping forces would be more appropriate to the Third World situation.

Peacekeeping is unfamiliar to most U.S. government personnel, who are trained for conventional war and especially offensive operations more appropriate for peacemakers. Peacekeeping requires considerable patience, for which the U.S. Army is not trained. Some countries, such as Norway, which maintain standing forces committed to peacekeeping, provide special schooling for soldiers assigned to that task, stressing that this is special duty requiring soldiers with special qualities. The United States does not have such a training facility, except for the military police. Therefore, it is questionable whether the U.S. Army in a time of declining resources is interested in training special peacekeeping forces.

The second and related problem is financial. Desert Storm was a temporary reprieve from the severe cutbacks that the U.S. military is being forced to absorb. Traditional military commitments (for example, in armor and airborne equipment) are now in competition with both one another and with domestic priorities. Furthermore, because peacekeeping has no constituency with which it might compete for funds, it is therefore not likely to succeed budgetarily in these hard economic times.

Third, there is uncertainty over whether American peacekeeping forces would be welcome in the Third World. Although, in theory, the U.N. Charter provisions on collective security provide for sending troops of Security Council permanent members into regional disputes, it is uncertain whether in practice the intrusion would be accepted by Third World countries. They may resent the presence of American peacekeeping forces in particular, viewing them as the "police officers" of Third World problems. Moreover, the U.N. Charter requires that peacekeeping arrangements be acceptable to all parties to a dispute. Long-term analysis of the U.S. intervention in Iraq to shield the Kurds from the Iraqi army may provide some clues about the acceptability of American peacekeeping efforts in the Third World.

CONCLUSION

Our discussion in this chapter has focused on counternarcotics, counterterrorism, and peacekeeping for several reasons. First, all three missions are at least partly North-South problems: the North consumes drugs produced in the South; most terrorism originates in the Third World; and peacekeeping is almost exclusively geared toward Third World problems. Second, each mission is designated by the U.S. Department of Defense as an important future concern. The questions are whether they should be important concerns and, in turn, whether they have military solutions.

From a geopolitical and strategic point of view, these are basically marginal concerns from the vantage point of American vital interests. As societal problems, illegal drugs, terrorism, and peacekeeping do not represent vital national interest for which the United States would be willing to enter a war. Of course, drug abuse is a serious societal problem in the United States. But terrorism against American citizens within the country has hardly even reached the nuisance stage, much less become a compelling governmental problem.

In other words, these are relatively small problems in comparison to the military issues underlying the Cold War. Declaring "war" on drugs is hyperbolic at best; declaring "war" on terrorism would be sophistical. Moreover, whether they are military problems at all is questionable (with the possible exception of peacekeeping). More clearly, they are highly specialized, unconventional missions that require not military but special forces.

Although it is assumed that military force can be applied in the eradication and interdiction of illegal drugs entering the United States, this too is unrealistic. Successful eradication of drugs can be carried out only by the governments of the countries in which the drugs are produced. As for interdiction, neither its effectiveness in the war on drugs nor its cost effectiveness in relation to other methods has been demonstrated.

For now, then, we are left without realistic solutions to the problems of illegal drugs, terrorism, and peacekeeping methods. Counternarcotics must address the demand for illicit drugs, and counterterrorism the misery in Third World countries. In addition, the peacekeeping forces must address the fact that certain countries do not have enough of a stake in peace to maintain it by themselves. Unlike the counternarcotics, counterterrorism, and peacekeeping efforts of today, which focus on only the symptoms of these problems, future efforts will have to shift focus to finding long-term cures.

CHAPTER 6

An Old Problem with New Teeth: Regional Conflict

Violence and instability among Third World nation-states are certainly nothing new. Many regional conflicts between Third World neighbors, which have occasionally led to war, predate the colonial experience. These conflicts resurfaced after World War II when independence was granted by the former European colonialists. In South America, for instance, there is the old ABC—Argentina, Brazil, Chile—rivalry, though it has weakened in response to increased democratization. North Africa has ongoing conflicts between Algeria and Morocco, Libya and Egypt, Egypt and Sudan, and Ethiopia and Somalia. In the Middle East, there is rivalry between Egypt and Israel (dormant since 1978), Israel and other Muslim states (Syria, Iraq, and Jordan), Syria and Iraq, Iraq and Iran, and Saudi Arabia and Iraq. On the Asian subcontinent, regional conflicts exist between India and Pakistan and India and China; in Southeast Asia, between Vietnam and China and Vietnam and Cambodia.

Regional conflicts in the Third World, however, have received far less attention from the West than did the Cold War conflict. Americans' vital national interests were in the U.S.–Soviet struggle during the Cold War period because that is where the greatest threats existed. Although at this same time the Third World was emerging from its colonial past, Western interests there were not considered as important.

The only importance the Third World did have to the West during the Cold War was in terms of its natural resources and as a place for the Cold War competition to grow. Those Third World areas with natural resources necessary for the industrial well-being of the First World were considered important. The mineral riches of southern Africa and the petroleum reserves of the Persian Gulf gave those areas value during the Cold War that they would not otherwise have had. In addition, the extension of the Cold War rivalry to the Third World created an interest in the mutual balancing of superpower influence in the region. For example, if the Soviets ventured into a certain geographical region of the Third World, the United States would seek to assure that its rival did not gain an upper hand there, or vice versa.

The end of the Cold War has changed how the First and Third Worlds think about and deal with one another, though it has not had a positive effect on Third World regional conflicts or on the potential for instability and violence. However, these conflicts may become a more important concern in the post–Cold War period. Indeed, they represent the most difficult problems facing the new world order. Solving them would mean a much more tranquil world than exists today.

Yet the problems of Third World political and economic development, which divide North from South, will not be easily resolved. In the past, the schism was regrettable but avoidable; the Third World did not really matter. Confronting the gap may be unavoidable in the new international system.

The Third World regional conflicts that exist today differ from those of the past in one significant way—they are potentially more lethal. Many developing countries have larger and more sophisticated arsenals than before: they have new, and potentially much sharper, teeth. These are the so-called NBC armaments—nuclear, biological, and chemical weapons—as well as ballistic means of delivering the weapons within the region and beyond. Iraq, of course, was considered the prototype until its humiliation in the Persian Gulf War. However, the Iraqi case does not make the NBC capability of Third World countries any less threatening.

Therefore, although regional conflicts have long existed in the Third World, they are now potentially more dangerous than ever before. The new world system, then, has an incentive for helping to further political and economic development, thereby engendering greater stability in the Third World.

OLD ROOTS: REGIONAL RIVALRIES
IN THE COLD WAR SYSTEM

Like internal wars within a Third World country, regional conflicts between countries are best understood in terms of the circumstances from which they emerge. In many cases, the disputes are old, deep, and have multiple causes related to history, culture, or religion. Moreover, each conflict has certain unique characteristics, which makes it difficult to generalize about regional conflicts.

Let us begin by looking carefully at some examples of regional conflicts. In the contemporary world, the most dangerous conflicts are in

South Asia and Southwest Asia, and in the Mediterranean Middle East. Through those examples we can better assess superpower behavior toward regional conflict in general during the Cold War period.

The Indian Subcontinent

One of the oldest and most difficult regional conflicts is in South Asia, the Indian subcontinent (see Map 6.1). The two major rivals, India and

Map 6.1 The Indian Subcontinent

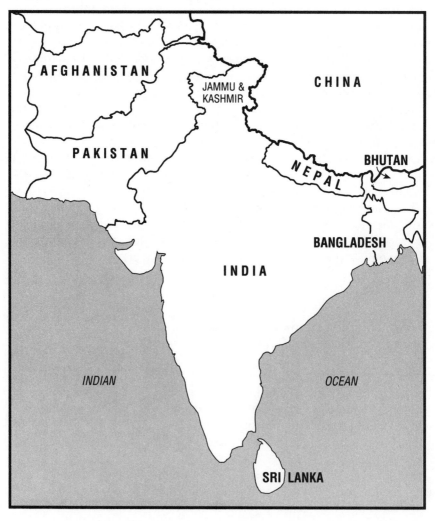

Pakistan, have fought two major wars (in 1965 and 1971) as well as a minor war (in 1947–48) at the time of the partition of the subcontinent.

At the heart of the conflict is the collision of Hindu and Muslim cultures and civilizations, which orginated about A.D. 1000 when Muslim invaders moved onto the subcontinent from Arabia and the Persian Gulf region. The two peoples differ from one another in multiple and fundamental ways—they are ethnically distinct, they speak different languages, they worship different deities and do so in different ways, and they are politically and historically diverse.

The rivalry was temporarily suspended during the rule of Great Britain (the British Raj). However, when British rule began to crumble under the pressures of Mohandas (also known as *Mahatma,* or "Great Soul"), Gandhi's Indian Congress, and Muhammed Ali Jinnah's Muslim League, the two sides temporarily took common cause in their mutual desire to be rid of colonial rule. The British, in their haste to accede to independence demands after World War II, agreed to a partition between Hindu India and Muslim Pakistan with boundaries drawn basically according to confessional habitational patterns.

The plan was drawn too hastily, and once the British were gone, the two sides realized that they had more at issue than in common. Moreover, the partition was defective in at least four ways: it left substantial members of each confession "trapped" in the wrong country; it did not decide the fate of critical parts of the old Raj (notably the princely states of Jammu and Kashmir); it created an untenable Pakistan with eastern and western sections divided by one thousand miles of Indian territory; and the border between the western section of Pakistan and India traversed the middle of the world's oldest river-based irrigation system—the Indus River system—without making provision to divide and distribute equally the critical waters from the river system.

In addition, both India and Pakistan were troubled by multinationalism, a periodic source of discord. Before the state of Bangladesh was created, the principal rivalry in Pakistan was between the light-skinned, warriorlike Punjabis of the western portion and the darker-skinned, more peaceful Bengalis of the eastern part. With partition accomplished in 1971, what is left of Pakistan (the western portion of the original country) continues to be divided along ethnic lines, mainly among the Punjabis, Baluchis, and various Afghan tribes.

The situation in India is similar. Despite efforts to divide Muslims from Hindus, a substantial Muslim population remains in India, constituting the majority in states such as Kashmir. At the same time, there is division among northern and southern Indian ethnic groups, and religious groups such as the Sikhs continue to present problems for the region.

Geopolitics has entered the scene as well. The India-Pakistan rivalry is augmented by a third party bordering on the region—the People's Republic of China. China and India are in dispute over the long border they share along the Himalayas. The border is of great geopolitical importance to India because it protects access to a narrow band of India's easternmost territory. The disputed territories also guard historic passes that have been used as invasion routes back and forth to the subcontinent. This particular aspect of the dispute is especially important because, by the year 2000, there will be 1.2 billion people living in China and 1.1 billion in India, representing over one-third of the total world population. Pakistan, especially since it was shorn of its eastern territories (Bangladesh), has thus nurtured a special relationship with China to counterbalance the overwhelming Indian population growth. The result is a geopolitical triangle with explosive potential.

Moreover, the area is not immune from the crisis of political and economic development that plagues the Third World. Politically, India is more developed than Pakistan, possessing what Indians proudly describe as the world's largest functioning democracy. At the same time, there is great factionalism within India that mars the uniform application of democratic principles. And the country's economy, while developing, has long strides to take before providing abundantly for its population. Pakistan has flirted with nascent democracy only to revert periodically to military rule, and its economy remains weak.

The regional balance is contested within this context. Among the states directly within the South Asian region—the two major powers plus Bangladesh, Sri Lanka, Bhutan, the Seychelles Islands, and Nepal—only India has the potential to be a regional hegemon, a role that it publicly denies an interest in occupying. At the same time, both India and Pakistan have nuclear programs on the verge of weapons production, as well as stores of ballistic missiles and other weapons of mass destruction.

The Persian Gulf

Bordering the Asian subcontinent at its western extremity, the countries along the Persian Gulf littoral (see Map 7.2, p. 182) have come to epitomize regional conflict and instability. At the vortex of the region's combustibility has been Iraq, which has fought an eight-year war with its Persian neighbor Iran, invaded and been expelled from Kuwait, and experienced numerous instances of internal instability, including the periodic brutal suppression of its Kurdish minority.

The regional powers of the Persian Gulf include Iran, Afghanistan,

Saudi Arabia, Kuwait, Oman, Yemen, Bahrain, and the United Arab Emirates. Of these, Iran is by far the largest in population and hence in potential power; in fact, Iran resembled a regional hegemon prior to the 1979 Iranian Revolution, which forced Reza Shah Pahlavi from the Peacock throne and brought the fundamentalist theocracy of Ayatollah Ruhollah Khomeini to power.

Since 1979, the Persian Gulf has been the most volatile region in the world. In November 1979, Iranian "students" stormed the American embassy in Teheran and held its inhabitants hostage for fourteen months, punctuated by the unsuccessful U.S. rescue mission known as Desert One. In December 1979, the Soviet Union, under the guise of the Brezhnev Doctrine, invaded Afghanistan to prop up a faltering Marxist government, an adventure that kept them militarily in the country for over eight years. In September 1980, Iraq attacked Iran to begin the draining eight-year conflict between those two Islamic rivals. This decade of violence was followed by the Iraqi annexation of Kuwait in August 1990 and their forceful expulsion in February 1991.

Several factors stand out in the Persian Gulf regional balance. The first, and geopolitically most important, is petroleum. The Persian Gulf region contains two-thirds of the earth's proven reserves of "black gold." To a world heavily dependent on petroleum as its primary energy source, the region is important to guarantee the continuing access of the First World to the oil fields. It is arguable that the world's interest would disappear in the absence of the petroleum incentive.

Second, the countries of the region are among the most heavily armed in the world. The stimulus to the regional arms race was the rivalry between Iran and Iraq, which in turn has caused other regional states such as Saudi Arabia to arm themselves heavily. What has made these levels of arms troublesome is that the arsenals contain chemical and biological weapons and ballistic means of delivery. Some of this concern ebbed with the apparently effective "defanging" of the Iraqi offensive military capability as part of the coalition effort to liberate Kuwait, and subsequent United Nations efforts. As long as rivalries simmer, however, the potential for additional rounds of the arms race persists.

Third, the Persian Gulf region contains considerable power imbalances. The states of the Arabian peninsula, where most of the oil is located, are small (except for Saudi Arabia) and relatively underpopulated (including Saudi Arabia). This imbalance leaves the smaller states reliant on the goodwill of the larger states for their independence, an infirm base as the Kuwaitis learned in 1990. Among the regional powers, Iran has by far the largest population at around 45 million, thus endowing it with the potential for regional dominance or influence.

Fourth, the region is also the collision point between the two major sects of Islam—Sunni and Shi'a Islam. Sunni is the majority sect within the Islamic world as a whole, but in the Persian Gulf region Iran's majority Persian population is Shiite, as is about 60 percent of the population of Iraq (though that country is ruled by the Sunni minority). Religious fundamentalism and revivalism are powerful forces within Shi'a Islam, giving nervous pause to the Sunni leaderships of the smaller, oil-rich states. Moreover, the holiest shrines of each sect are in the region: the Sunni holy places at Mecca and Medina in Saudi Arabia (in addition to Jerusalem) and the Shiite shrines at Karbala and an-Najaf in Iraq.

The Arab-Israeli Conflict

Prior to the emergence of the Persian Gulf as a world hot spot, the terms *Middle Eastern* and *Arab-Israeli* conflict were synonymous. The conflict between the Jewish state of Israel and the surrounding Islamic states (see Map 6.2) began in 1948, when Israel was born; subsequent major wars were fought in 1956 (the Suez War), 1967 (the Six Days' War), and 1973 (the Yom Kippur War). In each case, Israel prevailed over a coalition of states including, at different times, Egypt, Syria, Jordan, and Iraq. In addition to its "external" enemies, Israel is besieged by the Palestinian problem, the claim of the Islamic people who were the former rulers of Israel (or what they call Palestine).

The underlying issue dividing Israel and its neighbors is about real estate: Who is the rightful owner of Israel/Palestine? Both sides have a reasonable claim based on history and habitation, and the two groups even coexisted for a time between the world wars when the Jewish settlers were in the minority.

World reaction to the Holocaust and the perceived need to create a Jewish state after the war joined the conflict. After World War II, displaced Jews flooded Israel, despite unsuccessful attempts to limit their immigration. When the Jewish state was formally declared by the United Nations in 1948, and the surrounding Muslim states attacked vainly to destroy Israel, much of the Palestinian population panicked and fled, ending up in refugee camps in the surrounding countries. There are now sizable Palestinian minorities in most Middle Eastern states and a Palestinian majority in Jordan.

The plight of the Palestinians and the need for a Palestinian state carved out of some portion of Israel or the occupied territories—the Gaza Strip and the West Bank of the Jordan River are the most likely candidates—have provided a rallying cry for the so-called "Arab" states

Map 6.2   Israel, Jordan, and Lebanon

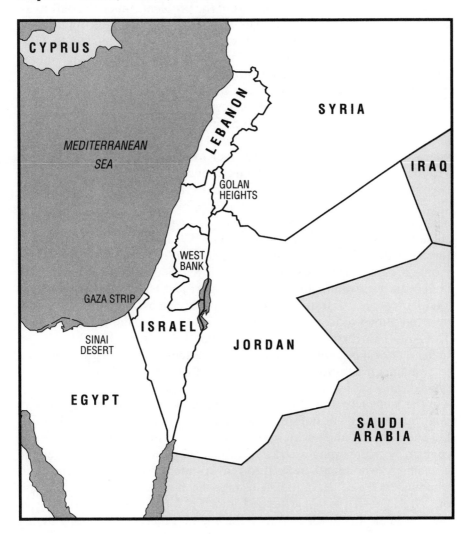

(technically, the term *Arab* is only applied to natives or descendants of people from the Arabian Peninsula), a sign of unity in an otherwise tumultuous and fractious condition. Arab unity with the dual emphasis of an Israel to hate and Palestinians behind whom to rally rhetorically is at least a hope; without either, that unity is a chimera.

The basic division between the sides is religious, and it comes to a head over Jerusalem, which houses some of the holiest shrines of three major religions—Christianity, Judaism, and Islam. Because of this, access by all religious groups is a major part of the problem. When the old city of Jerusalem was controlled by Jordan, Jews were denied access to their holy places, notably the Wailing Wall. With the old city in Israeli hands, Muslims can only visit the Mosque of Umar by passing through Israeli-armed checkpoints. It is not a very satisfactory situation, and it was made worse when Israel moved the capital from Tel Aviv to Jerusalem, thereby symbolically announcing their intention never to relinquish control.

The direct, bloody confrontation between Israel and the other states has been mute since 1978, when President Jimmy Carter negotiated a peace settlement between Israeli leader Menachem Begin and Egyptian President Anwar Sadat. The agreement ended the state of hostilities between the two states and recognized Israel's right to exist; in return, Israel agreed to negotiate a solution to the Palestinian question. That solution has remained elusive, however, despite the beginnings of face-to-face discussions between the parties in November 1991 in Madrid. The frustration for the Palestinians was expressed in the *intifada* ("uprising") and the more or less open Palestinian support for Saddam Hussein in the Persian Gulf War. The combination of that support and Israel's uncustomary restraint in the face of Iraqi Scud missile attacks against its cities temporarily diverted public concern away from the Palestinian claim to a homeland. The Arab-Israeli conflict will not, however, be concluded until the Palestinian question is resolved. American-led attempts at mediation continue to result in frustration, as the unsuccessful negotiations of early 1992 proved.

The final piece in the Arab-Israeli puzzle is the tragedy of Lebanon. A multicommunal state housing Christians and Sunni and Shiite Muslims, Lebanon existed in delicate balance throughout most of the Arab-Israeli conflict by maintaining a strict neutrality. Civil war broke out over the Lebanese government's refusal to redistribute power in conformance to communally-based demographic change dictated by the constitution, and the Arab-Israeli conflict extended into the fragile country. As long as there are Palestinians operating in the country, thereby prompting Syrian and Israeli occupation, there can be little hope for the restoration—or reconstruction—of a viable Lebanese order.

Our three examples are only the most prominent cases of regional conflict in the Third World; they are certainly not the only ones. In Southeast Asia, Vietnam has been in conflict with some of its neighbors, including Cambodia and Thailand. The two Koreas, as long as they remain separated, provide the potential for violence, as do the People's Republic of China and Taiwan. What will become of these conflicts in the future will be affected greatly by the changing nature of First World relations with the Third World.

THE COLD WAR FACTOR: THEN AND NOW

The Cold War rivalry between the United States and the former Soviet Union played a role in each of the regional conflicts just discussed. In South Asia, for example, the United States had a long relationship with Pakistan and a varying relationship with India, whereas the former Soviet Union concentrated its attentions on India. In the Persian Gulf, the United States sponsored Iran before the Iranian Revolution—in large measure an anti-American outburst—and the Soviet Union was the heavy sponsor of Iraq. In the Arab-Israeli dispute, the United States has been heavily associated with Israel and has nurtured relations with Egypt since 1975, as well as with Jordan. The Soviets were close to Syria and were the major supplier of arms to Egypt between 1955 and 1975.

The relative levels of Third World involvement by the two superpowers varied across time. The competition was largely joined at the Bandung Conference of 1955, which was dominated by anti-Western voices that created a wedge for Communist competition. Western dominance was thus challenged, and the competition for influence became the major way in which the Third World was viewed. The Soviets accelerated the competition in the 1960s and gradually moved to challenge American influence. In the wake of Vietnam during the 1970s, the American revulsion from foreign and defense affairs allowed the Soviets the upper hand. During the Reagan years, the United States became active once again.

A major part of the "new political thinking" on international relations implemented by former Soviet President Mikhail Gorbachev was noninterference in the affairs of other states. This entailed renouncing the Brezhnev Doctrine, which had been the justification for meddling in the Socialist countries of Eastern Europe and places like Afghanistan. It also meant backing away from the competition for influence in the Third World generally, a position necessitated by the Soviet need to focus their attention and resources inward.

The end of the Cold War thus marks a major change in how the North and the South interact. In one sense, the change will likely be positive: the Communist/anti-Communist lens through which the North viewed and distorted Southern problems will be removed. At the same time, the lack of competition may also reduce interest in the Third World, contributing to its further marginalization.

The Cold War Period: Competing Sponsorships

The historic attitude of the First and Second Worlds toward the Third World has been a sort of "good news, bad news" proposition. The good news was that the competition provided access to resources for the Third World that might not otherwise have been available. The bad news was that these resources were too often in the form of weaponry and excessive in terms of the legitimate defensive needs of Third World states. Moreover, since that assistance was provided from a motive of currying influence and favor, it was often what Third World governments wanted rather than what they needed to assist the process of development.

It is easy to overemphasize the geopolitical and hence instrumental base of American and Soviet interest in the Third World during the Cold War. However, the relationship was an extension of the worldwide rivalry defined by Americans in terms of the containment of communism and by Soviets as part of moving the historical dialectic of inevitable Communist victory ahead. The result was a kind of "scorecard" mentality in which one side "won" or "lost" by gaining regional followers in one place or the other.

Some countries—India was probably the master—played this competition to the hilt, managing to play one side off against the other. To some extent the former European colonizers, notably Britain and France, moderated the geopolitical game in their individual former colonies where they had historic interest and empathy. Nonetheless, the major emphasis was on the geopolitical contest.

There were at least two major reasons for transferring the Cold War competition to the Third World. First, it was a part of the world that was available for conversion to one or the other Cold War "faiths." In this regard, the Soviets and Americans each had advantages. From the American viewpoint, the colonialists had left behind nominally Western-style governmental systems that should have had affinity with the West; the problem was that often the new regimes were too inexperienced to make the systems work. The Communist advantage was that it offered a revolutionary blueprint in Maoism for throwing off the shackles of colonialism and an explicit game plan for development in Marxism-Leninism; the shortcomings were that the latter model did not work and that the Soviets lacked the financial resources to nurture achievement of Soviet-style "utopias."

The second reason Third World competition was attractive was that it was relatively safe. Direct East-West confrontation involved the most vital interests of each side; should confrontation devolve to violence, the results could be catastrophic. In the Third World, the interests were rarely vital; if confrontation occurred, one side could back away without great loss of national interest or prestige.

This tenor of the Cold War competition created certain implicit rules for the geopolitical game. First, the major interest of each side was limited to protecting the investment that it already had in a given government or to currying favor in places where the other side was not dominant. Second, direct challenges in countries where the other side was dominant were generally avoided on the grounds that such action might spill over and poison more important aspects of the central Soviet-American relationship. Third, whenever regional disputes boiled over into war, both sides had an active interest in avoiding escalation to the point that they might be drawn in on opposite sides.

These rules had two beneficial results. First, they placed a restraint on the level and intensity that regional conflicts might develop. The restraint was not, of course, solely out of an interest in the parties concerned, but to avoid superpower conflict. Thus, the Soviets restrained the Syrians from intervening in the Jordanian Civil War of 1970 and widening that conflict. In 1973, with the Egyptian army pinned against the Suez Canal and the road to Cairo unobstructed, the United States moved decisively to restrain the Israelis and avoid the danger of a threatened Soviet intervention. Although outside the Cold War context, Israeli restraint in the face of Iraqi Scud missile attacks during the Gulf War was certainly counselled by the United States.

The second beneficial effect was to maintain balances of power in regions that suppressed the emergence of regional powers with hegemonic ambitions. As long as there were rivals on both sides and neither the Soviets nor the Americans wanted the other's clients to reign supreme, there was a moderating effect on the realization of regional ambitions (such as those evidenced by Saddam Hussein before the Gulf War).

East-West Third World competition has been a victim of the Cold War's end. On one level, it was a simple matter of Soviet withdrawal from all but those places where interests were deep and long-standing, such as Angola, Cuba, and Afghanistan. In this case, the United States arguably emerged as the lone remaining superpower in what Charles Krauthammer (1990–91) calls a "unipolar" world system. On another level, the Soviet withdrawal reflected two realities confronting them. First, the competition was simply too expensive; a Soviet economy that could not provide for its own citizens could hardly afford a large subsidy to Cuba, for example. Second, the rewards of the competition were meager for both sides. Just as the motives for competing were instrumental rather than flowing from intrinsic interests, the commitments received were tentative, instrumental, and ephemeral. Often, the only gratitude for offering assistance was "What have you done for me lately?"

The Post–Cold War Period: Cooperative Action?

The end of the Cold War has left the U.S. and Russian policies toward the Third World uncertain. The basis for that policy can no longer be a competition that has ceased to exist. Whether the revised rationale will be captured in George Bush's "new world order" is debatable; whether the United States and the former Soviet Union will work together, independently, or at odds also remains conjectural.

The Third World will almost certainly be a more disorderly, difficult place to manage than it was during the Cold War period, particularly in terms of the major powers' ability to influence clients who no longer feel dependent. For one thing, the ability to influence through the supply of arms will be diminished; there are alternate private sources in the world for almost any category of arms, as well as an increasing availability of arms manufactured in Third World countries themselves. A lesson of the Gulf War may well be that large-scale interventions by major powers in the Third World are too expensive in human terms (for example, the mobilization of the American Reserves) to be undertaken often, despite the large subsidies for the U.S. effort.

Several trends are likely to emerge in the Third World. First, the vacuum created by the withdrawal of the superpowers will probably be filled by regional actors unfettered by Cold War restraints. In the Persian Gulf region, for instance, a resurgence of Iranian activism seemed plausible with a weakened Iraq after the Gulf War. India is almost certain to repeat its assertiveness in the Tamil uprising in Sri Lanka. Elsewhere, Egypt and Syria will emerge as major players in the Mediterranean Middle East, and Vietnam will almost certainly join Thailand as a major player in Southeast Asia. The availability or willingness of the United States and the former Soviet Union to provide a damper on regional assertiveness is uncertain at this time.

A second and related factor is likely to be a relative absence of regional organizations and structures to restrain regional competitions in the Third World. Such structures, as they existed in the Cold War period, were largely military alliances (for example, the old Central Treaty Organization [CENTO] and the Southeast Asian Treaty Organization [SEATO]) that had ceased to function prior to the end of the Cold War. The major remaining structure to which most Third World countries belong is the United Nations, though its ability to act decisively in regional situations is an open question.

A third unsettling factor is that one curious irony of the end of the Cold War is likely to be a new flood of weaponry to the Third World. As agreements such as the Conventional Forces in Europe (CFE) treaty and unilateral reductions by countries on both sides of the Cold War military competition result in smaller First World arsenals, there may be a flood of excess weaponry on both the public and private markets. Those weapons will go somewhere, and it is likely that they will find their way into the Third World, further overarming regional competitors.

Finally, the post–Cold War balance finds the principal Third World competitors armed with weapons of vastly greater lethality than ever before. The introduction of chemical and biological weapons and of ballistic means of delivering them make the existing regional balances especially dangerous. Moreover, as the physical range of missiles expands, the regional powers will almost certainly become able to menace the First World as well as one another. This is already a problem for the former Soviet Union, which borders on parts of the Third World; it can become a problem for the United States in the future as the regional powers gain global projection capability.

In the future, what roles will the former Cold War competitors play in the Third World? The Soviet role is likely to be modest because the former Soviet Union lacks the resources for sustained Third World activism, a realization the Soviets have grudgingly admitted. The largely rhetorical contribution that the Soviets made to the coalition effort in the Persian Gulf War is probably indicative of future actions. The republics of the old union will have to devote their resources toward restructuring the successor configuration of republics.

The future U.S. role in the Third World, however, is less certain. On the one hand, America's decisive leadership in the liberation of Kuwait suggests that it may play a major role in the new world order, which is certainly possible. On the other hand, a sustained U.S. commitment to mending the problems of the Third World will be problematic. In the history of U.S. foreign policy, periods of activism are usually interspersed with periods of introspection and withdrawal. As the United States struggles to confront its own domestic difficulties, then, the distant thunder of Third World problems may fade.

NEW DIMENSIONS: THE RISE OF THE "WEAPON" STATE WITH NEW CAPABILITIES

What many observers find most alarming about the problem of regional powers and regional conflicts is that many Third World countries have acquired sophisticated arsenals containing highly lethal weapons, which were once the exclusive preserve of the major powers. The result, according to columnist Charles Krauthammer (1990–91), is a rise in weapon states—"small aggressive states armed with weapons of mass destruction and possessing the means to deliver them." Currently, these states are primarily a threat to one another, but they are likely to pose a direct threat to the major powers in the future.

The problem of weapon states in the Third World has two important dimensions. The first is the growing armaments of Third World countries with NBC—nuclear, biological, and chemical—weapons. Although biological and chemical agents—what some call poor-man's nuclear weapons—are more prevalent, nuclear arms still pose a menacing threat in most cases. Second, the growing accumulation of ballistic missile means of delivering NBC and other weapons of massive destruction is a concern.

The extent of the threat posed by weapon states is serious and growing. As shown in Table 6.1, there are currently over twenty Third World countries that produce or are suspected of producing chemical or biological agents. The list of states possessing missile capability is growing in numbers as well. If some of these states also gain nuclear weapons capability, their potential ability to disrupt international relations will become a significant concern.

There are several observations that can be made about the fairly recent phenomenon of the Third World weapon state. First, we know that the NBC capabilities of these countries exist because they have been used effectively in war. For example, both ballistic missiles and chemical weapons were employed during the Iran-Iraq War, particularly by Iraq. In addition, the Iraqis hideously employed chemical weapons against their own Kurdish minority in 1987, and used missiles against Iranian cities to help push a war-weary Iranian population over the edge to sue for peace. How decisive the weapons were in that conflict remains controversial, but the efficacy of use was established.

Second, the proliferation of NBC capabilities among developing countries will be difficult to control, in part because the weapons are widely produced by the Third World itself. Chemical weapons are relatively easy to produce (they are made from commonly available materials) as well as to conceal. For example, a chemical plant that manufactures lawn fertilizer could be easily converted into one producing certain chemical weapons. The materials used in chemical weapon production are also used for legitimate manufacture, so controlling their availability is difficult at best. The only precedent for avoiding chemical weapons proliferation is in the model of the Nuclear Non-Proliferation Treaty (NPT), which attempts to prevent nuclear weapons spread. The problem here, though, is that sev-

Table 6.1   Status of NBC Proliferation in the Developing World[a]

	Nuclear	*Biological*	*Chemical*	*Missile*	*Strike Aircraft*
Africa					
Algeria	—	—	R&D	—	Deploy
Ethiopia	—	—	Prod	—	Deploy
Libya	R&D	R&D	Prod	Deploy	Deploy
South Africa	Prod	R&D	Deploy?	R&D	Deploy
Middle East and the Persian Gulf					
Egypt	—	R&D	Prod	R&D	Deploy
Iran	R&D	Deploy	Deploy	Deploy	Deploy
Iraq	R&D	Deploy	Deploy	Deploy	Deploy
Israel	Deploy	Prod	Prod	Deploy	Deploy
Saudi Arabia	—	—	—	Deploy	Deploy
Sudan	—	—	Deploy?	—	Deploy
Syria	—	R&D	Deploy	Deploy	Deploy
Yemen	—	—	Deploy?	Deploy	Deploy
Asia					
Afghanistan	—	—	Deploy?	Deploy	Deploy
China	Deploy	Prod?	Deploy	Deploy	Deploy
India	Prod	R&D	R&D	Prod	Deploy
North Korea	Prod	Prod?	Prod	Deploy	Deploy
South Korea	R&D?	R&D	Prod?	—	Deploy
Myanmar	—	—	Deploy?	—	—
Pakistan	Prod	R&D	R&D	Prod	Deploy
Taiwan	R&D	Prod?	Deploy?	Prod	Deploy
Thailand	—	—	Prod?	—	Deploy
Vietnam	—	—	Deploy	—	Deploy
Latin America					
Argentina	R&D	R&D	R&D	R&D	Deploy
Brazil	Prod?	R&D	Prod?	Prod	Deploy
Chile	—	R&D	Prod?	—	Deploy
Cuba	—	—	R&D	—	Deploy

[a]*R&D* = substantial research and development estimates; *Prod* = production capability or the capability to produce within one year; *Deploy* = deployed in combat forces or held in combat-ready storage. These estimates are based on material available in unclassified sources; they do not represent estimates drawn from U.S. government sources.

Source: John McCain, "Controlling Arms Sales to the Third World," *Washington Quarterly* 14, no. 2 (Spring 1991), p. 84.

eral of the chemical weapons-producing Third World states are not members of the NPT agreement, including Algeria, Argentina, Brazil, China, Cuba, Israel, Kuwait, and others.

Third, the NBC capabilities of the Third World are growing in sophistication. Although in the Persian Gulf War Iraq's obsolete Scud missiles were intercepted by Patriot missiles originally designed for antiaircraft purposes, the threat of Third World weapon states will grow in importance in the near future. India, for instance, successfully tested a missile for launching satellites into orbit; if tailored to ballistic missile weapons purposes, it would have a purported range of nearly 2,500 miles.

Fourth, the NBC capabilities of developing countries will increasingly place not only the Third World at risk but the First World as well. Parts of the former Soviet Union, for example, are vulnerable along borders shared with developing countries that possess NBC weapons. Although the United States itself is not currently at significant risk of a direct attack, American overseas military bases are potential targets. For instance, Libya's Muammar Qaddafi fired missiles at U.S. Mediterranean bases in retaliation for the 1986 air raid on Tripoli (though the missiles fell short of their targets, landing harmlessly into the sea instead).

Finally, growing NBC capabilities of Third World countries may spawn a whole new industry of countermeasures to protect nonpossessors from attack. The opening round of this new twist in the arms race was sounded by the Persian Gulf competition between Iraqi Scud missiles and American Patriot missiles directed over the Arabian desert. It is likely that countries at risk from and otherwise incapable of self-defense against NBC attacks will look to acquire defensive missiles to protect themselves.

The NBC Threat

The problems posed by deadly weapons are both old and new. The use of highly flammable substances goes back to the employment of Greek fire (burning oil) in ancient and medieval times. In more recent history, mustard gas was widely used by both sides during World War I in an attempt to find a way to break the system of entrenchments that strung from the English Channel to the Alps. During the Vietnam War, the United States used chemical defoliants (Agent Orange) to remove the jungle canopy beneath which the enemy hid from American bombardment. So-called "fuel-air" explosives, which spew forth a flammable mist, arguably fall within the realm of chemical warfare. Moreover, the Soviets probably experienced a serious biological accident when anthrax cultures escaped from a biological warfare plant in April 1979 and killed many in the surrounding community of Sverdlovsk.

The growing concerns about deadly weapons—whether nuclear, chemical, or biological—are not without precedent. The horizontal proliferation of nuclear weapons (that is, their spread to countries that previously did not possess them) led the superpowers to conclude the NPT agreement in 1968, and continues to be a priority of organizations like the Western Nuclear Suppliers Group (NSG), which seeks to control access to fuel-grade nuclear material. At the same time, international conventions prohibit the use of chemical and biological weaponry (also called *agents of biological origin* or ABO). Yet throughout most of the Cold War, the United States and the Soviet Union kept large, if not officially acknowledged, arsenals of both chemical and biological weapons to deter the other side. It was not until 1990 that they agreed to deactivate and destroy portions of those arsenals.

The spread of deadly weapons throughout much of the Third World, however, is a contemporary problem. The dread of nuclear proliferation, while still a potential nightmare, is less fearsome now than was predicted a quarter century ago. In 1964, China became the last acknowledged member of the nuclear "club"; although Israel, India, and possibly South Africa and Pakistan may have become nuclear powers, the list could be much longer. Thus, today's concerns about biological and especially chemical weapons proliferation are focused on Third World states. It is in the Middle East that the physical capability to produce these weapons is concentrated: in Iran, Iraq (before many of its facilities were destroyed in the Persian Gulf War), Syria, and possibly Israel. In addition, China, the Koreas, and Taiwan are probable members of the chemical weapons group.

The contemporary world is thus characterized by the emergence of highly lethal weapons states. According to Richard Barnet, they are "small states with large grievances or large ambitions." For example, Iraqi President Saddam Hussein developed and used chemical weapons during the 1980s, and in early 1990 he had nearly acquired nuclear weapons prior to the Persian Gulf War. When combined with ballistic means of delivery within the Gulf region, Iraq became a dangerous threat to the international community.

Much of the concern about NBC weapons derives from the question of why countries seek to obtain them. One reason may well be the pursuit of greater regional power at an affordable price. Certainly, a nation armed with chemical or biological weapons is recognized as more important militarily than a nation without them. Another reason for possessing such weapons may be deterrence. For example, if a country's regional rival possesses NBC weapons, the country may conclude that its only recourse against an attack would be to retaliate in kind. The same kind of reasoning underlies the idea of nuclear deterrence. In addition, chemical weapons possession may deter other nations, including the major powers, from a variety of actions.

Perhaps the most frightening reason behind a country's decision to obtain NBC weapons is to use them in the event of war. The world's experience with chemical weapons is at best mixed. Against military troops appropriately prepared, the results of chemical weapons are minimal (however, the bulkiness of antichemical suits can lower troop efficiency). These weapons may be more effective when used to terrorize unprepared civilian populations in crowded urban conditions. This is a problem in the Middle East, where large populations tend to be concentrated in a few urban areas, in which a maximum amount of damage could occur.

Chemical and biological weapons add several complications to already difficult regional conflicts. First, their potential use can add to heightened tensions before war occurs, panicking populations and making the decision to go to war more likely. Second, destroying these weapons before they are used would be a high priority of target states. Third, the use of such weapons can only increase the desperation of the participants as well as the motivation for revenge in the target population, thereby making it more difficult to end a war already begun.

The fourth problem is that chemical and biological weapons create more uncertainty in Third World regional conflicts. It is not clear whether the World War II experience in avoiding chemical weapons use through the fear of retaliation will apply to Third World situations. As a result, these weapons represent yet another (though more lethal) unpredictable variable in the regional conflict mix. Fifth, if chemical weapons possession is perceived as desirable or necessary, the proliferation of such weapons may be more difficult to control than even nuclear weapons. The key to nuclear nonproliferation has been denial of access to fuel-grade plutonium. However, the basic ingredients from which chemical weapons are produced are commonly available. A country that accumulates large stocks of these ingredients is probably intending to manufacture chemical weapons, but monitoring and controlling the situation is difficult.

Our recent experience with chemical weapons is limited to two cases, both involving Iraq. In the latter stages of the 1980–88 war with Iran, Iraq used chemicals against Iranian troops as well as its own Kurdish minority. It also engaged in terrorist missile attacks against Iranian cities. Experts disagree about how effective the chemical weapons were in these situations; some argue that the weapons were decisive, while others hold that they only convinced an already war-weary Iran of the futility of war.

However, experts agree that the Iran-Iraq War proved the ability to employ such weapons.

The other example is the Persian Gulf War, in which Iraq did not use its chemical weapons. Iraq may have judged their use ineffective, given how well the coalition forces were prepared for an attack. Or it may have feared reprisal in kind (some captured Iraqi troops had chemical equipment). Perhaps Iraq was only able to deliver its chemical warheads by means of limited-range artillery shells. Or perhaps Iraq was deterred by the fear that the coalition partners would escalate the war to the point of a nuclear attack.

In order to seek ways to limit or eliminate chemical and biological weapons in Third World regional conflicts, we must first understand the differences between the Iran-Iraq conflict and the war in the Persian Gulf. Some viable and effective deterrent over these agents must be developed so that it can act as the precursor to the elimination of such weapons.

The Role of Missile Delivery

Surface-to-surface missiles that can be delivered at ballistic velocity are yet another complicating element of Third World conflicts. Regardless of what these missiles carry (NBC or conventional explosives), they are potentially deadly if used against countries unable to defend themselves.

Most missiles in Third World inventories are less than state-of-the-art. Generally, they are either primitive superpower- or other Western-supplied weapons (such as the Scuds employed by Iraq against Israel and Saudi Arabia in the Persian Gulf War) or replicas of old First World designs produced in other Third World countries. Moreover, the missiles have limited ranges and even more limited accuracy. Nonetheless, they are still capable of menacing neighboring rivals and of terrorizing people living in cities. In addition, a new generation of relatively inexpensive but highly lethal cruise missile prototypes threatens to enter Third World arsenals.

Part of the problem are the kinds of Third World countries that possess missile capability. In the Middle East, for instance, the list includes Libya, Egypt, Syria, Iran, Iraq, Israel, Yemen, Kuwait, and Saudi Arabia. In addition, pairs of countries with historical animosities possess rockets: India and Pakistan, the Koreas, China and Taiwan, and Argentina and Brazil. A number of the possessors, such as China and Brazil, are also producers and sellers of rockets, thereby complicating efforts to control proliferation.

Missile technology, especially when combined with some form of NBC munition, changes Third World conflicts in several pernicious ways, particularly in the volatile Middle East. These weapons add to the lethality and flexibility of their possessors in that the missiles can travel long distances rapidly and attack with little warning. When the missiles can be accurately aimed at military targets, this gives the incentive to attack and destroy enemy forces before they are used, thus making war more likely to start. When they are inaccurate, they add to the terror created in urban populations.

In addition, most of the missiles and their launchers are also relatively primitive and vulnerable, thereby inviting preemptive attacks and therefore forcing possessors to engage in "use them or lose them" calculations (fire first or have your forces destroyed). The extent of this vulnerability varies, depending on the size of the arsenal and of the country possessing it. In Operation Desert Storm, for instance, a major problem facing the allied bombers in their attempt to destroy Iraqi Scud launchers was finding the numerous mobile platforms located in a country of 169,385 square miles. Identifying and targeting missiles in a small country like Kuwait or Yemen would presumably be a more manageable task.

Moreover, the missiles not only put Third World countries at risk but also the personnel and facilities of allied and friendly countries. The U.S. Patriot antiaircraft missiles employed in the Persian Gulf War were generally effective against the Soviet-made Scuds employed by Iraq. However, the Patriot missile is not perfect, as was demonstrated during the war when a Scud missile landed on an American base in Dhahran, Saudi Arabia, killing twenty-seven U.S. service personnel. The Scuds are primitive missiles, but Third World countries are likely to obtain more effective missiles that can avoid the Patriot.

Finally, there is a basic fear of missiles being available in the highly volatile Third World. Clearly, there is nothing new about missiles in military arsenals; the superpowers possessed them for over thirty years and have employed them with military effect. The utility of the sea-launched Tomahawk cruise missile in the Persian Gulf War is an example. The military decisiveness of missiles in regional conflicts has yet to be established, and conventional delivery of NBC or other explosives by airplane or cruise missile may be more appropriate to achieving military goals.

However, there are three bases of concern regarding missiles in the Third World, all of which are tied to the Iran-Iraq and Persian Gulf wars. First, this capability was possessed by someone like Saddam Hussein, whose sense of responsibility with the weapons was suspect at best. The prospect of missile proliferation raises the likelihood that future "Saddams" will obtain them. Second, it is not clear that all of the developing countries that may obtain missiles will treat them with the same restraint as First

World countries. Some experts speculate that certain cultures, particularly in the Middle East, which regard human life with less sanctity than others, may be more willing to use missiles in a potential *jihad,* or "holy war." Third, missile proliferation makes First World countries feel both guilty and impotent. The guilt arises because the Cold War antagonists were the original suppliers of missiles to the Third World, and indigenous industries in Third World countries take First World designs as starting points. The impotence comes from the perceived difficulty of halting the further spread of missile capability. Even if First World regimes can agree to quit supplying missiles, there are now other sources available. Moreover, the end of the Cold War has reduced the ability of either Cold War party to influence the behavior of former clients in this area.

However, efforts are under way, stimulated by the Persian Gulf War and President Bush's pursuit of the "new world order," to arrest or slow missile proliferation in the Third World. The major effort has been collaboration among the major First World producer nations under the guise of the Missile Technology Control Regime (MTCR). The goal of this voluntary organization, which contains most but not all missile producers, is to gain voluntary restraint on the export of missiles and missile technology. Its current limitations include (1) that not all producing nations—and especially not Third World producers—are members, (2) that it represents no legal or treaty obligation, and (3) that it allows collaboration on peaceful space programs that utilize many of the same technologies as weapons programs.

A control regime is vulnerable to the laws of supply and demand. As long as states believe that possessing ballistic missiles serves their interests, there will be other states and private entrepreneurs willing and able to service that demand. The spectacular success of U.S. rocket technology against Iraq has enlarged the market for American "smart" weapons, including rockets, which is testing U.S. government and industry resolve to resist proliferation in a time of trade deficits. For the Soviet successor states, especially Russia, weapons sales are their second largest source of hard currency after natural resources, and they are desperate for hard currency to underwrite economic reform. Even if the United States and the former Soviet Union abstain from the trade, others would gladly take their places.

Yet there are alternatives to resisting missile proliferation. One involves preemptive actions against worrisome proliferators, destroying their capability before it can be used or bringing international pressures to bear through organizations such as the United Nations. When the United States systematically destroyed the most lethal elements of Saddam Hussein's arsenal, the world did not raise an eyebrow. When a residual nuclear capability was discovered in Iraq, the United Nations moved forcibly to continue sanctions until the capability was dismantled.

Another approach involves developing defenses against ballistic missiles. The area of ballistic missile defense (BMD) in the Soviet-American nuclear relationship had a shady reputation, reflecting the suspicion that they could not deflect an attack made by the other. However, proposals emerged in early 1992 for joint Russian-American programs of cooperative defenses against Third World attacks.

Most experts agree that the technological task of defending against the relatively small missile attacks of Third World countries would be possible. As early as 1989, U.S. Senator Sam Nunn, chairman of the Senate Armed Services Committee, advocated redirecting the Strategic Defense Initiative (SDI) toward defending the United States against unauthorized, inadvertent, or small attacks by Third World countries. SDI gained considerable momentum after the Persian Gulf War and is now officially known as the Global Protection Against Limited Strikes (GPALS) program. Such defense programs could help to protect U.S. overseas facilities as well as the American homeland from ballistic attacks. More broadly, Third World countries, themselves locked in ballistic missile competitions or harassed by missile-possessing neighbors, represent a huge potential market for defensive systems.

Yet another possible way to slow or arrest missile proliferation is to apply the dynamics of bilateral nuclear deterrence, as it was developed in the U.S.-Soviet context, to the Third World. In most cases, a missile balance between foes already exists. However, it is uncertain whether the political and cultural contexts of the Third World will be similar to those of the East-West situation. Some experts argue that the Western intellectual base of deterrence is imbedded in a sanctity for human life that is greater than that of some Third World cultures. They hold that certain Third World values, such as martyrdom and a greater willingness to suppress or murder large numbers of citizens, presumably reduce the kinds of inhibitions that were present in the Soviet-American relationship. Whether this argument is valid or just an expression of cultural ignorance is uncertain.

MANAGING REGIONAL CONFLICT IN THE EMERGING INTERNATIONAL ORDER

Integrating a truly independent Third World into the international system will be one of the most challenging tasks of the future. The First World must lead this adjustment, for the vacuum created by the end of the Cold War competition requires the construction of a new set of arrangements. This adjustment, however, will take place in the experienced, mature, and relatively stable condition of long-standing relationships and political and economic stability in Europe.

Stability is missing in much of the Third World. The regional balances that will have to emerge lack long historical contexts, and the actors are inexperienced in constructing or maintaining balance. The Cold War provided a guiding and limiting hand in most Third World regions; it is now gone. Moreover, the general prosperity that underpins the stability—and can improve relations—in Central Europe is by no means universally present in the Third World.

At least three factors make Third World regional conflicts and efforts to create regional balances important to the international system. First, the current balances are potentially lethal—the major regional powers and their adversaries are already armed with NBC weapons and ballistic missiles, and others are nearing the same capability. The precedent for using these weapons in regional conflicts has already been set in the Middle East; because the weapons were used to military effect, they are likely to be employed again. This is an important concern of the international community. On humanitarian grounds, the use of such lethal materials is not a precedent that one wants to see reenacted. More geopolitically, the end of the Cold War may lessen the escalatory linkage between major powers and former Third World clients, but it will not sever these relationships altogether. Any use of NBC weapons carries some escalatory potential. In the worst possible case, for instance, if a Muslim state used NBC agents against Israel with great effect, Israel might retaliate with nuclear weapons. In addition, Americans and others who live and work on overseas bases might become the victims of such attacks. If so, what would Western governments do in response?

A second important factor is that it will be difficult to devise an overall policy toward Third World regions that is not so general as to be virtually meaningless in application. Each region in the Third World has unique elements that will require a different policy. The Middle East is important because of its petroleum resources, the southern portion of Africa is important because of its mineral resources, and Southeast Asia is important because it sits astride major oceanic trading routes. Different interests create different responses. Furthermore, the threats to Western interests vary. The Persian Gulf region is clearly the most volatile and unstable part of the world, inhabited by leaders most hostile to the West. South Asia has one major potential hegemon in India, whereas Southeast Asia wrestles with intrastate and interstate questions of human rights and self-determination in addition to development.

Third, Operation Desert Storm opened up the question of how appropriate Western involvement really is in settling regional conflicts. While the expedition was cloaked appropriately in response to aggression, guaranteed access to relatively inexpensive petroleum played a geopolitical role. What the world response would have been had Kuwait not possessed petroleum is uncertain. Moreover, the sheer extent of the American commitment in the Persian Gulf—of personnel, equipment, money, and national energy—though ending conclusively the Vietnam syndrome, raises questions about how often similar actions might be undertaken.

There are two major concerns for the future. The first has to do with forming and regulating regional balances, including the role of international organizations such as the United Nations and the major powers. The second has to do with whether or how to limit the acquisition and use of NBC weapons and ballistic missiles.

Devising Regional Balances and Stability

In systemic terms, the major international problem posed by the Third World is the stability of regional balances. The old Cold War restraints can no longer regulate, weapons are too freely available from multiple sources, and it is not clear there will be enough economic development capital available for development to occur.

At the nub of the regional stability question is the balance between states in regions. During the Cold War, balance meant that the superpowers ensured that the other's client did not become the hegemon; in the post–Cold War world, it means trying to avoid the emergence of regional hegemons. Saddam Hussein was the first regional actor to make a bid for hegemony; the question is whether some better way can be devised to blunt such ambitions than the military coalition that defeated Saddam.

There are two basic, overlapping approaches to stabilizing Third World conflicts. The first is the collective security agreement, in which a group of nations attempts to present enough force in opposition to aggression to successfully deter it. In the absence of broad-based collective security arrangements, the alternative is the formation of self-regulating regional balances, possibly coordinated through some extra-regional body such as the United Nations.

There are three collective security models available. The first is prescribed by the U.N. Charter; Chapter VII of that document, which was the legal source of the resolutions authorizing sanctions and force against Iraq, provides for a permanent U.N. force composed of the forces of the five permanent members of the Security Council and coordinated through the Military Staff Committee. However, these forces have never been formed or used. Historically, the reason for this was Soviet-American antagonism and rivalry that placed them on opposite sides of eligible disputes. Moreover, during the Cold War, the superpowers' joint operation would have been politically inconceivable.

Although the major barrier to U.N.-style collective security is gone, the model is still not likely to be workable in the short run. As Soviet-American political cooperation erased the last vestiges of the Cold War relationship, continued unrest and political adjustment will preoccupy the former Soviets for some time, precluding their dedication of armed forces to the United Nations. At the same time, neither country can afford financially to make the kind of commitment necessary to become "global police officers." Third, such an arrangement might well be unacceptable to the Third World, in which policing would have to occur and whose countries compose a majority of the voting membership of the U.N. General Assembly.

The second collective security model is implied by Operation Desert Shield/Storm. Although authorized under U.N. auspices, it was not a true U.N.-controlled operation, nor did it conform to the U.N. model. Rather, the operation was much closer to that prescribed under the old League of Nations, in which sanctions and actions were voted but enforcement fell on volunteers. This principle—known as the "hue and cry" approach to collective security—was invoked by Secretary James Baker as he assembled the Desert Storm coalition.

The coalition in the Persian Gulf held together—in terms of allegiance, commitment, and performance—well beyond many people's expectations and despite attempts by Iraq to splinter it (for example, by attacking Israel in the hopes of an Israeli response). As an approach, however, it suffered from the same difficulty that plagued the League of Nations: Without any permanent forces committed to collective security, deterrence depends only on the potential aggressor's assumption that a force will be formed; if the aggressor doubts that will happen, deterrence fails. Moreover, there is precedent from the League experience that states will depend on everyone else to participate, thereby justifying their own abstinence. If the League model had worked, the founding fathers of the United Nations would not have felt the need to change it.

The third model of collective security involves developing permanent U.N. forces from the smaller powers. The core of such forces could be those countries that have forces committed to U.N. peacekeeping activities. This approach, however, has two potentially fatal drawbacks. First, it is doubtful that a large enough pool of forces could be assembled from these countries to deal with anything more than small conflicts. Certainly, they could not match an army the size of Iraq's during the Persian Gulf

War. Second, a peacemaking force, such as that needed in Bosnia-Herzegovina in 1992, would be much more expensive. This is the kind of force proposed at the "summit" meeting of members of the U.N. Security Council in January 1992.

The alternative to managing regional conflicts through a global collective security arrangement is to devise a series of regional balances to manage their own individual regions. One clear advantage is proximity and, if military force was needed, greater ease and lesser expense in getting military force where it was needed. Thus, a regional balance formed around the states of the Indian Ocean littoral could have gotten Indian or Pakistani forces (or both) to the Persian Gulf much more quickly and cheaply than moving the American-based coalition. Because the regional actors are from the region, they presumably have a greater stake in how the balance operates and hence would be more willing to participate in necessary actions.

A series of regional balances has potential drawbacks. If the global world order became increasingly regionalized, as several economic analysts believe it would, there might be a tendency for the regions to become more parochial and introspective, rather than viewing increasingly global problems from a global perspective. The internationalization of the world economy can only be impeded by regionalized concerns, and transnational problems (such as environmental degradation) cannot be encompassed within several regional frameworks.

In addition, most Third World regions are beset by deep-seated regional conflicts that need regulating, and it is hard to see how those conflicts and regulatory mechanisms can be disaggregated. It is one thing to talk of a regional balance encompassing the Indian Ocean (IO) littoral, but how does one fit that into India's long-standing and unresolved conflict with Pakistan? Unless China, which is not part of the IO littoral, is included in the balancing mechanism, it is hard to imagine a coalition that could act if India was the protagonist.

Another problem with unrestricted regional balances is the regional hegemon that seeks to impose its values on less-than-enthused fellow regional states. Without the superpowers to dampen regional conflicts, the most powerful players are likely to be relatively more important than in the past. This could lead to a condition of more, not less, conflict within Third World regions.

A solution that combines regional and global collective security involves nurturing regional balances of power but overseeing and coordinating them through a universal organization such as the United Nations. Since almost all Third World nations are U.N. members and profess a great loyalty to the organization, the United Nations clearly is a candidate forum. With the U.N. organization proposing solutions to regional conflicts, which basically would be enforced regionally, the best features of both approaches—enforcement close to the problem without parochialism or hegemonic manipulation—would be utilized.

The United States clearly has a potential leadership role in such an arrangement. As the only remaining superpower with both global interests and means of power projection, the United States could play a key political and, where necessary, military role. The military role would not be of the style or size of Desert Storm every time a regional conflict broke out; rather, it would serve as a backdrop to the region-based forces, especially ground forces (particularly through the use of naval- and land-based air forces used to such devastating effect in Desert Storm) and for transporting regional forces to the theater, a role it already plays for transporting U.N. peacekeepers.

Deterring Regional Conflict with Deadly Means

Of course, the ideal solution to Third World regional conflicts involves promoting their peaceful resolution, especially in light of the potential dangers posed by lethal weapons. Thus, the problem of deterring the proliferation of deadly warfare agents and ballistic means of delivery is a major part of determining the health and stability of the global balance in the future.

But can deterrence be accomplished? Cultural differences may make it difficult to translate Western notions of deterrence to non-Westerners, and there are other problems caused by the unique circumstances of Third World regional conflicts. These are often much deeper and more bitter than the East-West conflict was; it has been argued that it was good that the nuclear arms race was between the United States and the Soviet Union, rather than between historic enemies, since they had no history of antagonism otherwise. The same cannot be said of most Third World regional conflicts, which have centuries of hatred and suffering behind them. Also, in areas like the Middle East, only short distances separate the antagonists from small, physically concentrated populations that make preemptive attacks more plausible and devastating than they ever could in a superpower world where thousands of miles separated the antagonists.

There are two important aspects to deterring Third World NBC and missile proliferation: (1) *deterring acquisition* (that is, persuading or coercing nonpossessing states not to acquire these weapons) and (2) *deterring employment* (that is, dissuading those states that possess the weapons from using them).

Two strategies have been employed to solve the problem of weapons acquisition. The first is persuasion, convincing Third World states that it is not in their best interest to obtain NBC weapons or ballistic missiles. The traditional vehicle for this strategy is the arms-control process, and the regime most frequently cited is the NPT. The major effort here is to reduce incentives to acquire such weapons through controlling or proscribing the acquisition altogether. As with NPT, the chief barriers include the potential proliferators' belief that they need the capability—either because a traditional enemy has it or to gain advantage over that enemy—and the failure to abstain by potential suppliers. If the NPT is any indicator, such efforts are most successful against the least offensive states—those not involved in regional conflicts or with minimal instability.

The other strategy for limiting weapons acquisition is coercive: threatening the proliferators' capability. Since those issuing the threats must have greater might than the proliferators, this is largely the approach of the First World. Coercion can take the form of economic sanctions (such as those sponsored by the United Nations against Iraq) or preemptive military strikes (such as the U.S. attacks on Iraqi weapons facilities during Desert Storm). However, this approach has two major shortcomings. First, there is the question of universality: Can any nation credibly threaten to destroy all instances of proliferation? Colonel Qadaffi and Saddam Hussein were both villainous, rogue leaders for whom few felt sorry and whose humiliation was broadly applauded; not all potential proliferators, though, are such obvious "bad guys." Moreover, this approach resembles vigilantism and, if widely practiced, would be condemned as such. Second, there is the question of detection: Although aspects of developing nuclear capability are relatively easy to monitor, other weapons capabilities are harder to determine (Saddam Hussein concealed much of his program before U.N. inspections in 1991).

The problems of deterring the employment of NBC and missile weapons are different but equally vexing. If a nation cannot be discouraged from developing a given weapons capability, the focus shifts to convincing that nation not to use it. As in the traditional bilateral Soviet-American nuclear deterrence, there are two approaches. The first and most common is to threaten retaliatory vengeance if a weapon is employed. Nuclear deterrence has worked because both sides feared that any attack would be met with a devastating counterattack. This is offensive deterrence, in which the threat of punishment operates to deter. But can this be transferred to Third World situations? If the deterrence relationship is between a major power and a Third World country, the evidence suggests that deterrence may hold. The only obvious example is the withholding of Iraqi chemical weapons in the Persian Gulf War, because of the fear of reciprocation or a lack of operational delivery means. If both opponents are Third World states, however, deterrence requires that both sides have the proscribed capability to allow reciprocal threats, which implies the need for further proliferation if only one side initially is so armed. At the same time, it requires forces to be adequately secure on both sides so that neither can calculate successful preemption. This is not always possible in Third World situations.

The other form of deterrence is defensive—the credible capacity to deny an attacker success by being able to intercept and destroy incoming weapons (active defense) or to successfully absorb attack without suffering devastating consequences (passive defense). In light of the spectacular success of missile defenses in the Persian Gulf War, there is likely to be considerable demand in Third World countries for the capability to defend against NBC-carrying missiles—the idea underlying the GPALS initiative. This approach, less destabilizing than the retaliatory approach, is only wasteful in that it diverts financial resources from other uses. The advantage of defensive deterrence—to the extent that the means are truly and unambiguously defensive—is that it is not provocative; it cannot be used to attack. Moreover, if one side gains an offensive capability, defending oneself checkmates the offensive strategy. If defenses become overwhelming, then they may become ineffective, irrelevant, and thus capable of being negotiated away. That was former President Reagan's hope for SDI.

However, the problem with defensive schemes is their effectiveness: Can they actually destroy an offensive attack? If a potential attacker is unconvinced that defenses work, then deterrence may fail. Moreover, one question that arose in the 1980s' debate over SDI was of "cost-effectiveness at the margins." Historically, defensive weapons have been more expensive to build than offensive weapons; thus, the way to overcome defenses was to buy more of the cheaper offensive weapons until the defender could not longer afford what the competition possessed. Until marginal cost effectiveness is achieved—defensive increments costing no more or preferably less than offensive increments—the offense has the advantage.

CONCLUSION

The end of the Cold War has repercussions for the Third World as well as for the First World. The internal crisis in the former Soviet Union forced it to abandon the competition both in Europe and the Third World (except in isolated situations with particular historical significance or where extrication takes time). The Soviets' impotence was demonstrated in their feeble attempts to mediate the Persian Gulf War before the ground phase began.

As the only remaining superpower, the United States has the opportunity to spread its influence and its values. However, without the Cold War, the rationale for activism in the Third World is no longer relevant. Indeed, there is a countervailing force seeking U.S. withdrawal from global obligations in order to allow the United States to deal with its own problems. The breathtaking success of the operation against Iraq stilled for a time the voices of introversion, but they will not remain silent.

How the United States and the West as a whole will treat the Third World will greatly affect how developing countries conduct their affairs as well as the stability of the post–Cold War system. The removal of Cold War constraints has left a power vacuum into which some force will be drawn. If it is not the United States—or some international force coordinated by the United Nations or another organization—then it may well be a series of regional powers with hegemonic pretensions.

The same will hold true for internal conflicts in Third World countries. The end of the Cold War also concluded ideological sponsorship of insurgencies and counterinsurgencies. Will there be any source of funds for movements in areas other than those that grow poppies or coca leaves? How will regional actors deal with internal struggles within their own regions?

Finally, the regional conflict problem is heightened by the acquisition of deadly NBC and missile weapons by Third World countries, a fairly recent problem. Solutions to the problem have not come from the First World; rather, it continues to build and sell many of the weapons being acquired by Third World countries. Moreover, as the range of ballistic missiles increases, North and South may be drawn together in unprecedented and unanticipated ways.

CHAPTER 7

Cases in Point: *Sendero Luminoso* and Desert Storm

One clear aspect of the transition from the Cold War international system to whatever pattern will replace it is that the nature of problems in the Third World will change. Internal turmoil will continue in many countries, occasionally spawning some form of insurgency against governments, and regional rivals will still threaten. What will be different, however, is the context in which Third World instabilities will occur as well as the kinds of Third World situations in which the international system will seek involvement.

The continuing existence of illegitimate governments in the Third World, offering their citizens less than is tolerable, will result in insurgencies. However, ideologically based conflicts between Communist insurgents and anti-Communist governments are unlikely to emerge. When the issues were framed in these Cold War terms, the responses were straightforward. This is no longer the case in the post–Cold War world.

In the new international system, different circumstances and questions will surround insurgent movements in the Third World. What missions will these insurgencies seek to accomplish? How will their missions affect the rest of the world? One factor is reasonably certain: the lack of appeal of Marxism-Leninism in either its Russian or Chinese variant. As the republics of the former Soviet Union struggle through their internal crises and the Chinese government seeks to suppress its own people so as to avoid another televised event like Tiananmen Square, it is difficult to imagine any future revolutionary movements taking the dream of a Marxist "utopia" as their model. Yet it is easy to imagine future insurgents adopting variations of Maoist politico-military strategy and tactics; however, these movements are not likely to support the political philosophy of the classic Maoist formulation.

Hence, if communism versus anticommunism will no longer form the base of insurgencies, what will? A likely candidate is national self-determination, through which insurgencies may attempt secessions from existing nation-states perceived as discriminating against them. The Eritrean revolt against Ethiopia and the Irish Republican Army (IRA) campaign against Great Britain may provide historical examples. Parts of the former Soviet Union and Yugoslavia (Bosnia-Herzegovina) provide examples. Kurdish misery bridges the past, present, and future.

The changing base of insurgent motivations raises this question: Who will sponsor and pay for future movements? In the past, the profession of communism or anticommunism was enough to open checkbooks and start the arms flowing. The Soviets have renounced such action, and the new republics hardly have the resources to revert even if they changed their minds. Moreover, since past U.S. involvement in insurgencies was usually tied to the Soviets' actions, the American motivation to get involved is also lessened in the post–Cold War climate.

The funding for insurgency, then, is an open question. Some movements may manage to be self-sufficient (for example, the new People's Army in the Philippines). Others may seek private supporters of particular causes (especially national self-determination) for funding (such as Irish-American support for the IRA). In addition, the union of narcotics traffickers and revolutionaries in the Andean nations suggests that criminal alliances and criminal behavior (for example, robbing banks or kidnapping for ransoms) may provide necessary funds.

With less predictability about sponsorship and goals, though, the insurgencies of the future are likely to be different in many ways. For instance, there may be hybrids of traditional low-level conflict (the alliance between insurgents and drug dealers and the small, isolated insurgent movements engaging in terrorism are two examples). The emergence of small, isolated, but persistent movements, with few realistic prospects of seizing power but which governments will be incapable of eradicating, is also possible.

The loss of the Cold War overlay will affect the pattern of Third World regional conflicts as well. These may still on occasion match Communists against anti-Communists (possibly between Thailand and Vietnam, for instance), but the Cold War competitive aspect of such conflicts will no longer play a role. More likely, regional conflicts will be rooted in historical animosities or in the ambitions of individual regional powers.

First World priorities will have to adjust to the new realities of Third World regional conflicts. Many observers argue that one future characteristic of regional conflicts and internal upheavals will be their uniqueness, which will require case-by-case assessments. If no common overriding principles apply to any one conflict, an ad hoc assessment will have to suffice.

Although this position may be overstated and presents an undesirable state of affairs, if the new international order is to regulate Third World violence, the amelioration of its causes and credible deterrence of would-be breachers of peace will be necessary. Treating all conflicts as *sui generis* amounts to saying there are no rules that can be broken; that was the kind of message apparently sent to Saddam Hussein. It is not the signal that one would hope for in the future.

The uncertainty about future patterns of insurgency makes it difficult to choose the best case studies for our analysis in this chapter. Ideally, our focus should be on the most typical kinds of problems that the new system will face in the future. However, given that we cannot predict the norm, the best we can do is examine the two worst possible cases that the system may face in the future.

Among the possible insurgencies, the Maoist war being waged by *Sendero Luminoso* in Peru is the best choice. The situation in Peru is intractable, the government is weak, the insurgents are fanatic, and narcotics trafficking is part of the problem. In terms of regional conflict, Operation Desert Storm is an extreme example. It was a large regional conflict. The presence of petroleum created interests in the Third World that might not otherwise have existed, the coalition's response represents one way of organizing such efforts in the future, the event may be unique in several ways, and its repetition is unlikely. A major question is whether Operation Desert Storm will represent the organization of the new order, as President Bush hopes.

SHINING PATH AND COCA: THE BATTLEGROUND FOR THE WAR ON DRUGS

High on the eastern slope of the Peruvian Andes is a remote valley named for the river that flows through it, the Upper Huallaga (see Map 7.1). Physically about two hundred miles from the Peruvian capital of Lima but politically much further removed from Peruvian life, this valley is the home of two forces of great consequence in the 1990s and probably beyond. One force consists of the peasants who grow over half the coca plants in the world, which are used to produce cocaine (60 percent of which is consumed by Americans). The other force is *Sendero Luminoso,* the Maoist Shining Path guerrilla insurgency described as akin to Pol Pot's Cambodian Khmer Rouge in terms of its program and potential for violence. Together, these two forces have created a "drug insurgency nexus"—the marriage of drug producers, traffickers, and insurgents in what would be one of the world's most marginal areas were it not for the active campaign against drugs

Map 7.1   Peru's Upper Huallaga Valley

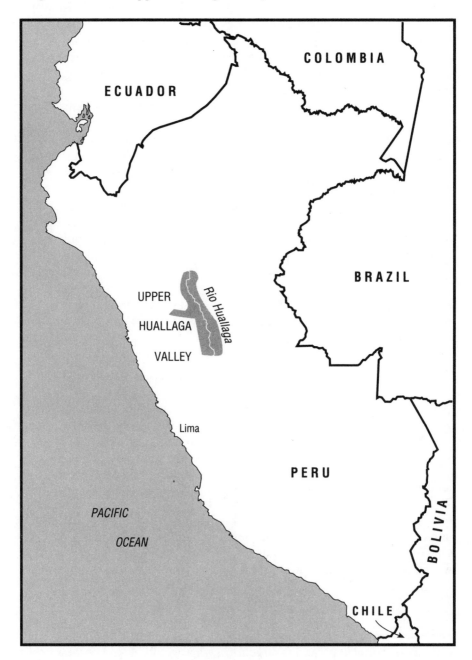

undertaken by the Bush administration. Shining Path has created one of the great challenges of the post–Cold War international system—a self-sustaining insurgency that finances its activities nationwide through protecting and "taxing" the Colombian narcotics traffickers (the *narcotraficantes*). Attempting to manage violence in this situation may represent one of the most difficult insurgency problems of the future.

We begin by looking at the background of *Sendero Luminoso* (SL), specifically its formation and involvement in coca cultivation, and then at the state of the narco-insurgency problem. The difficulties of countering the situation in the future can then be made clear.

Background: The Valley, the Farmers, Drugs, and SL

Throughout most of Peruvian history, the Upper Huallaga Valley was well removed both culturally and physically from Peruvian life centered in Lima. The only road leading into the valley (the *Cerreterra Marginal*) was built in the 1960s to entice unemployed and underemployed peasants to move from overcrowded urban areas and establish farms. When the immigrants, mostly of Indian and *mestizo* (mixed) background, arrived, they found that the best-growing crop in the Upper Huallaga Valley was coca, the plant from which cocaine is produced. Coca cultivation in this area of Peru and in a similar area in Bolivia predates the Spanish occupation. Chewing coca leaves, which produces a mild reaction, was part of the Indian culture and continued under the Spanish. The Indians worked in Spanish mines, so chewing coca made them more resistant to harsh weather and hunger. The coca culture was mostly limited to local production and consumption, though a small amount of coca was used for medicinal purposes by the pharmaceutical industry, thereby justifying its legality.

However, the isolation of the coca culture ended in the 1960s and 1970s, as large numbers of immigrants came to the Upper Huallaga Valley and the use of cocaine grew, especially in the United States. The immigrants increased the supply of coca producers, while the drug epidemic assured a continuing and growing demand for the end product, cocaine.

Coca cultivation thus made the Upper Huallaga Valley the economic mainstay of the region (today, over 90 percent of farm income is derived from coca production, the sole means of livelihood for many of the area's peasant farmers). In the process, the valley became the world's largest source of coca production.

Prior to the emergence of the Upper Huallaga as a primary source of illegal drugs, the government in Lima paid little attention to the problem, preferring instead to deal with higher priority issues within the coastal regions of the country. As a result, there was an economic and a political vacuum in the region. Into that vacuum came two different forces during the 1980s—the *narcotrafficantes* and *Sendero Luminoso*. Although the two groups have very different purposes and aspirations, the dynamics of drug production created for them a marriage of convenience.

The traffickers, of course, had a primarily economic interest in the relationship. They came from Colombia seeking a source of coca leaves and paste (the result of initial processing) at the best possible price, which they could take back home, refine into cocaine, and move into the United States. The Colombian traffickers brought money to pay for the coca, which in a currency-starved country like Peru was certain to attract the attention of a government desperate for foreign exchange. But the traffickers also brought a penchant for lawlessness and wild behavior. Because the government in Lima paid little attention to the region until 1983 (when martial law was declared and, for a time, enforced), the peasants were at the mercy of their benefactors, the traffickers.

The other group to arrive in the Upper Huallaga Valley—*Sendero Luminoso,* or Shining Path—was formed by an obscure philosophy professor named Abimael Guzman in the 1970s. It is a spinoff from other factions of the Peruvian Communist party, *Partido Communista del Perv Sendero Luminoso* (the Shining Path of the Peruvian Communist Party), which burst publicly onto the Peruvian political scene in 1980 with a series of terrorist attacks. Shining Path believes it is the last remaining pure Maoist movement in the world, referring to its program as the "Fourth Sword" (the other three swords belonged to Marx, Lenin, and Mao). The movement also believes that Maoism was effectively compromised in China during the Cultural Revolution of the 1960s, of which Guzman was apparently a personal observer.

The *Sendero Luminoso* (SL) program is anarchistic; it argues that all Peruvian institutions other than the lower peasantry are fundamentally corrupt and hence must be destroyed before a new, Maoist order can be established. Therefore, SL attacks all manifestations of the current order, including economic targets (by blowing up electric power pylons to disrupt electricity supplies, for instance) and human targets (for example, assassinations or bombing U.S., Soviet, and Chinese embassies).

Tactically, *Sendero Luminoso* is Maoist in orientation. Beginning as a small and weak group, its fighting strength in 1991 was estimated only at around five thousand guerrillas. It needed a safe base of operations in order to establish and expand its appeal. Beginning in about 1983, the area surrounding and including the Upper Huallaga Valley became the movement's sanctuary.

The *Sendero Luminoso* appeal in the region is also Maoist, though somewhat more terrorist than Mao probably would have preferred. Arriving in the Upper Huallaga Valley as an armed band, SL saw a situation that could be exploited: The peasant growers needed assistance to ensure fair treatment in their economic dealings with the *narcotraficantes* as well as to restore the law and order that were compromised by the actions of the traffickers. In addition, the traffickers could benefit from having the SL force physically positioned between themselves and the Peruvian authorities.

Thus, Shining Path bands swept into the valley, wresting political control from the traffickers and restoring order. Their methods were, and continue to be, brutal. In order to gain control of the villages, they assassinated government officials, except for those who joined the Shining Path cause. "Traitors and collaborators," to use Mao's phrase, were dealt with as well; a favorite method of execution involved first beheading and then sewing the severed head back onto the corpse backwards.

There are two other players in the Upper Huallaga Valley situation: the national government centered in Lima and the United States. Historically, the government in Lima has had little interest in the region; indeed, its neglect created the void into which SL has moved. The rise of the coca culture has increased the government's interest, though in contradictory ways. On the one hand, the trafficking of drugs is embarassing internationally and makes appeals for desperately needed outside assistance more difficult. On the other hand, the currency entering the country as payment for coca is its single largest source of foreign currency. As for the United States, Americans have no inherent interests in Peru or the Upper Huallaga Valley other than a humanitarian interest in the benefits of long-term stability. Of course, the sole U.S. interest is in destroying the coca crops that feed the American cocaine epidemic.

Narco-Insurgency: The Problem

Coca commerce in the Upper Huallaga and its control by Maoist radical insurgents are not problems according to those engaged in coca production—the peasants, the *narcotraficantes,* and the Shining Path protectors. They see themselves as managers of a commercial enterprise, and as such their only "problems" include setting the price for coca leaves, protecting the growers from some traffickers, and controlling the means by which law and order are maintained. Some of their basic problems are imposed by the Peruvian and American governments.

With the arrival of *Sendero Luminoso,* coca production benefits all three groups in the relationship. Although the alliance of SL, the traffickers, and the peasants is uneasy and occasionally fractious, it will be difficult for any outside force to staunch the flow of coca from the region unless at least one of the groups comes to view the relationship as dysfunctional.

The coca-growing peasants benefit from the relationship in two major ways. First, they can make more money growing and selling coca to the *narcotraficantes* than by cultivating alternative crops. The coca growers' per capita income is much greater than the national average, and their receipts are considerably higher than can be extracted from other crops suitable for growing in the region. (The price of coca fluctuates greatly, but until the government finds substitute crops that can bring a comparable income, there will remain little incentive for the growers to try a different crop.) Second, peasants receive cash for their crops from the traffickers and protection from *Sendero Luminoso*. SL protects the peasants not only from the traffickers but also from those who seek to eradicate the coca crop or interrupt its flow out of the country. Since the guerrillas maintain de facto control of the valley, government intrusion is inconsistent and subject to SL harassment, which seeks to guarantee the peasants' ability to grow the coca crop in relative peace.

The alliance also benefits Shining Path. SL does not approve of the drug trade beyond its poisoning effect in the "Colossus of the North." In particular, it has little sympathy with the *narcotraficantes,* whose members it holds in great personal disdain. As a dogmatically Maoist movement at the strategic and tactical levels, SL understands the necessity of having a sanctuary from which it can organize, recruit, and begin actions more directly against the government. The Upper Huallaga Valley's physical isolation from Lima and the army makes it an ideal place in this regard. Moreover, SL claims that its major appeal and support are concentrated among the Indian peasantry, who inhabit the region. SL terror is often directed at wealthy peasants and some confusion exists over which peasants are loyal to the cause, but generally the peasants represent the primary support base for *Sendero Luminoso.*

In addition, the reported $30 million annual income collected from the traffickers as a landing tax for trafficker aircraft permits SL to be financially independent and helps finance its operations in other parts of Peru. Without this support, SL would have to tax the peasants (which would weaken their support), find outside assistance in a world where aid is drying up, or limit its antigovernment actions.

The benefits of the relationship to the traffickers are obvious and straightforward. They need the peasants to grow the crop on which their illicit business is based. Although Shining Path may marginally cut into the traffickers' profits, SL makes the flow of coca more regular and predictable, despite the government's eradication efforts. In addition, SL provides the traffickers protection from Peruvian and American government efforts to interrupt their enterprise.

Hence, the "drug-insurgency nexus" is a mutually supporting and benefiting arrangement through which each group—the growers, traffickers, and *Sendero Luminoso*—gains from its relations with the others. The coca growers gain trafficker money and SL protection; Shining Path gains a base of operations and funds for its nationwide campaign against the government; and the traffickers gain a steady flow of coca.

Narco-insurgency is a major problem facing the governments of Peru and the United States. It is particularly troublesome for the Peruvian regime of Alberto Fujimori because it is both an insurgency and a source of illicit drug production. As long as SL maintains its base of support in the region, the government will continue to spend its scarce resources trying to control the problem. Moreover, the intransigence of SL ideology suggests that the government's only chance at countering the problem is by destroying the insurgency altogether. As long as SL exists, it is a problem for the government.

However, the government in Lima must not only crush *Sendero Luminoso,* it must also regain control of the Upper Huallaga and, ultimately, of the coca traffic. But it will have to drive SL out of the region before it can make any real attempt to eliminate coca production, and it will have to end coca production before it can significantly reduce the extent of the insurgency. At the same time, governmental stability is predicated on alleviating the crushing economic chaos in the country, which will be difficult to achieve without outside assistance (being withheld partly because of the coca problem). The Fujimori government—or a successor—then, is in a difficult position in that it will have to deal with both the insurgency and the narcotics problem simultaneously.

The United States has only one basic interest in the region: interrupting the flow of cocaine. Peruvians are well aware of this, and so it is a source of contention between the two countries.

Countering the Narco-Insurgency

Although the governments of Peru and the United States both seek to counter the narco-insurgency, each country has different ends in mind and different ideas about how to go about it. The U.S. government considers coca cultivation the main problem and eradication its only solution. The Peruvian government, however, sees the main problem as *Sendero Luminoso*'s control of the region and its solution as the destruction of the insurgency.

For the United States, then, the Upper Huallaga situation is a counternarcotics issue, not a counterinsurgency problem. The official U.S. government document states this position explicitly. Thus, it would be acceptable for the United States to eliminate the coca-growing trade while leaving SL intact. From the Peruvian perspective, it would be acceptable to destroy the SL insurgency while leaving coca cultivation alone. The real problem, however, must be addressed by both counterinsurgency and counternarcotics efforts.

The U.S. policy for dealing with the Upper Huallaga situation is part of the so-called "Andean Strategy." The primary aim of the strategy is to strengthen the resolve of the Andean governments (in Peru, Bolivia, and Colombia) to attack the drug problem by providing certain incentives, such as technical assistance, materials, money to aid drug-suppression activities, and more recently, counterinsurgency training. In Peru, the United States has emphasized crop eradication (through aerial spraying and slash-and-burn operations) by the Peruvian military and drug enforcement agencies assisted by the U.S. military (Special Forces) and the Drug Enforcement Agency (DEA).

However, this approach fails to address the center of gravity. It is argued that the center of gravity against which the war on drugs should be waged is the drug-taking population of the United States. Closer to the point, though, the problem is persuading the peasant population in Peru to cease cultivating coca. Eradication programs aimed simply at destroying the crop are akin to "shooting the symptoms"; the real key will be convincing the peasants to stop growing coca. How to accomplish that goal in a way that provides a durable solution to the peasants' dilemma must be addressed by the Peruvian and American governments.

For the Peruvian government to succeed, then, it will have to gain the support of the peasants, for they represent the center of gravity. SL relies on the peasants for its support base; the political loyalty of the peasants must be the focus of the government's efforts. Moreover, the peasants are potentially the weakest link in the alliance among growers, traffickers, and insurgents because they profit least from the arrangement and are the victims of violence in the region. The battle for their "hearts and minds" is the ultimate battleground.

Although it is clear that the government needs to win the peasants' loyalty, how to accomplish that goal is uncertain. The U.S.-preferred strategy of crop eradication may only further alienate the peasants by depriving them of their livelihood. Moreover, the strategy strengthens the role of the SL insurgents in providing the growers protection from Americans. Some SL writings suggest that the movement favors a physical U.S. invasion of the Upper Huallaga in order to solidify its support base.

Both the American and Peruvian governments recognize that the only realistic solution is crop substitution—offering the peasants an alternate way to earn an equivalent amount of money. Combined with land tenure reforms that would make it easier for peasants to own the land they till, the Fujimori government favors this solution. In principle, the U.S. government agrees. But crop substitution will not be easy to accomplish successfully for at least five reasons. First, there are not many crops that can be grown in the region, and among those that can be grown, none is as profitable as coca. Coffee, bananas, and citrus fruit have been suggested as alternative crops, but they are subject to considerable price fluctuations and would result in a decreased profit for the growers. Moreover, it would be difficult to move any of these crops in sizable quantities, given the region's primitive transportation system. Coca paste, unlike bananas, can be profitably transported out of the valley because only light aircraft are needed.

Second, government policy impedes crop substitution. In Peru, local laws make the process of incorporating a business difficult; until land tenure reform is enacted, setting up a legal farming business will not be a viable alternative for the coca grower. Although the United States would presumably be a major consumer of the substitute crops, it has quotas and other import restrictions on some of the suggested crops.

Third, obtaining the money needed to implement crop substitution is another problem. Since the new market would not by itself provide a profit equivalent to that of the coca market, grower incomes would have to be maintained through subsidies. But Peru's economy is weak, and the United States is not likely to be willing to provide the subsidies. Moreover, subsidies would drive up prices for American consumers, and some of the subsidized crops would compete with U.S.-grown produce (for example, citrus fruit).

Fourth, crop substitution is also hindered by strained relations between the Peruvian government and the coca-growing peasants. Years of government neglect have bred alienation and cynicism among the peasants about anything the government in Lima does. Government corruption has been rampant, and terrorist acts against the peasants by the Peruvian Army have often been more brutal than those of SL. In parts of the region, the army is reportedly more hated and feared than SL.

Fifth, crop substitution would receive serious opposition from SL and the traffickers. Shining Path would fight any government attempt to undercut its support base. Similarly, the traffickers would resist any attempt to eliminate the coca crop from which their livelihood is derived. Both groups would likely react vigorously to prevent the crop substitution program's success, and their drug-derived profits would provide them with considerable resources for doing so.

The government's battle for peasant support thus has a military aspect. The sword of protection from SL counteraction must be wielded in order to allow the shield of cultivating other crops to operate. Whether a successful counterinsurgency can be conducted by Peru alone or with U.S. assistance can be assessed by applying the counterinsurgency criteria discussed in Chapter 5: (1) developing an accurate assessment of the situation (What is the problem?); (2) determining the chances of success (Is there a viable strategy?); (3) considering an alternative to SL to regain the loyalty of the people (Does the government have a chance at winning?); (4) recognizing the inverse relationship between U.S. involvement and success (Does the United States realize the limits of its help?); and (5) establishing a means to gain American support for the operation (Will the American public support the effort?).

What is the problem? Two factors stand out in the effort to change the situation in the Upper Huallaga Valley: the cultivation and trafficking of coca continue in the face of failed suppression efforts, and *Sendero Luminoso* is still a viable insurgent group that has a large enough support base in the population to maintain effective rule. Moreover, these two factors are linked: peasant support of SL began when it restored some order to the region, which, in turn, aided the peasants' prosperity amidst a collapsing Peruvian economy. The eradication program associated with the Peruvian and American governments threatens the growers' prosperity and thereby elevates SL's status.

Reducing peasant support for SL will be critical to any solution. Shining Path engages in terror, which is not universally accepted. If the peasants came to be displeased with SL and the protection it provides, the insurgency would have a hard time sustaining itself.

Yet even if SL lacked overwhelming popularity, the peasants' relations with the government in Lima are troubled. The government is viewed with suspicion because of its historic indifference and brutality; American drug agents directly threaten peasant livelihood; and the unchecked traffickers upset the society. In these circumstances, the standards for SL's rectitude are relaxed; it does not take much to look better than the alternatives.

Is there a viable strategy? Devising a strategy to deal with the situation in Peru is key to solving the drug problem. The alternate strategies—eradication of coca production (the American emphasis) and defeating the insurgency (the Peruvian emphasis)—must be reconciled. The two emphases clash especially if the operation is treated as counternarcotics, the result of which will be to alienate further the coca growers, strengthen the appeal of SL, and make the success of the counterinsurgency more difficult. Furthermore, since the goals clearly commingle, the insurgency must be defeated before or at the same time as the success of eradication.

This commingling means that eradication will be slower than it would be in the absence of the counterinsurgency, since that is likely to be a long-term effort.

The problems of running a combined counterinsurgency-counter-narcotics effort are both substantive and jurisdictional. Substantively, eliminating SL requires an effective government counterinsurgency strategy that historically has not existed in Peru. To address the problem, the United States sent a small number of Special Operations Forces (SOF) to train Peruvian forces in counterinsurgency techniques. The Peruvian government clearly has jurisdiction here, and the Americans are not anxious to usurp that authority. The problem is whether the Peruvians have the means or will to mount the effort.

Conceptually, the problems surrounding the effort are threefold. First, since SL is well established and has the support or fear of the population, it will be difficult to dislodge. Many peasants will view efforts to destroy SL either as Yankee imperialism—a favorite theme of SL propaganda—or as attempts to destroy their prosperity. Second, SL guerrillas wear no identifying military uniforms and have no base camps, which makes them difficult to identify and to assault in masses. Moreover, they are notorious for avoiding direct combat, preferring strict Maoist mobile-guerrilla tactics. Third, there are jurisdictional disputes about priorities both within and between the United States and Peru. For example, the U.S. military prefers to concentrate on SL, whereas the DEA is more interested in eradication. A similar split exists among Peruvians.

Does the government have a chance at winning? Prior to the election of Peruvian President Alberto Fujimori, the government itself was a cause of concern, and this concern was reinforced when Fujimori suspended democratic rule in early 1992. Partially because of efforts by SL and other insurgent or terrorist groups, governance in Peru had broken down. The economy of Peru had slowed considerably, and today drug-related currency constitutes almost one-fifth of the country's GNP. Thus, since drug revenues are such an important element of the Peruvian economy, the government is less inclined to act against drug traffickers.

The problem is exacerbated by the friction between the Peruvian military and police over how to deal with SL and the drug trade. The military believes that an emphasis on eradication—which is the responsibility and emphasis of the police—will simply drive the peasants into the hands of the guerrillas by associating the government with loss of income. The relationship is so strained that there have been reports of military officials tipping off traffickers about police and DEA raid plans. Numerous reports charge that peasants and townspeople will regularly flee their houses and hide in the woods when a military patrol approaches, waiting until the soldiers have left before returning. Moreover, the amount of drug money available to corrupt officials poses a problem in an underpaid Peruvian military establishment.

The Fujimori government may provide some relief. It appears committed to honest reform and to programs aimed at weaning the peasants away from coca and from SL. The government has also shown an interest in U.S. assistance in the effort. Whether it will succeed is uncertain, but its involvement will be crucial to the success of the counterinsurgency. Moreover, the Peruvians understand this will be a long, slow process. At the San Antonio Andean summit meeting, Fujimori rejected President Bush's goal of a fifty percent reduction by the year 2000 as unrealistic.

Does the United States realize the limits of its help? The failure to slow the flow of coca out of Peru and defeat SL is frustrating the U.S. government. Americans want drug traffic stopped *now*. The dictates of counterinsurgency require firm but patient, long-term action. The two ends cannot be totally reconciled.

A compromise solution involves sending a small contingent of about fifty U.S. Special Forces into the Upper Huallaga Valley to train the Peruvians, as President Bush proposed in 1991. However, the impact of such a limited presence is questionable. Its potential for success is weakened by the lack of cooperation among Peruvian government agencies as well as the rivalry between the U.S. military and the DEA (which the introduction of American military forces would likely exacerbate). In addition, the presence of U.S. military forces, no matter how small, will be criticized by SL as a symbol of American imperialism in the region. Moreover, the history of SL terrorism makes it likely that Americans will be attacked almost instantly. Peruvian contract employees of the United States have already been executed by SL guerrillas; sending in U.S. Special Forces virtually assures American casualties. Finally, U.S. military forces in the region will be viewed—with the help of SL propagandists—as an open admission of the Peruvian government's impotence.

Will the American public support the effort? During Operation Desert Storm, the American public supported the use of military force in the Persian Gulf. Whether that enthusiasm would extend to an American military operation in the Peruvian Andes is uncertain. Moreover, there is the possibility that the U.S. military itself would oppose the effort.

The major question about U.S. intervention in the Peruvian insurgency is how long American support of the effort would last. Although SL is small and isolated, it will not be easily defeated because of the unique characteristics that comprise its support base. The American public would probably support an effort aimed at the eradication of cocaine, but whether it would tolerate American casualties is less certain.

The narco-insurgency is, *in extremis*, the kind of insurgency the United States will face in the future. The situation will not be another Vietnam—the massive insertion of American forces into a large-scale insurgency. Peru will be more like El Salvador—a small, nagging, persistent, and protracted affair that makes reasonably small demands on American resources but which defies definitive resolution. The United States has been involved in El Salvador since 1980, and only the withdrawal of outside Communist aid made a solution of the insurgency conducted by the Farabundo Marti Liberation Movement seem attainable in early 1992; the narco-dollars underwriting SL are unlikely to dry up. How much of a commitment are the American people likely to make?

One element likely to weigh in negatively is the U.S. military. In light of its recent successful military exploits in Panama and Iraq, the prestige of the military is at a peak, making its leadership less inclined to get involved in situations that may fail (such as in Peru). The military leadership may thus be more conservative about using force. Moreover, top military leaders are typically suspicious of this kind of operation as well as of the special forces necessary to carry it out. Thus, the fact that the operation in Peru would be handled by special forces may add to the military's reluctance.

OPERATION DESERT SHIELD: REGIONAL CONFLICT IN THE NEW WORLD ORDER?

On August 2, 1990, Iraqi military forces poured across the frontier and quickly occupied the tiny oil-rich state of Kuwait (see Map 7.2). President Bush quickly declared the annexation of what Iraqi President Saddam Hussein called the "nineteenth province of Iraq" an unacceptable act of aggression. Reviving the moribund collective security provisions of the United Nations, Bush called on the nations of the world to join the Americans in reinstating Kuwaiti sovereignty. Secretary of State James Baker was dispatched to enlist volunteers; in the end, a coalition of thirty states stood opposite the Iraqi lines. Standing rhetorically with the coalition was the former Soviet Union.

The Iraqi invasion of Kuwait was the first traumatic act of the post–Cold War period. As such, it was widely portrayed as precedent-setting for what President Bush called the "new world order." Many disagreed (and continue to disagree) with his typification, and Bush subsequently abandoned the term; most agreed that the international reaction would send a loud message to any other Saddams who might be lurking in the shadows.

Map 7.2   The Persian Gulf

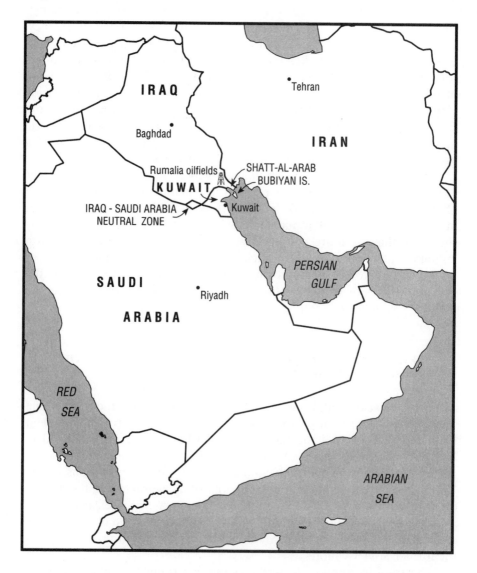

   The symbolism was enhanced by Iraq's status. A country of only about fifteen million that would otherwise not be of great import except for its location in the middle of Persian Gulf oil reserves, Iraq had become the quintessential weapon state. Iraq possessed and had employed chemical weapons against its own Kurdish minority and against Iran, and was thought to be capable of producing biological agents. Thanks to very lax enforcement of restrictions on the export of equipment necessary for nuclear bomb fabrication—including actions by the United States—the Iraqis were perilously close to joining the nuclear weapons club, a status confirmed by U.N. inspectors in late 1991 as U.N.-ordered sanctions attempted to dismantle the Iraqi bomb program. Moreover, the Iraqis possessed Soviet-supplied Scud ballistic missiles in numbers badly underestimated by intelligence reports before the war began.

Saddam Hussein clearly appeared to have hegemonic ambitions. He had long coveted the mantle of leader of the Arab movement, left vacant since the death of Egyptian President Gamal Abdel Nasser. A weakened Iran, his natural counterweight, made the aspiration thinkable. The appearance of Saddam himself made this prospect especially forbidding, and his actions throughout the crisis only reinforced his image. Whether it was patting the head of a hostage British schoolchild early in the crisis or a defiant declaration that the coalition invasion of Kuwait would create the "mother of all battles," Saddam appeared to the outside world a caricature of evil.

All of this makes the Persian Gulf War a fitting example of regional conflict. Some argue it is akin to most evolving Third World conflicts, in the sense of being a case all its own and thus difficult to generalize about, and that may well be. It is, however, almost certainly an instance of the worst case that the new international system will face, and it does, to some degree, represent a precedent for the new international order.

Background to the Invasion

Iraq's sudden, largely unanticipated invasion of Kuwait and the crushing American-led reversal of that invasion can only be understood in the context of the broader, Byzantine-style politics of the Persian Gulf region. As detailed in Chapter 6, the Persian Gulf region has been the most unstable area of the world for over a decade. The year 1979 symbolizes that unrest because it brought the triple traumas of the Iranian Revolution, the American hostage crisis in Teheran, and the Soviet invasion of Afghanistan; Iraq's September 1980 invasion of Iran was the exclamation point.

Although the perspective of the past decade makes it difficult to remember, prior to 1979 Iraq had been considered by most outsiders the most unstable state in the region, and its leader Saddam Hussein was viewed as the region's most unsettling force. Before 1979, the United States had supported and trumpeted the Iran of Reza Shah Pahlavi as the bulwark in the region, the moderating force opposing the pariah state,

Iraq. Only the ascendancy of the radical fundamentalist Shiite regime in Iran, of which Ayatollah Ruhollah Khomeini was the symbol, made Iraq seem more acceptable by comparison. When Saddam attacked Iran in 1980, many Arabs who had deeply opposed him put their hatred and suspicion aside as he did their bidding to staunch the spread of Shiite revivalism.

The Iran-Iraq War was a respite in Iraq's relations with the region and the rest of the outside world, and Saddam played it to the hilt. Because he opposed the Iranians, he became the incarnation of the old saying "the enemy of my enemy is my friend." In the process, he reestablished diplomatic ties with the United States that had been broken by Iraq in 1958 and strengthened his relations in the region. As payment for his sacrifice in opposing the Iranian fanatics, he was rewarded with huge amounts of assistance, notably weaponry. His stock rose to the point that, when an Iraqi missile slammed into the *USS Starke*, killing several Americans on a Kuwaiti reflagging mission, there was hardly a murmur of condemnation. Likewise, when he gassed Kurds within his own territory, the international system treated the act with disingenuousness, as a doubtful occurrence but an internal act under any circumstances.

The end of the Iran-Iraq War left Iraq with an impressive arsenal of weapons and credits and orders for more. The same Saddam Hussein who a decade earlier had been a reckless lunatic was now a world statesman. The problem was that Saddam had not changed; the world's view of him had changed.

Of more immediate import, the war had also left Iraq in a perilous economic condition. Although Iraqi military expenses had been largely underwritten by other Sunni Arab states—including Kuwait and Saudi Arabia—the war had massively disrupted the Iraqi oil industry that formed the lifeblood of the economy. The Iraqis owed their neighbors $39 billion (which Kuwait and Saudi Arabia refused to forgive), and Saddam wanted $30 billion more in credits (which were not forthcoming). With the war ended, Saddam's political well-being—some argue even his political existence—demanded a restoration of prosperity. The vehicle for this had to be regulating the flow to keep oil at as high a price as possible.

Kuwait, among others, opposed the plan. Saddam called for a slowing of production to raise prices per barrel that had been lowered because of a glut on the market. Kuwait and others ignored this advice and continued to produce at the accustomed levels. Moreover, the Iraqis accused Kuwait of tapping petroleum from the Rumalia oil fields partly in the Neutral Zone and partly in Iraq, thereby effectively stealing Iraqi oil needed for the reconstruction effort.

The world turned a blind eye as Saddam and his emissaries made, reiterated, and escalated his demands of the Kuwaitis. No one believed that Saddam would actually do anything like invading Kuwait. Although the diplomatic record remains confused, did the world encourage Saddam's adventure? Clearly his capacity to attack his neighbor was underestimated. Former U.S. Ambassador to Iraq April Glaspie, who was in the eye of the controversy, explained to the Senate Foreign Relations Committee in March 1991 that the reason for ignoring Saddam's warnings was that "we foolishly did not realize he was stupid" and "impervious to logic and diplomacy." Had he made the same threats in 1978, of course, everyone would have believed him.

The fact that the bullying was directed at Kuwait and its imperious Emir made ignoring the escalating rhetoric easier. The Kuwaiti al-Sabah royal family, one of the most traditional in the region, was widely viewed as both anachronistic and arrogant, dispensing its oil riches to other Arab states as if giving alms to the poor. The Emir himself was one of those characters "one loves to hate." If he were made to sweat a bit, so what?

The Iraqi Invasion

Despite the spiral of warnings and the massing of Iraqi forces along the Kuwaiti border in the immediately preceding days, the world was visibly surprised when Iraqi forces moved across the border and steam-rolled the tiny Kuwaiti armed forces. The Emir, Sheik Jaber al-Ahmed al-Sabah, and his entourage rapidly fled to Saudi Arabia, ultimately taking up quarters in a plush Sheraton hotel. As much of the Kuwaiti forces as could, along with many civilians, fled into exile. The invasion was over almost before it began; as the occupation was consolidated, the major question was whether Iraq would stop with Kuwait or whether it would continue south into Saudi Arabia, possibly capturing the rich Saudi oil fields along the Gulf.

Worldwide reaction was swift and almost universally negative. Saddam had broken two rules: (1) he was the first U.N. member to conquer another member, and (2) he broke an unwritten rule of the Arab world by forcibly changing area borders established after World War I. After furtive discussions with the Saudis, on whose borders the Iraqis now stood, President Bush announced that American forces would be sent to Saudi Arabia to draw an unambiguous line in the sand, and the coalition-building effort began in earnest. Among those most loudly denouncing the invasion was the Soviet Union, Iraq's primary armorer for over thirty years.

The diplomatic issue quickly moved to the United Nations. The Americans and Soviets took the lead in introducing a series of resolutions under

Chapter VII of the U.N. Charter, which authorizes collective security actions. The initial motion, under Article 42, called for economic sanctions against Iraq and demanded Iraq's total and unconditional withdrawal from Kuwait. A subsequent resolution was passed under Article 43, authorizing the forming of—but not using—forces to dislodge the Iraqis. Finally, on November 29, 1990, the Security Council voted Resolution 678 without dissent—China abstained—to authorize the use of force under Article 44. It was the first time that such a vote had been taken. The post–Cold War order appeared to have passed its first test.

The method by which the U.N. force was to be formed did not conform to the provisions of Chapter VII. Rather than calling on standing U.N. forces that did not exist, the method was to call for volunteers, the hue-and-cry method of the League of Nations. Leading the call was the United States, which initially committed over 200,000 troops, and doubled that allocation to over 400,000 in November.

The coalition was a remarkable assemblage, both for who was and who was not a part of it. Thirty states ultimately joined the physical effort, ranging from American allies like Great Britain to an assembly of Muslim states that included major contingencies from Saudi Arabia, Egypt, Turkey, and even a Syria motivated by the intense hatred of Syrian President Hafez al-Assad for Saddam Hussein. The Kuwaitis fielded volunteer forces, and contingents came from as far as Morocco and Bangladesh.

There were some notable absences. The Soviets lent verbal support but did not provide any soldiers or materials. Originally, this was justified because the Soviets had several thousand military technicians in Iraq, and later Soviet absence was excused because of the Soviet Union's well-publicized internal difficulties that necessitated keeping its forces and resources close to home.

Other absentees were more troubling. Although no one expected Germany or Japan to join the military effort, their reticence was conspicuous. The Japanese first volunteered to send hospital units that never materialized and then pledged money that was slow in arriving, while Japanese politicians debated whether they should be involved at all. Germany pledged economic support to help defray costs, but participation created a lively political debate rather than the expected show of solidarity with the coalition effort.

The real losers were those Middle Easterners who remained neutral or backed Iraq, notably Jordan and the Palestinian Liberation Organization (PLO). Jordan's King Hussein attempted to act as a mediator as the crisis grew, but his neutrality appeared to tilt toward Iraq, thereby angering Islamic members of the coalition. PLO leader Yasir Arafat openly supported Saddam, which cost both him and his organization dearly after the war. Other expatriate Palestinians were also the targets of derision and attack, at least partly because of reports that Palestinians within Kuwait collaborated with the Iraqi occupiers. Both Jordan and the PLO have been supported financially by both Saudi Arabia and Kuwait, neither of which renewed that support after the hostilities.

Support for Operation Desert Shield was initially very high in the United States, but the mounting operation became politically charged in the fall. Two points of contention predominated the debate. First, there was the intransigence of Saddam Hussein in the face of the economic sanctions and the growing military forces arrayed against him. This sparked an active debate about whether the sanctions would force Iraq's withdrawal from Kuwait. The debate became partisan, with Republicans generally backing President Bush's hard-line rhetoric and Democrats generally counseling caution, suggesting that the sanctions be given adequate opportunity to work.

The debate was further enlivened by the second point of contention: In November 1990, President Bush announced that the number of U.S. troops in the Gulf region would be doubled to over 400,000, including the activation of a significant number of reserve units. Critics claimed that the expansion would only escalate the crisis, virtually precluding letting the sanctions do their job and committing the coalition to early military action, because it precluded rotation of forces back to the United States.

The clouds of war gathered and darkened in December. Congress debated authorizing military action by the president and, after long and rancorous discussion, narrowly passed a resolution in support of a vote of fifty-two to forty-eight in the Senate. Combined with Resolution 678, the die was cast.

Operation Desert Storm

U.N. Resolution 678 ordered Iraq to leave Kuwait no later than January 15, 1991. As the deadline neared, no Iraqi withdrawal appeared to begin, and a flurry of diplomatic activity produced no progress. On the weekend before the deadline, the Soviet Union, in an effort that may have been the first highly visible sign of its decline on the world stage, made a last effort at mediation. It was brushed aside. Speculation turned from whether there would be a coalition attack to what kind of attack and when.

The answer came during the nightly American network news programs on Wednesday night, January 16. At approximately 6:55 p.m. EST (about 4 a.m. the next morning in the Persian Gulf area), the sky over

Baghdad came ablaze with the Iraqi antiaircraft fire and the thuds and explosions of American bombs. The air portion of the war had begun.

Commanded by American General Norman ("Stormin' Norman") Schwarzkopf, the war was to be a classic application of Western technology wedded to the air-land battle concept for fighting in Europe, for which the United States and its NATO allies had been preparing for years. In one sense, the Kuwaiti and Iraqi deserts were the ideal place to apply the concept. Once equipment had been adapted to withstand the corrosive effects of Persian Gulf sand, the desert made the perfect environment for precision bombardment and the *blitzkrieg* style of maneuver on which the strategy was based. Unlike Europe, no foliage, no villages or towns, and no topographical barriers impeded the application of maximum force.

The war began with a massive air campaign designed to disrupt and degrade the Iraqis. Its first purpose was to destroy Iraq's access to the sky by knocking out its early warning systems and as many aircraft as it could. The result was to establish from the outset coalition air superiority to conduct the unopposed application of strategic airpower.

With air superiority achieved, the campaign was directed at Iraq's ability to conduct war against the coalition. Of first priority was the destruction of Iraqi NBC capabilities and potentials, which were rapidly degraded, if not totally destroyed, without any adverse international reaction. The campaign then turned toward isolating the Iraqi Army and the supposedly elite Republican Guard on the battlefield. This was done by attacking the communications network to the occupied territory and systematically taking out roads and bridges necessary for an Iraqi retreat, as well as pummelling Iraqi forces on a 24-hour-a-day basis.

As the six-week air campaign continued, its emphasis changed to direct attacks on the Iraqi armed forces in the desert. The supposed heart and soul of the Iraqi strength was its heavy armor, principally tanks and field artillery. These were the target of relentless attacks, as were Iraqi forces dug into fortifications erected throughout Kuwait. The purpose was to attrite and demoralize Iraqi units to the point that they would lose military cohesion and hence effectiveness.

The campaign succeeded brilliantly. By knocking out Iraqi communications capabilities in the first wave of the attack, coalition technological superiority was accentuated. Heat-seeking sensors revealed dug-in Iraqi tanks, allowing them to be attacked and destroyed by very accurate and deadly American bombers. Unable to anticipate when and where the Americans, British, and others would attack through the air, Iraqi units fell prey to devastating attacks that, in the end, killed thousands of soldiers. The U.S. government has declined to estimate how many Iraqis died; Iraq either does not know or will not say.

The air war also prepared the way for the ground phase of the war, Desert Sword, in two ways. First, the destruction of Iraqi communications and reconnaissance capabilities meant the Iraqis could not detect any movement of land forces unobservable by direct sight, a debilitating disadvantage. As a result, Schwarzkopf was able to have his troops execute his "Hail Mary" maneuver that covertly moved large numbers of American and French troops around the Iraqi flank, leaving the Iraqis prey to having their flank rolled up when the ground fighting began, and allowing the coalition to get behind the Iraqi forces and block their means of escape.

Second, the air war clearly broke whatever cohesion the Iraqi forces in the field had. As the coalition moved forward, there was only isolated resistance to their advance. In most cases, the Iraqi defenders, shocked by the brunt of the air attacks, lacking incentive to fight, and, in many cases, hungry and thirsty, surrendered in huge numbers. Others fled before the advancing coalition troops. Saddam Hussein's "mother of all battles" turned out in the end to be little more than supervised surrender.

In some ways, the war was as remarkable for what did not happen as for what did. A great fear before fighting began was that the Iraqis would use chemical weapons against coalition forces, and elaborate precautions were taken to protect against chemical attacks. No such attack occurred. A second fear, underestimated in prewar intelligence reports, was the use of ballistic missiles. The Iraqis employed Scud missiles—in much larger numbers than intelligence agencies had guessed they possessed—in terrorist attacks against Saudi Arabia and Israel. These attacks failed in their basic mission, which was to provoke an Israeli retaliation that would split the Islamic states away from the coalition. Finally, the great bloodshed that many feared would be exacted by the large, battle-tested, and supposedly battle-hardened Iraqi Army proved a chimera.

In the end, an assessment must ask and attempt to answer whether the lightning success of the coalition was the result of an extraordinarily competent, even brilliant performance by the American-led coalition, an overwhelmingly incompetent performance by a badly overrated Iraqi force, or both. At the same time, one can ask why the pundits inside and outside of government did not more accurately predict what would happen, as only a handful did. The definitive answer will undoubtedly be some time in coming.

The Persian Gulf War was custom-made for both American doctrine and preparations. As stated, the air-land battle concept, wedded to technological superiority in the "offset strategy" devised by then-Secretary of Defense Harold Brown in the 1970s, had been in place for a decade. During the funding-rich first half of the 1980s, the U.S. armed forces had developed substantial stores of the kinds of weapons to execute the strategy, and the forces were well trained for its execution. Transferring the battle to the desert required some adaptation in terms of equipment and creature comforts, but it added the advantage of carrying out a *blitzkrieg* without natural or manufactured obstacles.

Should Saddam Hussein have seen this coming? As the noose tightened around his neck, he seemed oblivious to the signs of impending doom. Known as a man who dealt harshly with rivals and those bearing contrary messages, is it possible that he really believed that he could prevail? Or even more modestly, that he could put up enough of a fight to retain some measure of respect? In any case, his military judgment proved wrong.

The Lessons of Desert Storm

What the Persian Gulf War represents for the new international system, and more specifically for regional conflicts and regional balances, will depend on three interrelated issues. The first is whether the war was in fact the first clash of the new order with precedent-setting effects that will help shape the way the new system performs in the face of challenges by would-be regional hegemons. President Bush clearly hopes so; others believe that the experience was so unique that its generalizability is limited.

The second concern is with whether the action succeeded in its purpose of reconstructing some semblance of a stable balance. Once again, such an assessment may be prejudiced by the highly complex and idiosyncratic circumstances of the region that restrict the ability to extrapolate to other regions and other conflicts. Third, one important part of the coalition action was to destroy Iraqi NBC and ballistic missile capability, and the U.N. terms for a permanent cease-fire demanded full destruction of the stockpiles and the supervised dismantling of production capabilities and monitored sanctions on arms sales to the country.

Each issue must be viewed independently. According to President Bush, reaction to the Iraqi invasion was a necessary part of constructing the new world order. A resolute international reaction would set the rules for aggressive behavior and provide a warning for other regional leaders with similar aggressive ambitions. This view was shared publicly by former Soviet leader Mikhail S. Gorbachev in a January 1991 speech, when he stated, in support of authorizing military action against Iraq, that "our unity in condemning it and our shared concern at the outcome of the crisis are also a sign of radical change in our mode of thinking and in the understanding of the goals and means of world politics."

The potential beneficiary of the new construction, of course, is the

U.N. system, which was the forum in which condemnatory actions were adopted. Thus, if Desert Storm was a precedent-setting event, then we can presumably expect the international system to react to other attempts to rearrange regional balances by force. Some observers disagree with this conclusion. They argue that the situation in the Persian Gulf was a unique case, so there are no other Saddam Husseins to receive the message sent forth by the new order. Others hold that the real message is that the system reacts only when the world's access to petroleum is threatened. They ask what the world's reaction to the invasion would have been if Kuwait was not an oil-rich country, and they conclude that the system would have wrung its hands but taken no other action. Moreover, the importance of the region has been increasing—nearly 90 percent of the increase in oil production since 1985 has been from the Persian Gulf region.

The other major concern about Operation Desert Storm is whether the outcome contributed to the restoration of a balance of power in the region. Given the physical devastation of both Kuwait and Iraq, this question will not be fully answered for some time. However, we do know that the war opened up prospects for change with important regional and international repercussions.

The first set of changes surrounds Iraq itself. Its forces were thoroughly routed and defeated in the war, but the coalition did not elect to destroy them entirely, deciding instead that some remaining Iraqi military capability was necessary to provide a counterweight to Iran and to restore order in Iraq. Unfortunately, when civil unrest broke out in Iraq in March 1991, as the Kurds revolted in the north and Shiite Muslims rebelled in the south, the Iraqi forces were employed ruthlessly to smash the insurrections while the coalition stood by, unwilling to become involved beyond shielding Kurds in the precedent-setting Operation Provide Comfort.

Both rebellions were crushed, and although Saddam Hussein survived and even strengthened his hold on the country, long-term change could take two directions. First, the possibility exists that the country may fracture, with an independent Kurdistan in the north and a free Shiite state in the south, leaving Iraq a diminished participant in the balance of power (a prospect strongly opposed by the Bush Administration). Second, the possibility also exists that Shiite cousins of radical fundamentalists in Iran, who constitute 60 percent of the Iraqi population, might actually seize power from the Baathist Sunni minority. The prospect of another Shiite state sent shivers through Sunni countries such as Saudi Arabia. Moreover, the stationing of American forces in Iraq to protect the Kurds from their own government offered a possible precedent regarding future infringements of sovereignty against states that mistreat minority populations.

The reduced stature and military power imposed on Iraq by the U.N.-sponsored permanent cease-fire agreement returned some of the regional focus to Iran. After its de facto defeat in the Iran-Iraq War, Iran had adopted a lowered profile regionally. A weakened Iraq returns Iran to the center stage of Persian Gulf politics. Although the Iranian government of Hashemi Rafsanjani is not the firebrand that the Khomeini regime was, the danger that the Shiite government will again become actively evangelical poses a threat to the Sunni oil-rich states.

The Third World order question unleashed by the Persian Gulf War was the movement toward greater political participation within the major oil states, notably Kuwait and Saudi Arabia. The proximity of these populations to the American forces undoubtedly helped fan the desire for greater democracy instead of the benevolent patriarchies that preexisted. At the same time, the haughty stand of the Emir of Kuwait in delaying his return to the country after its liberation and his very public insistence on refurbishing his palaces while the needs of the average citizen were held in abeyance only added to the pressures. At the same time, King Fahd of Saudi Arabia made a first step toward broadening his support base by appointing a Consultative Council of Citizens in March 1992.

In the long run, the winds of political change could be the most far-reaching. There are no practicing political democracies within the Islamic world, and it is not clear how sectarian Islam and secular political democracy can be reconciled, if they can be reconciled at all. Regardless, it is unlikely that the near feudal political structures that preceded the war can remain intact.

Another major concern raised by Operation Desert Storm is the proliferation of deadly weapons and indefensible means of delivery. Saddam Hussein had both NBC weapons and ballistic missiles, and there was great speculation that, once backed into a corner, he would employ one or both. In fact, he never resorted to using NBC warheads, and there is little indication that serious preparations were made for their use. The Scud launchings against Israeli and Saudi urban targets were made exclusively with conventional bombs. When push came to shove, the quintessential weapon state pulled its punches.

There are potential precedential outcomes on all three dimensions of dealing with NBC weapons and missiles—deterrence, defense, and destruction. The fact that Saddam Hussein did not use NBC weapons but did employ missiles gives some indication that deterrence worked. Whether the absence of NBC attacks is attributable to the fear of retaliation or the lack of appropriate means of delivery is important. Their introduction would clearly have changed the nature of the war, something that Saddam was apparently unwilling to do. The use of ballistic missiles, in contrast, hardly threatened a qualitative change in the treatment to which Iraq was being subjected, since the bombing of Iraq was massive anyway. The worst that could have happened was the removal of a few targets from the proscribed list; at best, Israel might have been lured into the war, fracturing the coalition. The ability to counteract any escalation of weaponry may thus have been a lesson of the war.

Defenses against missile attacks were also highly effective in minimizing the destruction caused by the Scud attacks. In a sense, both the attacking and defending weapons were rather primitive devices. The Scuds were older and less capable than state-of-the-art designs; the Patriots were actually anti-air rather than antiballistic missile weapons. The experience, however, is almost certain to spur interest in effective ballistic missile defenses against the kinds of light attacks that Third World countries can mount—the problem for which GPALS is designed. Such systems are much more technologically feasible than former President Reagan's SDI because they do not have to deflect the enormous attack force for which SDI was intended.

The Persian Gulf War also suggests the kinds of uses for which defenses will be put in the future. Clearly, there will be a market in countries facing ballistically armed neighbors. At the same time, the Scud attack on Dhahran suggests that U.S. military facilities in regions where missiles are present will be attractive targets. As the range of Third World rockets achieves intercontinental status, a thin defense of the United States may seem necessary as well.

The stiff U.N.-imposed prohibition on Iraq's NBC and missile capability suggests the horror in which the international community holds the possession of these weapons by dangerous leaders. The intention to destroy them was a very public priority of the U.S. government, and it was met with no objections elsewhere in the world. This is not the first time that preemption has occurred against Iraq in this regard. When Israel destroyed a reactor in 1981, there was some loud but short-lived criticism; this time there was none. While the destruction in 1991 came in the middle of a war, when many restrictions are lifted, it may still represent a precedent.

CONCLUSION

It would be imprudent to extrapolate too much on the basis of only two cases. However, both cases—Shining Path in Peru and Saddam Hussein in Kuwait—are extreme, "worst case" scenarios around which policy is often shaped. Hence, if it is possible to deal with SL and the drug problem, any future problems of lesser magnitude can probably be handled as well. Conversely, the inability to solve the drug problem in Peru does not mean that a counterinsurgency is not possible.

The situation surrounding the Persian Gulf War is similar. Iraq was the archetype of the weapon state and Saddam Hussein the caricature of villainy; moreover, the fact that the Iraqis snatched a small state sitting on an oil dome and threatened to disrupt the world's flow of petroleum made the invasion important. In these circumstances, the rallying cry was sent forth and an impressive array of members of the international community heeded the call.

As the post–Cold War world unfolds, however, many challenges will likely be of a lower magnitude than the two events examined in this chapter. How the challenges of the future are dealt with will depend to a large extent on the quality of North-South interactions within the new international system. The debate about the appropriate American role in the new world order is already under way as a result of the Persian Gulf experience. The shape of that debate is our focus in Chapter 8.

CHAPTER 8

Distant Thunder or Siren's Call?

As events since 1989 demonstrate, the geopolitical map for the remainder of the twentieth century will differ markedly from the Cold War system that preceded it. In the current transitional period, it is not possible to make precise predictions about the nature of the rules and relationships that will characterize the new world order. However, several factors that are likely to influence the shape of the future international system can be discerned.

One certain factor is continued conflict in the Third World. The violence and instability that have dominated life in the Third World since the start of decolonization in the late 1940s will remain until their causes—political, economic, social, national—are addressed in meaningful ways. In some cases, life in the Third World is getting worse, not better. And at this point in time, there is no real indication that the prosperous members of the international system will choose the strategy of maximum development to foster long-term stability in the Third World.

If the pattern of Third World conflict has changed, it has changed only in terms of the new post–Cold War context. In the Cold War international system, Third World conflicts were a part of the larger East-West struggle that dominated international politics. As noted in earlier chapters, the Cold War overlay had both good and bad effects on Third World conflicts. Positively, superpower participation in the Third World created interest there and brought resources that may not otherwise have been available. In addition, the fear that the conflicts could escalate to war, thereby engaging the superpowers, created some restraint. Negatively, of course, the Cold War distorted the true basis of Third World conflicts by contorting issues into the Cold War mold.

Cold War influence in the Third World has faded, but what will take its place? By renouncing the Brezhnev Doctrine, the Soviets moved rapidly to liquidate their interests in the Third World, and in the wake of the messy situation in the Persian Gulf, the United States may do the same.

One result of the end of the Cold War, then, could be a power vacuum. The absence of Cold War constraints probably helped embolden Saddam Hussein to attempt the takeover of Kuwait. Whether an invigorated United States or some international body will emerge to serve as regulator of the emerging world order is one of the major challenges facing the system today.

Another factor that will influence the shape of the evolving international system is the changing perception of the importance of Third World conflicts. Some observers argue that the dissolution of Cold War-based interests leaves the First World with few interests in Third World countries other than those related to obtaining petroleum. In this view, the retreat of the First World will continue, leaving the Third World even more "marginalized" in the new international structure than it was in the old one.

While increased marginalization of the Third World is indeed possible in areas such as developmental assistance, the opposite may occur in the area of national security. The international emphasis here is likely to shift to the Third World because of the absence of major conflict in the North. The end of the Cold War has reduced greatly the danger of conventional war in Europe as well as the probability of strategic nuclear war. The only First World-related problems with major security implications center around the outcomes of change in the former Second World, and especially the playing out of nationalist forces suppressed under Communist rule, as in Bosnia-Herzegovina. Third World conflict will rise in stature only because of the lack of alternative conflicts.

In addition, the kinds of conflicts that will mark the Third World will be very different than those of the old East-West competition. In retrospect, the Cold War system had a comfortable intellectual simplicity that the new system will not possess. It was easy then to pinpoint the enemy and to define what made him the enemy. Potential Cold War conflicts were conventional and straightforward; the center of gravity was clear and the means of conducting war were based on European-style warfare as it had evolved since the Napoleonic wars. Certainly the weapons were more deadly, but preparing for the next war was simply a matter of preparing for a larger World War II.

Warfare in the Third World is likely to be more complicated than the wars of the past. Although there may be occasions when conventional means can be applied, as in the Persian Gulf War, these will represent the exception, not the rule. Third World conflicts are not simple or straightforward. Distinguishing enemies from friends is difficult because they are always changing positions. Thus, it is unlikely that many relationships between Third World states will endure in the manner that NATO has.

Moreover, the kinds of conflicts and their resolutions that characterize the Third World situation are not clear-cut; rather, they are people-oriented conflicts in the sense that the center of gravity is often the support of target groups. In these circumstances, political and military imperatives intermix liberally and sloppily, so sorting out influences and solutions is intellectually complex. When political scientist John Mearsheimer suggests that we may come to regret the end of the Cold War, he means we may miss the conceptual tidiness of the period.

Therefore, we can venture only tenuously into the future to see if involvement in Third World conflict will be characterized by distant thunder or the call of the siren. First, we need to examine the factors in the international environment that will influence the system and to review the kinds of problems that remain endemic in the Third World. This will lead us to an assessment of the new world order. Finally, we will speculate on some ways that the United States may choose to involve itself in Third World problems and situations.

FEATURES OF THE NEW INTERNATIONAL ENVIRONMENT

The events of the late 1980s changed the context of developments within the Third World as well as the relations between Third World and First World countries. All of the changes are likely to contribute to continued turmoil and uncertainty within the region and in its relations with the rest of the world.

Two positive changes stand out clearly. First, there is a small but growing movement toward democratization that was stimulated by the events of 1989. This movement is more pronounced in some Third World areas than in others, but it is a rising force that will eventually be felt throughout the developing world, though it will have varying and unpredictable results. Second, the internationalization of economic activity that fueled the prosperity of the First World began to spill over into some Third World countries during the 1980s; as it continues to do so in the future, it may help to alleviate some incipient Third World ills.

In addition, three negative changes are notable. First, the end of the Cold War will almost certainly create a temporary power vacuum in Third World areas; until the void is filled, conflict and friction are likely. Second, unless generally effective means of regulation can be crafted, the weapon states will continue to create regional instability. Third, until a new order is established (*if* one is established), the Third World is likely to experience continued, even expanded disorder and disarray.

The Positive Dimensions: Democratization and Economic Internationalization

The most glaring difference between the developing and developed worlds is the absence of political and economic development in the former. With a few notable exceptions, Third World governance remains authoritarian or chaotic and corrupt, or both, and economic life is marked by poverty, a noncommodious life-style, and maldistribution of available resources.

However, there are signs of improvement. At the political level, fledgling, tentative, and fragile democracies emerged during the 1980s in South America and, to a lesser extent, in Central America, as well as around the Pacific Rim. Even where authoritarianism continues to hold sway—from the People's Republic of China to the Persian Gulf littoral—pro-democratic movements are beginning to emerge and are demanding greater political participation.

In the long run, greater political democracy will likely be a positive stabilizing force. In the short run, however, this may not be the case, as the disintegration of the Soviet Union demonstrates clearly. One major result of the Soviet odyssey was to give voice to demands for national self-determination that was stifled under authoritarian rule in the Soviet Union and in Eastern Europe. This phenomenon will be relevant to the Third World as developing countries begin to democratize. Nationalism remains a primordial demand and, unfortunately, it often does not express itself within the lines drawn on Third World political maps. People will demand freedom, including the right to live in political communities of their ethnic and national choosing. To do so will require the redrawing of many national boundaries, and though the process may be slow and painful, it may also be a prerequisite to long-term stability in the region. The phenomenon will also extend to those countries trying to maintain the old trappings of power: Can there be any doubt that change and self-determination will not, for instance, encompass the People's Republic of China in time?

The relationship between political and economic development is intimate and reciprocal. Political democracy creates the freedom and openness in which economic enterprise flourishes; this, in turn, helps create a willing, self-interested, and self-motivated work force that nurtures economic prosperity. However, democracy unaccompanied by economic well-being will remain fragile and tentative. Economic well-being provides the nurturing ground of contentment and the seedbed for further political growth. The two phenomena together form the long-term foundation for stability.

There are some hopeful signs that political and economic development will increase in the Third World. The great economic expansion of the Pacific Rim countries suggests that the proper government policies can entice private investment in the Third World. In this case, economic progress was accompanied by political expansion, which, in turn, produced a sense of well-being (though not identical to the Western notion of participatory democracy).

The increasing internationalization of economic activity can provide opportunities for the Third World. In the 1980s, true international business firms emerged, the so-called "stateless corporations." These entities have become so international in ownership, management, work force, and production that they are increasingly difficult to tie to any individual state of origin, and they are spreading their activities worldwide (wherever labor or market conditions seem ripe). The exponential expansion of instantaneous telecommunications capabilities means no part of the globe is so remote that its location is a disqualifying factor.

Third World states will not automatically qualify for inclusion in the expanded international economic activity. The process that can lead to their participation will require the demonstration of political and economic stability and responsibility; however, these traits will be difficult to nurture in conditions of privation and despair. Where the conditions for inclusion can be met, the prospects are good. First World governments may provide the resources that Third World countries need to take advantage of these opportunities in order to help create stability and prosperity in the region.

The Negative Dimension: Disengagement, Weapon States, and Disorder

The process of furthering development in Third World states will itself be destabilizing while it is occurring, so instability in the region is likely to rise during the remainder of the twentieth century. Although some areas will face more severe problems (the Persian Gulf) than others (South America), the process of change will be characterized by significant difficulties.

One source of uncertainty relates to the East-West disengagement. The recently concluded conflict in the Persian Gulf exhibits the extremes of the process of change. Saddam Hussein was probably emboldened to invade Kuwait because he assumed that the international system would not respond forcefully to his actions. In what may have been the last gasp of the old Cold War system (or the first flexing of its replacement), the international order rose to enforce order in the Persian Gulf. With Kuwaiti independence restored, however, the system was confused and indecisive as Saddam Hussein crushed the Kurdish and Shiite revolts against him. Is internal suppression based on the principle of sovereignty still all right in the new world order? If not, who will be deputized to enforce the new values? The world has not yet decided.

The pattern of disengagement will continue to be differential between the superpowers. Parts of the Soviet Union (Russia) remain a major political force because of a history of involvement in the Third World, but it is not likely to be a military force except possibly in small ways near its borders. The United States emerges from the end of the Cold War in a condition of relative strength unparalleled since 1945. The American economic colossus may be under challenge, but the United States is the only military and economic superpower and the only country with unquestionable global reach.

How will the United States provide leadership? It is clear that the American public will not support for long the U.S. role of global police officer if it appears that the United States is acting as a mercenary for the rest of the First World. The problem for the United States is how to replace the stability of the Cold War system with a new form of stability that combines military power and political leadership. Fashioning such a role will be the chief challenge of American Third World policy in upcoming years. One viable approach is for the United States to provide military support up to and including the engagement of American naval and air forces, but not ground forces, in support of regional ground efforts to deal with threats to peace (similar to the strictures of the Nixon Doctrine).

As Iraq demonstrated in 1990 and 1991, the possession of significant military arsenals can make otherwise small and geopolitically insignificant states much more of a problem than they would otherwise be. A major systemic effort will be made to arrest or slow the spread of NBC weapons and ballistic missiles to Third World countries, but controlling the weapon states will remain a problem.

The key to managing Third World proliferation of weapons of mass destruction is to rearrange the incentive system that makes these weapons attractive. Clearly, as long as Third World states feel the need to own these weapons, there will be a demand for them that will attract suppliers. Nuclear weapons proliferation has been much slower than many observers predicted a quarter century ago because obtaining nuclear materials has generally been difficult, if not impossible. In addition, many Third World states have concluded that nuclear weapons are dysfunctional to them. It is this disincentive that needs to be tapped to minimize the NBC and ballistic missile problems.

Providing incentives for Third World countries not to obtain chemical and biological warfare agents and missiles is even more important than discouraging nuclear weapons proliferation. Obtaining the basic building blocks for NBC weapons is easier; many chemical weapons are fabricated from commonly available materials. In addition, evading prohibitions and international norms is easier for the NBC manufacturer. For example, if a state begins to stockpile in large quantity certain combinations of chemicals, it is likely that they will be used for chemical weapon production. Monitoring the flow of these materials, however, is difficult. Central monitoring mechanisms simply do not exist. Furthermore, there are so many chemical manufacturers that even a presumably airtight system of monitoring would be implausible.

Moreover, there are multiple sources of NBC and missile capabilities. As noted in Chapter 6, production of these kinds of weapons has penetrated the Third World itself; it now represents a lucrative business to public and private sources. If the demand exists, suppliers will come forward, and attempts to limit the supply are likely to suffer the debilities of cartels.

Therefore, unravelling buyer incentives may be the only effective method of limiting NBC weapons. The problem is similar to nuclear proliferation. Countries obtain nuclear weapons either because their enemies have them or because they feel they can gain advantage over an enemy. The seedbed of demand is insecurity. A truly effective security system is hence the best bet against proliferation.

Unfortunately, however, the new international system is likely to be marked by greater disorder than the old order. Until a replacement system fills the void left by the end of the Cold War, opportunism will flourish.

One unsettling aspect of the new disorder is the wave of forced immigration that is occurring as a result of conflicts. Even before the end of the Cold War, there was considerable movement of people from the Third World to the First World for economic reasons. This problem is now augmented by large numbers of people dislocated by wars; often their own governments are responsible for their flight. During the 1980s, Afghan refugees clogged Pakistan; more recently, Kurdish Iraqis fled persecution by Saddam Hussein's forces. The global refugee count in 1991 stood at over fifteen million.

The problem will likely worsen as national self-determination increases. Nationalism, after all, often has the dark side of excluding those who are not of like nationality. Because populations have become intermixed throughout most of the world, any nationalism efforts will almost certainly involve population exchanges. This problem is greatest in the former Soviet Union, where an estimated sixty to sixty-five million former Soviet citizens live outside their "national" homelands. In 1989, the problems that surfaced between Azeris and Armenians within the Armenian enclave of Nagorno-Karabakh in Soviet Azerbaijan and reappeared in 1992 may be a harbinger as the movement toward secession and self-determination continues.

Another unsettling factor is the potential for continued, even enhanced, Third World regional conflicts conducted without Cold War restraints. The Korean peninsula, Southeast Asia, the Asian subcontinent, and the Persian Gulf and Levant portions of the Middle East are all areas with potential for renewed violence. Given the combination of heavy armament, simmering disagreement, and a lack of outside restraints, the potential for explosive conflict is clearly present.

ONGOING THIRD WORLD PROBLEMS

While there are agents of change in the emerging order, there is also some continuity. In the Third World, the overriding and ongoing problems are the dual crises of legitimacy and authority as well as the need for development and modernization. As long as these conditions persist—and especially if they worsen—the prospects for a more tranquil international system in the future will remain elusive.

The Dual Crises

Both the political problems associated with the crises of legitimacy and authority and the socioeconomic ills impeding economic development can create barriers to the emergence of stable political systems in the Third World. More importantly, however, they tend to interact and to make one another worse; a politically bankrupt Panama, for instance, finds it hard to rebound in conditions of economic destitution, and economic chaos plagues the political odyssey of the former Soviet Union, worsening the process of adjustment to new separatist realities.

The causes of the ongoing political crisis are numerous. In the Afro-Asian world (including the Middle East), the greatest single barrier to the emergence of democratic political governments remains multinationalism. In situations where multiple national groups cannot transfer their primary loyalty to the nation-state, the political struggle will inevitably pit nation against nation, and the spoils will be suppression of the weaker by the stronger. The dreadful carnage in Iraq after Operation Desert Storm is only one example.

Multinationalism is not, of course, the only reason that regimes feel the need to impose themselves by force. In some cases, regimes are imposed so that one group can gain economically or otherwise at the expense of others, as in El Salvador. Authoritarian rule may result from corruption, malfeasance, or the simple incompetence of those who rule. For example, given the enormous amounts of money involved, it is not likely that Manuel Noriega will be the last person to rule for drug profits.

The socioeconomic crisis exacerbates the political problems. Most Third World countries are not in good economic shape to provide a decent and dignified life for all or most of their people—the kind of life that would maximize the prospects of loyalty transfer to the state and government. Population growth outstrips economic growth, infrastructural deficiencies create a situation where adequate food is grown but cannot be distributed, and dizzying inflation robs the poor of their meager buying power. For many in the Third World, standards of living actually declined in the 1980s.

The ability of Third World countries to deal with these problems unilaterally or as a group is limited. If one had to choose the most detrimental effect on developmental progress, it would be the enormous debt run up by the Third World and the crushing weight that servicing that debt has on what little developmental capital is available. As bad economic conditions worsen, capital flight adds to the net outflow of capital from South to North.

Dealing with these crises creates dilemmas of its own. One is the order in which problems are addressed. Although it is generally agreed that what most Third World countries need is to attract outside public and private capital, there is no agreement about how an economically impoverished and politically unstable country can change its image. This problem is made worse when necessary economic and political actions have contradictory short-term effects.

To make a country attractive to outside assistance generally requires putting national economies in order. Specifically, this entails curbs on governmental spending, enforcement of higher savings rates through austere fiscal policies, allocation of resources away from social programs and toward infrastructure development, and passage of legislation creating a favorable climate for outside private investment (such as education laws and tax incentives). Most of these initiatives are likely to be politically unpopular in ways that may be suicidal for governments lacking a broad legitimate base. Most involve so-called "belt-tightening" measures that force reluctant citizens to defer consumption for the promise of future benefit. To those who have already suffered for a long time, that promise may ring hollow and evoke an antigovernment reaction.

Starting with political reform is initially easier for a government not so embedded in the old system of privilege and benefit that it cannot bring itself to change. Providing greater political participation does not require additional economic resources and can, for a time, evoke additional support for regimes. If economic benefits do not follow political reform, however, that freedom rapidly can turn to overt criticism of the government, which is difficult to suppress. This was the tortured experience of Mikhail S. Gorbachev in the former Soviet Union, and it is being relived in places as diverse as Violetta Chamorro's Nicaragua and the Philippines. Whether a future generation of reformers will risk political reform without the prospects of economic success will hinge on these and similar experiences.

The most difficult problem posed by the dual crises is that they are so closely intertwined. There is little disagreement about the end state that is desired: free societies that choose, within their own historical and cultural heritages, political and economic circumstances that they can support. From a Western viewpoint, this can best be achieved within the framework of political democracy and market economics—the choices that free people from Western civilization have made. Freedom of choice is a universal desire, as is the hope for prosperity and comity of life. Both conditions are necessary for a stable world order.

What Can or Should Be Done?

There is considerable disagreement about how to bring about development in the Third World, including how active the North should be in the process and how much change can be induced by outside interference. Arguments range from the advocacy of great activism to virtual passivity.

The aggressive intervention approach to the developmental process starts from one or both of two assumptions. From the Third World's viewpoint, there is the belief that the First World, by virtue of the colonial experience, "owes" massive assistance to the Third World. From this perspective, the imposition of the West created the desire for development along Western lines and then impeded that growth through colonial bondage. Hence, there is an obligation to engage in some "catch up" to correct the situation. The other assumption is that large-scale involvement can bring about the desired effects. If, for instance, the major impediment to Third World development is a simple paucity of economic resources, then the application of assistance should be the palliative.

However, this assumption is not universally accepted. The other approach to Third World development is more cautious and even passive. In this view, the problems of most Third World areas are part of a natural evolution that cannot be materially sped up without worsening the consequences. Europe, after all, went through a long, divisive, and violent evolution that lasted several hundred years and from which it is now emerging. It may be that the the colonial experience simply suppressed a similar natural evolution in the Third World.

The other side of the argument for a more passive approach arises from the availability of resources to engender change. Certainly the post–World War II powers are in no position to finance aggressive action to induce major Third World change, and there is reason to question their resolve to disengage regional conflicts in other than select cases.

There are alternatives between the two extremes. Total passivity is probably made impossible by modern telecommunications, which makes us too vividly aware of human misery to ignore it entirely. Whether the disasters are natural or manufactured, the great tragedies of the Third World will not be played out in some Darwinian fashion. Instead, the public scrutiny that modern worldwide television provides ensures that the world will be made aware of tragic events. Cable News Network (CNN) and other American television networks, for example, certainly played a role in encouraging the United States to provide Kurdish relief in 1991.

Another force moderating against a "natural" evolution of the Third World is the speed with which things occur in the modern world. The electronic, high technology revolution clearly has had much to do with shrinking the globe both physically and temporally. Whether one takes active steps to spread the application of advances in microelectronics or biotechnical engineering, the structure of the international system means that impacts will be felt. The effect will be to accelerate the rate of change occurring in the Third World. That is inevitable; less certain is whether the pace of change will be directed and systematic or random. The answer is probably a bit of both.

A final influence militating against sheer passivism in the Third World is enlightened self-interest. It is generally agreed that international economic activity, sometimes expressed in terms of power, will be much more important in the new international order than before. For the general prosperity that blossomed in the 1980s to maximize its impact and to avoid serious conflict among the economic giants, it must expand, and the obvious place for its expansion is in the Third World.

The prospect is a positive-sum outcome for international activity in which all or most players profit. From a First World perspective, the Third World offers labor pools that can produce the goods designed by the high technologists in the First World but at lower prices. The great untapped markets for most goods are in the Third World, and can benefit from the addition of investment and jobs through increased prosperity and decreased poverty and misery. So that cries of economic imperialism do not blot out the benefits, the participation of Third World countries and enterprises in the economic order can create the partnerships of the future.

THE "NEW WORLD ORDER"?

Whether the First and Third Worlds will find ways to collaborate economically and thus share the general prosperity will in large part determine the nature of the new international order. The shape of that order and how it will affect the Third World are uncertain.

There has evolved a tendency, certainly encouraged by the revolutions of 1989, to presume that the new international system—President Bush's "new world order"—will be very different than the old Cold War system. However, this presumption is premature. These are convulsive times; there are changes occurring now that were not foreseen or that would have seemed ludicrous only two or three years ago. Whether these changes are fundamental or transitory is a judgment only history can make. Still, we can make several observations about changes in the evolving world order that are likely to affect future relations.

First, the Cold War is over and will not return. The process of change in the former Soviet Union will remain volatile for the foreseeable future as the newly independent republics struggle to create stable internal systems and relations among themselves. In this process, the Commonwealth of Independent States is almost certainly a transitional device. What will supersede the Commonwealth is uncertain; that the successor will be diminished in power compared to the old Soviet Union is very likely. The question is how much it will be diminished.

The least likely outcome is a revival of the old Soviet-American ideologically based military confrontation. The weapons of mass destruction—notably nuclear weapons—will remain in smaller numbers, but their role will likely be to deter third parties in possession of NBC weaponry; the theoretical ability of the United States and the former Soviet Union to decimate one another will remain the rationale for keeping the arms, but it will seem increasingly farfetched.

The end of the Cold War also terminates the system of international relations and rules that derived from the competition. The new system, then, will feature a much more fluid and unpredictable system of relationships. In the short run, the result is likely to be increased fluidity in events, marked by the impermanence of relations and the "ad hocracy" of situations. The Operation Desert Storm coalition was an important harbinger in this regard; the coalition brought together a diverse set of nation-states, each with individual interests and agendas that happened to coincide, for the purpose of reversing the actions of Iraq's Saddam Hussein in Kuwait. When that purpose had been achieved, the coalition ceased to operate.

Moreover, in this period of fluidity, a search for a new basis for international and national security will be necessary. The Cold War alliance system is shattered and increasingly irrelevant and dysfunctional. The Warsaw Pact no longer exists as a military entity at all, and the successor states to the Soviet Union are rapidly jettisoning their security relationships elsewhere. The United States and the other members of NATO cling tenaciously to that organization to provide some solace against the uncertainties of the future. In the long haul, however, it is difficult to see how NATO, formed for the specific task of deterring a Communist thrust westward, will endure in the absence of the problem for which it was created without substantial alterations in purpose, structure, and membership.

If the old structure lies in tatters, what will follow? In the initial euphoria surrounding the Desert Storm experience, the United Nations seemed a likely candidate for the organizational foundation for security. There are, however, at least three cautionary notes about the likely future U.N. role. First, the Persian Gulf operation was not typical of likely future situations. In one sense, it was conceptually a very easy action around which to rally an international consensus: The Iraqi action was a clear violation of international law and norms of behavior, and Saddam Hussein was a clearly villainous character who invited punishment. In retrospect, the absence of a strong international coalition would have been more surprising.

Second, the Persian Gulf action taken under U.N. auspices did not fulfill the letter of the Charter. Rather, the United Nations acted in the Persian Gulf in the way prescribed in the League of Nations Covenant: the hue-and-cry. Had Iraq's naked aggression not been so obvious—or had Kuwait not been located on an oil dome—the reaction could have resembled the League's tepid acquiescence to the similar rape of Ethiopia by Italy in 1936 or the U.N. response to the conflict in Bosnia-Herzegovina in 1992. Future actions sponsored by the U.N. require the continuing agreement among the permanent members of the Security Council. A consensus was reached in 1990, but it was the first and only time. Whether such agreement will persist in the future is uncertain. The early 1992 agreement to form permanent U.N. peacekeeping forces offers some hope.

Third, the United Nations has been the major preserve of the Third World, the one place where its voice could be loudly heard. If the primary focus of concern in the new international order is Third World conflict, the transformation of the United Nations into the vehicle for collective security will make it the regulator of its most basic supporters. While the Third World has no veto within the Security Council that authorizes collective security actions, can the world organization act in ways contrary to the perceived interests of the majority of its membership?

Given these circumstances, a far more likely outcome is a system of regional balances, each with slightly different values, that uses the United Nations as the vehicle through which they organize regional peace. The United States, as the sole remaining state with global reach and interests, will clearly have a major leadership role, minimally through its U.N. veto power. At the same time, the veto will also assure that even a Russia in decline can cling to the illusion of a superpower's role in evolving world affairs.

The final influence will be the search for a new order in relations generally. The old system had as its anchor the confrontation between East and West, communism and anticommunism. No such obvious dichotomy exists in the new order; communism will continue to wither until it virtually disappears, and there is unlikely to be a publicly acknowledged ideological differentiation by which "sides" can be drawn.

The central threat to the new order exists in the Third World, specifically in the grievances of the miserable against the wealthy. The most serious cases will be those Third World states that aspire to greater status and that find utility in ever-greater armament to achieve their ambitions. The specter of weapon states armed with agents of mass destruction and advanced means of delivering them to their adversaries will be a central problem facing the new order in its attempt to prove itself a better alternative to that which preceded it.

THE AMERICAN RESPONSE TO THE NEW ORDER

Because the United States has emerged from the Cold War as the only remaining military *and* economic superpower, the role that Americans play will be critical. Although the staccato pace of unforeseen events since 1989 makes prediction a fool's errand, one can at least point to several themes that will influence American action and that American policy will, in turn, seek to influence.

One fairly obvious theme is continued collaboration and cooperation between the U.S. and the Soviet successor states (notably Russia) in the Third World. The Cold War competition was a costly and ultimately feckless pursuit from which neither side benefited in any material way even vaguely resembling the costs. In the future, both countries, but especially the Russians, will be resource-constrained in terms of what they can spend in the Third World; moreover, their prior experience can only counsel restraint.

"Superpower" Cooperation in Third World Matters

Russian-American accord is likely to be manifested in at least two distinct ways. The first is in the approach to settling wars in the Third World. Neither country, especially the former Soviets, wants to become personally involved with ground forces very often or in very large numbers. They must deal with internal strife. The American public will not support the frequent use of the U.S. military as the world's police officer. Especially if a U.S. military role was financed abroad, Americans would see themselves as little more than mercenaries for, say, the Germans or Japanese.

It seems likely, then, that the two countries will find common cause in emphasizing the role of the United Nations. In the short run, this will probably mean promoting hue-and-cry collective security efforts, though the bulk of the forces will come from countries in the affected region. At some later time, peacemaking forces will likely come from nonaligned, small powers (following the U.N. model of peacekeeping forces). Should major power involvement be needed, it will probably come in the forms of supply, transportation and logistics, intelligence reconnaissance, and possibly a limited employment of naval or air forces.

The second area of cooperation is likely to be in controlling arms in the Third World. Collaboration in this area goes back to the 1968 joint cosponsorship with Great Britain of the Nuclear Nonproliferation Treaty (NPT), which was an overt attempt to persuade and commit Third World countries into foregoing the nuclear weapons option. NPT, admittedly, has been less than a total success. Many Third World states that pose the most alarming threat in terms of nuclear capability are not members of the treaty. Nonetheless, the spread of NBC weapons and ballistic missile capabilities to more Third World countries will activate further efforts.

In some ways, conventional arms control may be even more important than controlling nuclear proliferation. The world worried about Saddam Hussein using chemical weapons during the Persian Gulf War, but the size and equipment of the Iraqi armed forces also created a serious concern about coalition casualties. While that fear did not materialize, due to the low morale and quality of the Iraqi forces, numerous other weapon states (for example, Vietnam and North Korea) still pose a threat.

Conventional arms control efforts will face problems of their own. Since both the United States and former Soviet Union produce conventional arms competitively and in great quantities, efforts to limit the flow of arms to Third World countries will be economically damaging. But for conventional arms control to be successful, other weapons merchants, including armorers in the Third World itself, will also have to honor the limits. Moreover, adding to the problem are the excess weapons flooding the market as a result of the end of the Cold War.

Involvement in Third World Conflicts

Unilateral U.S. policy in the Third World is likely to be cautious, selecting carefully the conflicts in which to become involved. Caution will be exercised in order to choose those conflicts that provide opportunities for American activity, because of the U.S. track record in these situations and because of the legacy of the Persian Gulf War.

The kinds of conflict that will persist in the Third World will likely be internal conflicts (insurgencies and counterinsurgencies) and regional disputes between states. Experience has shown that third-party involvement in internal conflict is only rarely decisive and frequently long and frustrating. Moreover, the traditional guise for direct involvement—countering a Communist movement that was sponsored by or affiliated with the Soviets—will no longer apply in the post–Cold War world. In terms of regional conflict, then, the United States may be willing to provide assistance to states against whom aggression has been committed, but the assistance will be much more limited than in the past.

In addition, U.S. policy in the Third World will exercise restraint because of the limited American success in these situations in the past. The United States has only limited expertise for dealing with Third World insurgencies, and the U.S. military leadership has made only a modest effort to develop counterinsurgency techniques. Special operations and low-intensity conflict (SOLIC) has always held a low priority within the armed services, and the Bush administration's procrastination in implementing the Nunn-Cohen legislation dealing with SOLIC has not been criticized by the military leadership. Moreover, the military's recent successes in Iraq and Panama make it less likely to seek involvement in situations that may fail and tarnish its image. The style of warfare prevalent in much of the Third World is simply not practiced by the U.S. military, which may explain why the United States has never shown any marked aptitude for non-European style warfare.

The U.S. experience in the Persian Gulf is likely to influence future involvements in the Third World. Although the effort was highly successful and the number of American casualties was small, the war was a very expensive and emotional undertaking. Other nations' pledges to underwrite the effort covered the monetary costs, but there was also the human cost of committing such a large force in the region. Moreover, the current reductions in military forces will make it physically difficult for the United

States to mount a similar operation in the future. In order to do so, the U.S. Reserves would have to be mobilized, which the American public is not likely to support for long.

In addition, the Persian Gulf War is increasingly viewed as a unique situation that is unlikely to recur. The war was fought over oil-rich land and because of the aggressive actions of a hegemon, both of which are not likely to occur again. In 1991, General Colin Powell, chairman of the Joint Chiefs of Staff, said that he "would be very surprised if another Iraq occurred. Iraq has spent somewhere in the neighborhood of $50 billion to $60 billion over the past ten or twelve years [for arms]. Whether that kind of wealth is around and whether anybody wishes to invest [it] in hardware for war [are] unlikely."

Finally, the aftermath of the war's violence demonstrates the complexity and intractability of Third World conflict. If the war had ended after 100 hours of combat, if Saddam Hussein had been overthrown, and if the United States had been able to bring home its forces quickly, the war would have had implications for future Third World involvement. However, Iraq's bloody suppression of the Kurdish and Shiite rebellions and the U.S. commitment of aid to the refugees demonstrate the need for caution in Third World conflict, which often has unforeseen ramifications.

The Basis of American Policy

How the United States views Third World problems will also be affected by the general orientation of U.S. foreign policy. It has always been based on the promotion of American values and ideals as well as the dictates of geopolitics. During the Cold War, geopolitics provided the prism for viewing the world, and Third World situations were, accordingly, viewed in Communist versus anti-Communist terms. With the collapse of communism, however, this perspective is no longer relevant to the Third World.

In the early euphoria surrounding the revolutions of 1989, Western politics and economics seemed to be the decisive waves of the future. Thus, a U.S. foreign policy based on the promotion of freedom, democracy, and market economics was no longer hopelessly Pollyannaish, as geopoliticians had long maintained. Now that there has been some time for the events of 1989 and 1990 to take effect, a greater balance appears to be emerging. The former Soviets' movement toward Westernization, while not derailed, has been made more unpredictable by the chaotic process of national self-determination within the republics. Similarly, Saddam Hussein remains in power, demonstrating that there are still hegemons in the world whose aggression will require forceful responses.

Can the two perspectives of U.S. foreign policy—promoting American values and geopolitics—be reconciled? As the world's only super-power, the United States cannot ignore geopolitical realities. But its geopolitical perspective is not adequate enough to do anything more than simply managing the disorder; it cannot solve the underlying problems that occasionally lead to violence. If political ideology is decreasingly the demarcating line between peoples, it is being replaced by the economic yardstick. As long as the world is divided between the rich and the poor and the gap continues to widen, the potential for Third World instability and violence will remain.

It may be possible to combine the concepts underlying U.S. foreign policy with the idea that bringing general prosperity to the Third World is good geopolitics. The desire for freedom is universal: political freedom from repression as well as economic freedom from poverty and misery. Free people may differ in the ways they choose to use their freedom, but they rarely choose to settle their differences through violent means.

The emerging international economic order provides some hope for an improved distribution of wealth in the Third World. Technology is shrinking the globe, making it possible for the poor to contrast their situation with that of the rich; the result is sometimes relative deprivation.

Dealing with a Complex World

The emerging world order will have to be more intellectually and physically challenging than the Cold War system. The simplicity of the Cold War competition made it easy, in most regards, to organize reality.

The new system, specifically those parts that emphasize the Third World, will be more difficult to organize for three reasons. First, the Third World is remote and generally not well understood by Americans. Because the United States has largely dominated international politics over the past half-century, Americans have enjoyed the luxury of insularity. Occasionally, our lack of understanding of the Third World has caused us to bumble into situations where we had no business and where we could not devise successful solutions. Vietnam is the classic example; the Operation Provide Comfort aftermath of Desert Storm is another case in point.

Second, almost all Third World situations involve greater subtleties and innuendos than did the Cold War. The latter was a confrontation between Western ideas and Western nations. The Third World, in contrast, is separated by a chasm of history, experience, values, and cultural differences that is misunderstood by most Americans and thereby hampers an understanding of Islamic cultures as they are practiced in the

Middle East. In addition, counterterrorism efforts by the United States are ineffective largely because of the American cultural heritage, which makes Americans unwilling to engage in some types of terrorist acts that Third World terrorists apply.

Third, relations among Third World countries typically lack the permanence that characterizes the relations among Western nations. In the Third World, alliances are often transitory, especially in the Middle East.

In the evolving post–Cold War world, U.S. foreign policy in the Third World will face great challenges. Historically, Third World problems have not been of great importance to the United States—they represented only distant thunder within the larger international context. As conflict shifts from an East-West to a North-South axis, it will be interesting to see whether Third World problems become instead a siren's call that cannot be ignored.

BIBLIOGRAPHY

Albright, Madeleine K., and Allan E. Goodman. 1990. U.S. foreign policy after the Gulf crisis. *Survival* 32, no. 6. (November–December): 533–42.

Anderson, Harry. 1990. The next nasty war? *Newsweek,* May 21, 36–37.

Arab hearts, Arab minds. 1991. *The Economist* 318, no. 7694 (Feb. 16): 11–12.

Art, Robert J. 1991. A defensible defense: America's grand strategy after the Cold War. *International Security* 15, no. 4 (Spring): 5–33.

Attali, Jacques. 1990. Lines on the horizon. *New Perspectives Quarterly* 7, no. 2 (Spring): 4–12.

Bacevich, A. J. et al. 1990. New rules: Modern war and military professionalism. *Parameters* 20, no. 4 (December): 12–23.

———. 1989. *American military policy in small wars: The case of El Salvador.* Cambridge, Mass.: Institute for Foreign Policy Analysis.

Bailey, Kathleen C. 1991. Ballistic missile proliferation: Can it be reversed? *Orbis* 35, no. 1 (Winter): 5–14.

Baritz, Loren. 1985. *Backfire: A history of how American culture led us into Vietnam and made us fight the way we did.* New York: William Morrow.

Barnet, Richard J. 1990. Reflections (the age of globalization). *New Yorker,* June 16, 46–60.

Bell, Daniel. 1987. The world and the United States in 2013. *Daedalus* 116, no. 3 (Summer): 1–31.

Belonogov, Aleksandr M. 1990. Soviet peacekeeping proposals. *Survival* 32, no. 3 (May–June): 206–11.

Bergsten, Fred. 1990. The world economy after the Cold War. *Foreign Affairs* 69, no. 3 (Summer): 96–112.

Bissell, Richard E. 1990. Who killed the Third World? *Washington Quarterly* 13, no. 4 (Autumn): 23–32.

Blacker, Coit D. 1990–91. The collapse of Soviet power in Europe. *Foreign Affairs* 70 (1): 88–102.

Blaufarb, Douglas S., and George K. Tankam. 1989. *Who will win? A key to the puzzle of revolutionary war.* New York: Crane Russak.

Blodgett, John Q. 1991. The future of U.N. peacekeeping. *Washington Quarterly* 14, no. 1 (Winter): 207–20.

Borden, William Liscum. 1946. *There will be no time: The revolution in strategy.* New York: Macmillan.

Brenner, William M. 1991. New terms of engagement. *SAIS Review* 11, no. 1 (Winter–Spring): 11–26.

———. 1990. Finding America's place. *Foreign Policy* 79 (Summer): 25–43.

Brinton, Crane. 1965. *The anatomy of revolution.* Rev. ed. New York: Vantage.

Broad, Robin, John Cavanaugh, and Walden Bello. 1990–91. Development: The market is not enough. *Foreign Policy* 81 (Winter): 144–62.

Brodie, Bernard. 1946. *The absolute weapon: Atomic power and world order.* New York: Harcourt.

Brooke, James. 1990. U.S. will arm Peru to fight leftists in new drug push. *New York Times,* April 22, 1.

Cable, Larry E. 1986. *Conflict of myths: The development of American counter-insurgency doctrine and the Vietnam War.* New York: New York University Press.

Campbell, Curt C., and Thomas G. Weiss. 1991. The Third World in the wake of Eastern Europe. *Washington Quarterly* 14, no. 2 (Spring): 91–108.

Carus, W. Seth. 1990. *Ballistic missiles in the Third World: Threats and response.* (CSIS Washington Papers no. 146.) New York: Praeger.

Chailand, Gerard, 1982. *Guerrilla strategies: An historical anthology from the long march to Afghanistan.* Berkeley, Calif.: University of California Press.

Chipman, John. 1991. Third World politics and security in the 1990s: 'The world forgetting, by the world forgot?' *Washington Quarterly* 14, no. 1 (Winter): 151–68.

Claude, Inis L. Jr. 1971. *Swords into plowshares: The problems and progress of international organization.* 4th ed. New York: Random House.

Clutterbuck, Richard. 1990. *Terrorism and guerrilla warfare: Forecasts and remedies.* London: Routledge.

Cranston, Maurice. 1990. Is the Gulf America's business? *National Review* 42, no. 23 (December 3): 40–44.

Crawford, Malcolm. 1990. After Saddam Hussein—What? *The World Today* 46 (November): 203–205.

DeBray, Regis. 1967. *Revolution in the revolution? Armed struggle and political struggle in Latin America.* New York: Monthly Review Press.

Dietz, Henry. 1990. Peru's *Sendero Luminoso* as a revolutionary movement. *Journal of Political and Military Sociology* 18, no. 1 (Summer): 123–49.

Douglass, Joseph D. Jr. 1990. The war on drugs: Prospects for success. *Journal of Social, Political, and Economic Studies* 15, no. 1 (Spring): 45–57.

Egan, Jack. 1990. Business without borders. *U.S. News & World Report* 109, no. 3 (July 16): 29–31.

Epstein, William. 1990. Conference a qualified success. *Bulletin of the Atomic Scientists* 46, no. 10 (December): 45–47.

Ferrell, William Regis. 1982. *The U.S. government response to terrorism: In search of an effective strategy.* Boulder, Colo.: Westview Press.

Friedberg, Aaron L. 1991. Is the United States capable of acting strategically? *Washington Quarterly* 14, no. 1 (Winter): 5–26.

Fukuyama, Francis. 1989. The end of history? *The National Interest* 16 (Summer): 3–18.

Gaddis, John Lewis. 1991. Toward the post–Cold War world. *Foreign Affairs* 70, no. 2 (Spring): 102–22.

Garthoff, Raymond L. 1990. Changing realities, changing perceptions. *Brookings Review* 8, no. 4 (Fall): 13–20.

Giap, Vo Nguyen. 1962. *People's war, People's Army.* New York: Praeger.

Gigot, Paul A. 1990–91. A great American screw-up. *The National Interest* 22 (Winter): 3–10.

Goldberg, Arthur C. 1991. Challenges to the post-Cold War balance of power. *Washington Quarterly* 14, no. 1 (Winter): 51–60.

Gorbachev, Mikhail S. 1991. *Perestroika* is marked by pitfalls: Political and economic conditions in the U.S.S.R. *Vital Speeches of the Day* 57, no. 7 (January 15): 194–200.

———. 1990. U.S.S.R. and U.S. relations: The European communities. *Vital Speeches of the Day* 57, no. 5 (December 15): 130–32.

———. 1987. *Perestroika: New thinking for our country and the world.* New York: Harper & Row.

Gorritti, Gustavo. 1990. The war of the philosopher-king. *New Republic* 3, 935 (June 18): 15–23.

Greentree, Todd R. 1990. *The United States and the politics of conflict in the developing world.* Washington, D.C.: U.S. State Department Center for the Study of Foreign Affairs, August. (Also released by the Center for Low-Intensity Conflict, Langley AFB, Va.)

Guevara, Ernesto "Che." 1961. *Guerrilla warfare.* New York: Monthly Review Press.

Gurr, Ted Robert. 1970. *Why men rebel.* Princeton, N.J.: Princeton University Press.

Haass, Richard N. 1991. Regional order in the 1990s: The challenge of the Middle East. *Washington Quarterly* 14, no. 1 (Winter): 181–88.

———. 1990. *Conflicts unending: The United States and regional disputes.* New Haven, Conn.: Yale University Press.

Hamilton, Kimberly A., and Kate Holder. 1991. International migration and foreign policy: A survey of the literature. *Washington Quarterly* 14, no. 2 (Spring): 195–211.

Harkavy, Robert E., and Stephanie Neuman, eds. 1985. *The lessons of recent wars in the Third World: Approaches and case studies.* Vol. 1. Lexington, Mass.: Lexington Books.

Hatfield, Mark O., and William F. McHugh. 1991. After containment: A new foreign policy for the 1990s. *SAIS Review* 12, no. 1 (Winter–Spring): 1–10.

Hazleton, William A., and Sandra Woy-Hazleton. 1990. *Sendero Luminoso* and the future of Peruvian democracy. *Third World Quarterly* 12, no. 2 (April): 21–35.

Head, Ivan L. 1989. South-North dangers. *Foreign Affairs* 68, no. 3 (Summer): 71–86.

Heller, Mark A. 1991. Ballistic missile proliferation: Coping with it in the Middle East. *Orbis* 35, no. 1 (Winter): 15–28.

Hellman, John. 1986. *American myth and the legacy of Vietnam.* New York: Columbia University Press.

Hilsman, Roger. 1990. *American guerrilla: My war behind Japanese lines.* Washington, D.C.: Brassey's.

Hoffman, Stanley. 1991. Avoiding new world disorder. *New York Times,* February 25, A19.

———. 1990–91. The case for leadership. *Foreign Policy* 81 (Winter): 20–38.

———. 1989. What should we do in the world? *Atlantic Monthly* 264, no. 4 (October): 84–96.

Holstein, William J. 1990. The stateless corporation. *Business Weekly* 3159 (May 14): 98–105.

Hormats, Robert D. 1989. The economic consequences of the peace—1989. *Survival* 31, no. 6 (November–December): 484–99.

———. 1988. The international economic challenge. *Foreign Policy* 71 (Summer): 99–116.

Hunter, Shireen. 1989. Terrorism: A balance sheet. *Washington Quarterly* 12, no. 3 (Summer): 17–29.

Husbands, Jo L. 1990. A buyer's market for arms. *Bulletin of the Atomic Scientists* 46, no. 4 (May): 14–19.

Hyland, William C. 1990. America's new course. *Foreign Affairs* 69, no. 2 (Spring): 1–12.

———. 1988–89. Setting global priorities. *Foreign Policy* 73 (Winter): 22–40.

International Peace Academy. 1984. *Peacekeeper's handbook.* New York: Pergamon Press.

Jervis, Robert. 1984. *The Illogic of American nuclear strategy.* Ithaca, N.Y.: Cornell University Press.

Kaiser, Karl. 1990. From nuclear deterrence to graduated conflict control. *Survival* 32, no. 6 (November–December): 483–96.

Karsh, Efraim, and Inari Rautsi. 1991. Why Saddam Hussein invaded Kuwait. *Survival* 33, no. 1 (January–February): 18–30.

Katz, Mark N. 1991. Beyond the Reagan doctrine: Reassessing U.S. policy toward regional conflicts. *Washington Quarterly* 14, no. 1 (Winter): 169–79.

Kemp, Geoffrey. 1990. Regional security, arms control, and the end of the Cold War. *Washington Quarterly* 13, no. 4 (Autumn): 33–51.

Kissinger, Henry. 1991. False dreams of a new world order. *Washington Post,* February 26, A21.

Klare, Michael T., and Peter Kornbluh, eds. 1990. Wars in the 1990s: Growing firepower in the Third World. *Bulletin of the Atomic Scientists* 46, no. 4 (May): 9–13.

———. 1988. *Low intensity warfare: Counterinsurgency, proinsurgency, and antiterrorism in the eighties.* New York: Pantheon Books.

Kober, Stanley. 1990. Idealpolitik. *Foreign Policy* 79 (Summer): 3–24.

Krauthammer, Charles. 1990–91. The unipolar movement. *Foreign Affairs* 70 (1): 23–33.

Kristol, Irving. 1991. After the war, what? *Wall Street Journal,* February 22, A10.

Laqueur, Walter. 1977. *Terrorism.* Boston, Mass.: Little, Brown.

Lewis, Bernard. 1990. The roots of Muslim rage. *Atlantic Monthly* 266, no. 3 (September): 47–54.

Lewis, Flora. 1990. The return of history. *SAIS Review* 10, no. 2 (Summer–Fall): 1–11.

Livingstone, Neil C., and Terrell E. Arnold, eds. 1986. *Fighting back: Winning the war against terrorism.* Lexington, Mass.: Lexington Books.

Lodge, Juliet, ed. 1988. *The threat of terrorism.* Boulder, Colo.: Westview Press.

Luttwak, Edward N. 1990a. Kuwaiting game. *New Republic* 3946 (September 3): 25–27.

———. 1990b. The shape of things to come. *Commentary* 81, no. 6 (June): 17–25.

MacDonald, Scott B. 1989. *Mountain high, white avalanche: Cocaine and power in the Andean states and Panama.* (CSIS Washington Papers no. 137.) New York: Praeger.

MacFarquhar, Emily. 1990. The Kashmir question. *U.S. News & World Report* 108, no. 23 (June 11): 42–44.

MacKinlay, John. 1989. *The peacekeepers: An assessment of peacekeeping operations at the Arab-Israeli interface.* Boston, Mass.: Unwin Hyman.

MacQuarrie, Kim, and Keefe Borden. 1990. The comrades. *Third World* 24 (February): 12–13.

Mahnken, Thomas G. 1991. The arrow and the shield: U.S. responses to ballistic missile proliferation. *Washington Quarterly* 14, no. 1 (Winter): 189–203.

Mandelbaum, Michael. 1990–91. The Bush foreign policy. *Foreign Affairs* 70 (1): 5–22.

Manwaring, Max G., ed. 1991. *Uncomfortable wars: Toward a new paradigm of low intensity conflict.* Boulder, Colo.: Westview Press.

Martic, Milor. 1975. *Insurrection: Five schools of revolutionary thought.* Cambridge, Mass.: Dunellen.

Maynes, Charles William. 1990. America without the Cold War. *Foreign Policy* 78 (Spring): 3–25.

McAfee, Kathy. 1990. Why the Third World goes hungry: Selling cheap and buying dear. *Commonweal* 117, no. 12 (June 15): 380–85.

McGeorge, Harvey J. 1990. Bugs, gas, and missiles. *Defense and Foreign Affairs* 17 (May–June): 14–19.

McMahon, Bernard F. 1990. Low-intensity conflict: The Pentagon's foible. *Orbis* 34, no. 1 (Winter): 3–16.

McNaugher, Thomas L. 1990. Ballistic missiles and chemical weapons: The legacy of the Iran-Iraq War. *International Security* 15, no. 2 (Fall): 5–34.

Mead, Walter Russell. 1990. The world economic order: Perils after Bretton Woods. *Dissent* (Summer): 383–93.

Mearsheimer, John J. 1990. Why we will soon miss the Cold War. *Atlantic Monthly* 266, no. 2 (August): 35–50.

Metz, Steven. 1989. An American strategy for low-intensity conflict. *Strategic Review* 17, no. 4 (Fall): 8–16.

Moran, Theodore H. 1990–91. International economics and national security. *Foreign Affairs* 69, no. 5 (Winter): 74–90.

Myers, Norman. 1989. Environment and security. *Foreign Policy* 74 (Spring): 23–41.

Neuman, Stephanie G., and Robert E. Harkavy, eds. 1987. *The lessons of recent wars in the Third World: Comparative dimensions*. Vol. 2. Lexington, Mass.: Lexington Books.

Nolan, Janne E. 1989. Ballistic missiles in the Third World—The limits of nonproliferation. *Arms Control Today* 19, no. 9 (November): 9–14.

———, and Albert D. Wheelon. 1990. Third World ballistic missiles. *Scientific American* 263, no. 2 (August): 34–40.

Norton, Augustus R., and Thomas G. Weiss. 1990. Superpowers and peacekeepers. *Survival* 32, no. 3 (May–June): 212–20.

Novak, Michael. 1990. The collapse of the alternatives. *Freedom at Issue* 114 (May–June): 18–20.

Nye, Joseph S. Jr. 1990. *Bound to lead: The changing nature of American power*. New York: Basic Books.

O'Neill, Bard E. 1990. *Insurgency and terrorism: Inside modern revolutionary warfare*. Washington, D.C.: Brassey's.

Palevitz, Marc S. 1990. Beyond deterrence: What the U.S. should do about ballistic missiles in the Third World. *Strategic Review* 17, no. 3 (Summer): 49–58.

Paschall, Rod. 1990. *LIC 2010: Special operations and unconventional warfare in the next century*. Washington, D.C.: Brassey's.

Pastor, Robert A. 1991. Preempting revolutions: The boundaries of U.S. influence. *International Security* 15, no. 4 (Spring): 54–86.

Peters, Ralph. 1989. *Red Army: A novel of tomorrow's war*. New York: Pocket Books.

Pfaff, William. 1990–91. Redefining world power. *Foreign Affairs* 70 (1): 34–48.

Pipes, Richard. 1990–91. The Soviet Union adrift. *Foreign Affairs* 70 (1): 70–87.

Pires, Claudia. 1990. Critical condition. *Third World* 24 (February): 7–12.

Potter, William C., and Adam Stulberg. 1990. The Soviet Union and the spread of ballistic missiles. *Survival* 32, no. 6 (November–December): 543–57.

Powell, Colin L. 1991. Statement of the Chair of the Joint Chiefs of Staff before the Subcommittee on Defense, Committee on Appropriations. U.S. House of Representatives, February 19.

Psychological operations in guerrilla warfare. 1985. New York: Vintage.

Ra'anan, Uri, Robert L. Pfaltzgraff, Richard H. Shultz, Ernst Halperin, and Igor Lukes, eds. 1986. *Hydra of courage: International linkages of terrorism; the witnesses speak*. Lexington, Mass.: Lexington Books.

Ramasamy, T. K. 1990. The Third World as moral arbiter: Testing the unity of the South. *World Press Review* 37 (December): 20–21.

Ravenal, Earl C. 1990–91. The case for adjustment. *Foreign Policy* 82 (Winter): 3–19.

Ravenhill, John. 1990. The North-South balance of power. *International Affairs* [London] 66, no. 4 (October): 731–48.

Rice, Edward E. 1988. *Wars of the third kind: Conflict in the underdeveloped countries*. Berkeley, Calif.: University of California Press.

Rizopoulos, Nicholas X., ed. 1990. *Sea changes: American foreign policy in a world transformed*. New York: Council on Foreign Relations Press.

The road to war. 1990–91. *Foreign Affairs* 70 (1): 1–4.

Rosen, Stephen. 1982. Vietnam and the American theory of limited war. *International Security* 7, no. 1 (Fall): 83–113.

Rosenau, William. 1990. Poor Peru. *American Spectator* 23 (December): 11–18.

Rostow, W. W. 1990. The coming age of regionalism. *Encounter* 74 (June): 3–7.

Rothstein, Robert L. 1991. Democracy, conflict, and development in the Third World. *Washington Quarterly* 14, no. 2 (Spring): 43–62.

Rubin, Uzi. 1991. Ballistic missile proliferation: How much does it matter? *Orbis* 35, no. 1 (Winter): 29–39.

Russett, Bruce, and Alan D. Romberg. 1991. The U.N. in a new world order. *Foreign Affairs* 70, no. 2 (Spring): 69–83.

Sarkesian, Sam C. 1984. *America's forgotten wars: The counterrevolutionary past and lessons for the future.* Westport, Conn.: Greenwood Press.

Sayigh, Yezid. 1990. *Confronting the 1990s: Security in the developing countries.* (Adelphi Papers no. 251.) London: International Institute for Strategic Studies.

Sendero Luminoso: Peruvian terrorist group. 1989. *Department of State Bulletin* 89, no. 2153 (December): 49–52.

Shafer, D. Michael. 1988a. *Deadly paradigms: The failure of U.S. counterinsurgency policy.* Princeton, N.J.: Princeton University Press.

———. 1988b. The unlearned lessons of counterinsurgency. *Political Science Quarterly* 103, no. 1 (Spring): 57–80.

Shultz, Richard H. Jr., 1989. Low intensity conflict: Future challenges and lessons from the Reagan years. *Survival* 31, no. 4 (July–August): 359–75.

Simpson, Charles M. III. 1983. *Inside the Green Berets: The first thirty years.* Novato, Calif.: Presidio Press.

Simpson, John, and Darryl Howlett. 1990. The 1990 NPT review conference. *Survival* 32, no. 4 (July–August): 349–60.

Smith, W. Y. 1991. Principles of U.S. grand strategy: Past and future. *Washington Quarterly* 14, no. 2 (Spring): 67–78.

Snider, Lewis W. 1991. Guns, debt and politics: New variations on an old theme. *Armed Forces and Society* 17, no. 2 (Winter): 167–90.

Snow, Donald M. 1991a. *National security: Enduring problems in a changing defense environment.* 2d ed. New York: St. Martin's Press.

———. 1991b. *The shape of the future: The post–Cold War world.* Armonk, N.Y.: M.E. Sharpe.

———. 1991c. *Third World conflict and American response in the post–Cold War world.* Carlisle, Pa.: U.S. Army War College Strategic Studies Institute.

———. 1987. *The necessary peace: Nuclear weapons and superpower relations.* Lexington, Mass.: Lexington Books.

Sorensen, Theodore C. 1990. Rethinking national security. *Foreign Affairs* 69, no. 3 (Summer): 1–18.

Spector, Leonard S., and Jacqueline R. Smith. 1990. Deadlock damages nonproliferation. *Bulletin of the Atomic Scientists* 46, no. 10 (November–December): 39–44.

Stanfield, Rochelle L. 1991. The other war zone. *National Journal* 23, no. 5 (February 2): 258–61.

Stephan, Robert B. 1989. *Counterinsurgency in the Philippines: Problems and prospects.* Langley AFB, Va.: Army-Air Force Center for Low-Intensity Conflict.

Sterner, Michael. 1990–91. Navigating the Gulf. *Foreign Policy* 81 (Winter): 39–52.

Stokes, Bruce. 1991. Help on hold. *National Journal* 23, no. 5 (February 2): 262–66.

Summers, Harry G. Jr. 1982. *On strategy: A critical analysis of the Vietnam War.* Novato, Calif.: Presidio Press.

Sun Tzu. 1963. *The art of war.* Translated by Samuel B. Griffith. Oxford, Engl.: Oxford University Press.

Szafranski, Richard. 1990. Thinking about small wars. *Parameters* 20, no. 3 (September): 39–49.

Tarazona-Sevillano, Gabriela, with John B. Reuter. 1990. *Sendero Luminoso and the threat of narcoterrorism.* (CSIS Washington Papers no. 144.) New York: Praeger.

Taylor, Maxwell. 1988. *The terrorist.* London: Brassey's Defence Publishers.

Thompson, Loren B., ed. 1989. *Low-intensity conflict: The pattern of warfare in the modern world.* Lexington, Mass.: Lexington Books.

Thompson, Sir Robert. 1989. *Make for the hills: Memories of Far Eastern wars.* London: Lee Cooper.

Tse-Tung, Mao. 1967. *Selected works of Mao Tse-tung.* Vols. 1–4. Peking, China: Foreign Languages Press.

Tucker, Robert W. 1990. Why war? *New Republic* 3960 (December 10): 22–26.

Uhlig, Mark A. 1990–91. Latin America: The frustration of success. *Foreign Affairs* 70 (1): 103–19.

Urquhart, Brian. 1990. Beyond the "sheriff's posse." *Survival* 32, no. 3 (May–June): 196–203.

Van Evera, Stephen. 1990. The case against intervention. *Atlantic Monthly* 266, no. 1 (July): 72–80.

Vuono, Carl E. 1991. Desert Storm and the future of conventional force. *Foreign Affairs* 70, no. 2 (Spring): 49–68.

Weiss, Thomas G. 1990. Superpowers and peacekeepers. *Survival* 32, no. 3 (May–June): 212–20.

Wheat, Andrew. 1990. Shining Path's "fourth sword" ideology. *Journal of Political and Military Sociology* 18, no. 1 (Summer): 41–55.

Wicker, Tom. 1990. This is where I came in. *New York Times,* April 12, A19.

Wiseman, Henry, ed. 1983. *Peacekeeping: Appraisals and proposals.* New York: Pergamon Press.

Wolf, Charles Jr. 1990. The Third World in U.S.-Soviet competition: From playing field to player. In *Rand Paper P-7625.* Santa Monica, Calif.: RAND Corporation.

Ziemke, Caroline F. 1991. Military planning beyond the Cold War: Lessons for the 1990s from the 1920s and 1930s. *Washington Quarterly* 14, no. 1 (Winter): 61–80.

INDEX

Afghanistan, 10, 14, 15, 78, 140, 141,
        145, 147, 183
Agent Orange, 152
AIDS, 39, 118
Algeria, 136, 152
Al-Sabah, Sheik Jaber al-Ahmed, 185
Amazon Basin, 21, 38
American Revolution, 58, 82
an-Najaf, 142
Andean nations, 47, 176
Angola, 10, 15, 147
Antiterrorism, 128
Aquino, Corazon, 62
Arab-Israeli conflict, 142–145
Arafat, Yasir, 186
Argentina, 19, 20, 40, 49, 96, 136, 152
Armenia, 13, 201
Assistant Secretary of Defense (ASD)
        for Special Operations and Low-
        Intensity Conflict, (SOLIC) 57,
        107
Azerbaijan, 28, 29, 201, 202

Bahutu, 89
Baker, James, 161, 181
Ballistic missiles, 20, 49, 137, 141, 149,
        150, 155, 159, 164, 166, 190,
        192, 200, 209
Bandung Conference, 145
Bangladesh, 40, 44, 139, 140, 186
Barry, Marion, 123
Begin, Menachem, 144
Beirut, 131
Bennett, William S., 118, 119
Biafra, 28
Biological weapons, 20, 141, 149
Bolivia, 71, 72, 96, 115, 120, 124, 176
Bosnia-Herzegovina, 16, 131, 133, 162,
        168, 196, 207
Brazil, 19, 20, 34, 36, 40, 49, 96, 146,
        152

Brezhnev Doctrine, 10, 141, 145, 195
Brinton, Crane, 11, 59
Brown, Harold, 112, 189
"Brushfire Corollary," 46, 99, 103–104,
        109
Bulgaria, 9, 11
Burundi, 28, 89
Bush, George, 1, 53, 86, 108, 117, 119,
        132, 148, 169, 171, 180, 181,
        185, 187, 190, 206

Cable News Network (CNN), 205
Cambodia, 19, 20, 21, 136, 144
Camp David Accords, 134
Canada, 16, 132
Capital flight, 41, 203
Carter, Jimmy, 112, 144
Castro, Fidel, 14, 64, 71, 78
Center of gravity, 77, 79–80, 89, 93–97,
        110, 129, 176, 196, 197
Central America, 37, 198
Central Intelligence Agency, 92, 108
Central Treaty Organization
        (CENTO), 48, 148
Chamorro, Violetta, 15, 204
Chemical weapons, 20, 114, 141, 149
Chile, 20, 136
China, People's Republic of, 16, 23,
        32, 36, 48, 49, 67, 76, 136, 140,
        144, 152, 153, 162, 198
Coca, 40, 115, 174, 177, 178, 180
Cocaine, 47, 117–124, 171, 172
Cohen-Nunn Act of 1986, 107, 108, 210
Cold War, 2–4, 6, 14, 17, 18, 23, 43,
        46, 48, 55, 65, 85–87, 90, 105,
        109, 112, 113, 131, 136, 145–
        148, 153, 157, 159, 161, 165,
        166, 195–197, 199–201, 206, 212
Collective security, 3, 53, 134, 160, 181
Colombia, 115, 120, 124, 172, 176

Commonwealth of Independent States, 9, 12, 53, 206
Contras, 47, 58, 72, 78, 84, 98, 109
Conventional Forces in Europe (CFE), 10, 113, 149
Counterinsurgency, 44, 59, 66, 81, 85–111, 124, 176, 178, 179, 180, 210
  American approach to, 105–108
Counternarcotics, 47, 115, 117–124, 135, 176, 178
Counterterrorism, 21, 47, 115–117, 125–131, 135, 213
Coup, military, 45
Crop substitution. See drugs
Crystal methamphetamine, 115, 122
Cuba, 13, 23, 71, 78, 121, 147, 152

DeBray, Regis, 88
Debt service, 33–35, 203
Decolonization, 26
Democratic contradiction, 98, 109
Democratization of Third World, 197, 198–199
Desert One, 141
Desert Storm, 15, 18, 28, 50–52, 81, 105, 114, 131, 133, 134, 156, 159, 161, 163, 164, 169, 180, 181–193, 202, 206, 212
Dien Bien Phu, 69
Drug Enforcement Agency, U.S., 120, 176, 179, 180
"Drug-insurgency nexus," 169, 175
Drugs
  crop substitution and, 124, 177
  eradication of, 119–121, 124, 135, 175, 176, 178, 179
  interdiction of, 116, 119, 121–122, 123, 124, 135
  legalization of, 119

Egypt, 131, 136, 142, 148, 186
El Salvador, 41, 88, 89, 90, 100, 104, 181, 203
Environment, 21, 42–43
Eritrea, 38, 89
Ethiopia, 28, 38, 42, 45, 89, 136, 168
European Community (EC), 6, 7, 54

First World, 1, 13, 19, 25, 26, 31, 36, 38, 43, 125, 146, 152, 157, 158, 164–166, 197, 200, 204, 205
Foco, 71, 96
France, 2, 16, 49, 69, 92, 146
Fujimori, Alberto, 40, 96, 120, 175, 177, 179, 180

Gaza Strip, 142
Germany, 2, 3, 4, 15, 50, 186
Giap, Vo Nguyen, 58, 65, 66, 69–71, 75, 78, 86
Glaspie, April, 185
Global Protection against Limited Strikes (GPALS), 158, 165, 193
Goldwater-Nichols Defense Reorganization Act, 107
Gorbachev, Mikhail S., 5–11, 14, 32, 33, 53, 98, 145, 190, 204
Great Britain, 2, 16, 49, 132, 146, 168, 186, 209
Green Mountain Boys, 58, 83
Green revolution, 37
Grenada, 2, 104
Guerrilla war, 57, 75–76
Guevara, Ernesto (Che), 64, 66, 71–72, 87, 88, 96
Gurr, Ted Robert, 60
Guzman, Abimael, 64, 172

Haiti, 45, 90
Hausa-Fulani, 28, 89
High-Intensity Conflict (HIC), 114
High technology, 6, 7, 22, 205
Hilsman, Roger, 58
Ho Chi Minh, 64, 78, 92, 93
Horn of Africa, 28, 38
Hussein, King of Jordan, 18, 186
Hussein, Saddam, 13, 18, 19, 21, 29, 49, 50, 84, 114, 131, 144, 147, 153, 156, 160, 164, 169, 181, 196, 199–201, 207, 209, 211

Ia Drang Valley, 100
Ibo, 28, 89
India, 19, 20, 36, 42, 44, 48, 49, 136,

138–140, 145, 146, 148, 153, 159, 162
Congress Party, 48, 139
Indirect approach, 66, 67
Indonesia, 40
Indus River system, 139
Infrastructure, 41–42, 54, 203
Insurgency, 20, 24, 41, 44, 46, 57–84, 88, 89, 115, 117, 210
International economic change, 4, 6–8, 162, 197, 198–199, 205
Intifada, 144
Iran, 19, 20, 28, 47, 50, 127, 140–142, 145, 153, 182, 183, 191, 192
    Revolution of 1979, 141, 145, 183
Iran-Iraq War, 44, 48, 150, 155, 156, 184, 192
Iraq, 17, 18, 20, 28, 29, 49, 50, 52, 53, 104, 106, 113, 114, 127, 136, 137, 140–142, 148, 153, 161, 181–193, 200, 202, 210
Irish Republican Army (IRA), 126, 127, 168
Irredentism, 27, 28–29, 44
Islam, sects of, 42
Israel, 17, 21, 42, 48, 49, 89, 131, 136, 142–145, 152, 153, 159, 161, 189

Japan, 2, 3, 6, 7, 50, 54, 69, 186
Jerusalem, 143–144
Johnson, Lyndon B., 68
Jordan, 18, 136, 142, 145, 186, 187
    Civil War, 48, 147

Karbala, 142
Kashmir, 21, 42, 48, 139
Kennedy, John F., 86, 107
    Center at Ft. Bragg, 107
Khmer Rouge, 19, 169
Khomeini, Ayotollah Ruhollah, 141, 184
Khrushchev, Nikita, 5, 14, 58
Korea, Democratic People's Republic of (North), 23, 49, 209
Korea, Republic of (South), 3, 20, 22, 40, 49, 115, 122, 144, 153
Kuomintang, 58

Kurdistan, 28, 29, 191
Kurds, 134, 140, 150, 154, 168, 182, 191, 200, 201
Kuwait, 13, 29, 49, 53, 106, 113, 141, 149, 152, 156, 181–193, 196, 199, 207

League of Nations, 161, 186, 207
Lebanon, 31, 42, 89, 144
Legitimacy, 43, 45, 85, 90, 94, 95, 126
    and authority, 26, 27, 29–33, 202–204
Libya, 47, 127, 130
Liddell Hart, Sir Basil, 66, 80
Low-Intensity Conflict (LIC), 57, 105, 115, 210
    Board, 107, 108

Malayan insurgency, 96, 98, 101, 102
Mao Tse-Tung, 64, 66, 67–69, 74, 75, 78, 86
Marion, Francis, 58, 83
Mecca, 142
Medina, 142
Mexico, 34, 36, 62, 96, 121
Mexico City, 38
Middle East, 42, 115, 154, 157, 159, 163, 202
Middle-Intensity Conflict (MIC), 114
Migration, 35, 201
Military Staff Committee, 133, 160
Missile Technology Control Regime (MTCR), 157
Mobile-guerrilla warfare and strategy, 59, 65, 70, 72–77, 82, 98, 99, 103, 109, 179
Moldava, 29
Morocco, 132, 136, 186
Mozambique, 10
Mujahadin, 14, 47, 58, 78
Multinationalism, 27–29, 45, 85, 89, 202
Muslim League, 48, 139

Nagorno Karabakh, 202
Najibullah, 15
Namibia, 15

"Narcodollars," 74
Narco-insurgency, 173–178, 181
Narcotraficantes 171–174
Nationalism, 27, 198, 201
Nation-building, 31–32, 85
Nation-state, definition of, 27
National Security Council, 107
New People's Army (Philippines), 20, 59, 74, 97, 168
New Political Thinking, 9, 145
"New World Order," 1, 148, 157, 181, 194, 206–208
Newly industrialized countries (NICs), 6, 40, 42, 56
Ngo Dinh Diem, 41, 92, 93, 110
Nicaragua, 15, 72, 78, 204
Nigeria, 19, 28, 34, 40, 89
Nixon Doctrine, 52, 87, 200
Non-Proliferation Treaty (NPT), 150, 152, 164, 209
Noriega, Manuel, 123, 203
North Atlantic Treaty Organization (NATO), 4, 5, 10, 12, 15, 113, 114, 196, 207
North Vietnamese Army (NVA), 76, 80
Norway, 16, 132, 134
Nuclear, biological, and chemical (NBC) weapons, 137, 150, 152– 155, 159, 164, 166, 188, 190, 192, 200, 201, 206, 209
Nuclear Suppliers Group (NSG), 153
Nunn, Sam, 158

Offset strategy, 189
Ogaden, region of Ethiopia, 28
Operation Provide Comfort, 191, 212

Pacific Rim, 6, 17, 33, 40, 42, 56, 198, 199
Pahlavi, Reza Shah, 141, 153
Pakistan, 40, 44, 45, 48, 49, 136, 139– 140, 162, 201
Palestine Liberation Organization (PLO), 186, 187
Palestinians, 42, 48, 89, 127, 142–144, 187
Panama, 104, 181, 202, 210

Partisan war, 57
Patriot missile, 152, 156, 193
Peacekeeping, 16, 115, 116, 117, 131– 134, 135, 161, 163, 207, 209
Peacemaking, 16, 131–134, 162, 209
"People's War," 58
Persian Gulf, 13, 17, 19, 21, 37, 136, 140–142, 145, 148, 159–160, 182, 195, 199, 207
Persian Gulf War, 50, 52, 84, 111, 113, 114, 137, 139, 144, 147, 149, 152, 153, 155–157, 165, 166, 181–193, 196, 209, 211
Peru, 120–124, 169–181
Philippines, 62, 74, 115, 122, 204
Pol Pot, 19, 20, 169
Population, growth in, 35–37, 203
Posse comitatus, 124
Poverty, in Third World, 38–39
Powell, General Colin, 124, 211
Privatization, of economic activity, 7, 54
Proliferation, nuclear, 49, 153, 200

Qaddafi, Muammar, 116, 127, 152, 164

Rafsanjani, Ali Akbar Hashemi, 19, 192
Reagan, Ronald, 46, 98, 112, 118, 165
Doctrine, 47
Regional conflict, 14, 18–19, 47–49, 136–166, 168, 202, 205, 210
Relative deprivation, 60–62, 63, 64, 95, 212
Revolutions of 1989, 1, 3, 8, 9, 11, 22
Romania, 9, 11, 29
Rumalia oil fields, 184
Russia, 16, 133, 200, 208
Rwanda, 28, 89

Sadat, Anwar, 144
Sahel, region of Africa, 38, 40
Sanctuary, and insurgency, 73
Sandinistas, 62
Saudi Arabia, 20, 141, 142, 155, 184, 185, 186, 191, 192
Schwarzkopf, General Norman, 188, 189

Scud missile, 144, 147, 152, 155, 156, 183, 192, 193
"Search and destroy," 100
Second World, 1, 6, 13, 146, 196
Sendero Luminoso, 47, 59, 74, 92, 96, 120, 123, 169–181
Shaba Province, of Zaire, 20
Shining Path. See *Sendero Luminoso*
Sierra Maestra Mountains, 78
Sikhs, 42, 89, 139
Sinai Peninsula, 116
Six Day War, 132, 142
Small war, 57
Somalia, 28, 136
South Africa, Republic of, 49, 62, 153
Southeast Asia Treaty Organization (SEATO), 48, 148
Soviet Union, Former, 1–5, 9, 11, 12, 13, 15, 18, 22, 23, 26, 28, 29, 32, 33, 35, 38, 46, 48, 49, 51, 53, 62, 74, 113, 114, 127, 141, 145, 148, 149, 152, 153, 157, 163, 165, 167, 168, 181, 185, 187, 198, 201, 202, 204, 206, 207, 209
Special Forces, 86, 105–106, 115, 124, 146, 179, 180
Special operations, 57, 210
Sri Lanka, 140, 148
Stateless corporations, 7, 199
Strategic Arms Reduction Treaty (START), 5, 6, 114
Strategic Defense Initiative (SDI), 158, 165, 193
Strategic hamlets, 102, 124
Sudan, 42, 45, 89, 136
Sukarno, Achmed, 64
Sun Tzu, 57, 66–67, 69, 70, 75
Syria, 17, 18, 29, 42, 47, 48, 127, 129, 136, 145, 148, 153, 186

Taiwan, 22, 115, 144, 153
Tamils, 148
Telecommunications, 39, 55, 199, 205
Terrorism, 24, 44, 47, 65, 90, 116, 125–131
Tet offensive, 71, 77, 80
Thailand, 20, 144, 148, 168

Thompson, Sir Robert, 98
Thurmond, General Max, 116
Tiananmen Square, 167
Tomahawk cruise missile, 156
Transnational problems, 21, 162
Transylvania, 29
Turkey, 28, 120, 186

United Nations, 16, 18, 131–133, 141, 148, 157, 158, 160, 161, 185, 207, 208, 209
  Charter of, 3, 15, 133, 134, 160, 186
  Emergency Force (UNEF), 131–132
  Security Council, 16, 53, 133, 186, 207
United States, 2–5, 10, 15, 16, 26, 36, 41, 46, 48–51, 53, 57, 71, 81, 82–87, 93, 98, 103, 111–115, 118, 121, 123, 132, 134, 135, 145, 147, 148, 152, 153, 157, 163, 173, 175, 179, 181–184, 186, 188, 195–197, 200, 205–213
United States Army, 86, 105, 107, 115
  Field Manual (FM) 100-5, 106
  Field Manual (FM) 100-20, 79, 107
Upper Huallaga Valley, 93, 120, 121, 169, 171–178, 180

Viet Cong, 70, 77, 80
Viet Minh, 70, 78
Vietnam, 2, 14, 19, 20, 37, 41, 52, 69, 76, 77, 78, 81, 86, 90, 93, 100, 102, 104, 106, 110, 130, 144, 145, 168, 181, 209, 212
Vietnam War, 76–77, 82, 92, 112, 127, 152
Vital interests, 52, 135

Wars of national liberation, 14, 58, 86
Warsaw Pact. See Warsaw Treaty Organization
Warsaw Treaty Organization (WTO), 4, 5, 6, 9, 15, 113, 114, 207
Watutsi, 89
Weapon states, 150, 153, 182, 197, 200, 208

Weinberger, Caspar, 107, 108
West Bank, occupied, 142
Westmoreland, General William, 57
World Bank, 41

Yeltsin, Boris, 12, 53
Yugoslavia, 1, 11, 23, 168

Zaire, 132